SOFTWARE ENGINEERING SERIES

Designing Flexible
Object-Oriented
Systems with UML

Charles Richter

MACMILLAN
TECHNICAL
PUBLISHING
U·S·A

Designing Flexible Object-Oriented Systems with UML

By Charles Richter

Published by:
Macmillan Technical Publishing
201 West 103rd Street
Indianapolis, IN 46290 USA

Copyright © 1999 by Macmillan Technical Publishing

Library of Congress Catalog Card Number: 98-85556

ISBN: 1-57870-098-1

2001 00 99 8   4 3 2 1

Interpretation of the printing code: The rightmost double-digit number is the year of the book's printing; the rightmost single-digit, the number of the book's printing. For example, the printing code 98-1 shows that the first printing of the book occurred in 1998.

Trademark Acknowledgments

All terms mentioned in this book that are known to be trademarks or service marks have been appropriately capitalized. Macmillan Technical Publishing cannot attest to the accuracy of this information. Use of a term in this book should not be regarded as affecting the validity of any trademark or service mark.

Postscript™is a registered trademark of Adobe Systems.

The UML symbol™is a registered trademark of Rational.

Windows™and Microsoft™are registered trademarks of the Microsoft Corporation.

Warning and Disclaimer

This book is designed to provide information about designing object-oriented systems. Every effort has been made to make this book as complete and as accurate as possible, but no warranty or fitness is implied.

The information is provided on an "as-is" basis. The authors and Macmillan Technical Publishing shall have neither liability nor responsibility to any person or entity with respect to any loss or damages arising from the information contained in this book or from the use of the discs or programs that may accompany it.

Feedback Information

At Macmillan Technical Publishing, our goal is to create in-depth technical books of the highest quality and value. Each book is crafted with care and precision, undergoing rigorous development that involves the unique expertise of members from the professional technical community.

Readers' feedback is a natural continuation of this process. If you have any comments regarding how we could improve the quality of this book, or otherwise alter it to better suit your needs, you can contact us at networktech@mcp.com. Please make sure to include the book title and ISBN in your message.

We greatly appreciate your assistance.

Publisher
David Dwyer

Executive Editors
Ann Daniel

Linda Engelman

Acquisitions Editor
Karen Wachs

Development Editor
Thomas Cirtin

Managing Editor
Gina Brown

Project and Copy Editor
Laura Loveall

Proofreader
Elise Walter

Indexer
Tim Wright

Layout Technician
Amy Parker

Team Coordinators
Amy Lewis

Jennifer Garrett

Manufacturing Coordinator
Brook Farling

Book Designer
Gary Adair

Cover Designer
Karen Ruggles

About the Author

Charles Richter has been teaching and applying object-oriented methods and techniques for over 10 years. He is the founder of Objective Engineering, Inc., a company that provides training and consulting in object-oriented analysis, design, and programming. He is also an instructor for the Software Quality Institute of the University of Texas at Austin, where he teaches object-oriented design and Java programming. He has presented tutorials on object-oriented design and the UML notation at several conferences.

Prior to forming Objective Engineering, Charles was engaged in object-oriented development and research at MCC, a research consortium in Austin, Texas. He has been a project leader and software engineer on various commercial software development projects. He is currently a member of the IEEE and the ACM.

Charles has a B.S. degree in computer science from Purdue University (home of the 1999 NCAA women's basketball champions) and an M.S. degree in computer science from the University of Texas at Austin. He is a past member of the editorial board of the IEEE Computer Society Press. He lives in Austin with his wife, Dion, his daughters, Jennifer and Jessica, and his two tabby cats, Moonbeam and Silverado. In his spare time, he enjoys snorkeling, cooking, and collecting wine. Charles can be reached at `crichter@oeng.com`.

About the Technical Reviewers

These reviewers contributed their considerable practical, hands-on expertise to the entire development process for *Designing Flexible Object-Oriented Systems with UML*. As the book was being written, these folks reviewed all the material for technical content, organization, and flow. Their feedback was critical to ensuring that *Designing Flexible Object-Oriented Systems with UML* fits our reader's need for the highest quality technical information.

Laura Paterno is a real-time systems programmer, until recently, working at the Fermi National Accelerator Laboratory (Fermilab). She received her B.S. degree at the Rensselaer Polytechnic Institute. She has been responsible for the critical review of all the OOAD, Java, and C++ courses given at Fermilab. She has designed and developed a wide array of software products, ranging from graphical user interface design to interprocess communication and real-time control systems for a multimillion dollar experiment.

Laura has been involved with software reviews for, and OOAD mentoring of, physicists at Fermilab. She first met the author while reviewing his course in object oriented analysis and design. She has been working with object-oriented technology for the past 7 years.

Marc Paterno is a physicist-turned-software designer working at the Fermi National Accelerator Laboratory (Fermilab). He received a Sc.B. in physics from MIT and an M.S. and Ph.D. in physics from the State University of New York at Stony Brook. He spent 10 years working on high-energy physics experiments, with much of his time spent developing customized software for the analysis of multi-terabyte data samples.

He has been programming in Smalltalk since 1989 and in C++ since 1991, and he has been involved with the production of object-oriented systems at Fermilab for the past 7 years. He has contributed to the design, development, implementation, and review of C++ class libraries, which will be used by more than 800 physicists in the two largest experiments at Fermilab, in the collection and analysis of more than 100 terabytes of data per year.

Phil Price is a vice president of software with Qualcomm Incorporated, where he was one of the initial system designers on the Globalstar project and then led a research department responsible for investigating the application of new technologies and techniques to practical applications. In addition to technical roles, for the past 6 years he has been involved in promoting software process improvement efforts and object-oriented methodologies for application on very large projects within the company.

Phil is also active with local universities, especially in the areas of software engineering and design methodologies. Prior to joining Qualcomm, Phil spent 5 years working for Hughes Network Systems on a next-generation digital cellular system, and 5 years prior to that at the European Space Agency working on redesigning the low earth orbit control system.

Dedication

To my wife, Dion, who makes all of my endeavors possible.

Acknowledgments

Writing this book has been a much more difficult process than I imagined it possibly could be, and I am extremely grateful to several individuals who have assisted me during the journey. I thank all the people at Macmillan Technical Publishing who through their faith and hard work have brought this book to fruition. Special thanks go to Ann Daniel, who convinced me to undertake this venture; to Jen Garrett, who handled web page creation and other technical logistics; to Laura Loveall, who managed the technical production; and especially to Tom Cirtin, who shepherded me through the review and revision process. I especially appreciate Tom's patience because I'm sure there were times when he wondered if I would ever finish the book.

The material for this book is drawn largely from an object-oriented analysis and design course I teach. I am grateful to the hundreds of students I have had in my courses and tutorials over the years who have contributed greatly to my understanding of object-oriented development through their many questions, comments, and suggestions. I am also indebted to Phil Price and Laura and Marc Paterno, the technical reviewers of this book, for their many thoughtful suggestions. As an occasional reviewer myself, I know how much time and effort a careful review requires.

Finally, I can never adequately express my appreciation to my daughters, Jennifer and Jessica, and especially to my wife, Dion, for their unending patience. Dion has been extremely supportive, doing everything she could to relieve me of other burdens. Because this undertaking was important to me, my wife and daughters never complained, even though most of my writing occurred during what otherwise would have been family time. I don't think they asked me, "When will the book be finished?" more than a handful of times.

Contents at a Glance

Table of Contents

Introduction

Object-oriented development is the process of turning an idea or a problem specification into an object-oriented program. That program consists of a group of objects that communicate with one another. The objects are created as the program executes, and they are instances of classes that exist in the program's source code.

An early step in the development process is *object-oriented analysis (OOA)*. OOA transforms a glimmer of a product into an object-oriented model of that problem. A definition of the functional requirements of the system to be developed and a description of the classes in the problem domain are included in a typical object-oriented analysis model. Some analysis models also include a definition of the high-level system components (such as subsystems) and their interactions, as well as the general interactions among instances of the problem domain classes.

Object-oriented design (OOD) entails transforming the analysis model into a feasible design. Much of design involves refining the analysis model through the introduction of classes and algorithms that define exactly how certain required features are realized.

Another common design activity is the development of an overall system architecture. This entails organizing the system as a set of major building blocks, such as subsystems or components. For a *concurrent system*, the architecture includes the basic task or process structure. For a *distributed system*, it includes the organization of hardware in terms of processors and their interconnections.

Once the design reaches a sufficient level of specificity, it is translated into an implementation through *object-oriented programming*. This task can be either relatively straightforward or rather challenging, depending upon the amount of detail in the design (and perhaps on other factors, too).

This book describes the concepts and notation required to specify an object-oriented analysis model or object-oriented design. It also discusses a set of approaches that one can use when practicing OOA and OOD.

Why Object-Oriented Anything?

Projects making a transition from a more traditional development approach, such as structured analysis and structured design (SA/SD), to object-oriented development are likely to encounter several impediments. When completed, the object-oriented software must coexist with legacy software that is not object-oriented, often requiring that the two types of software communicate with one another. Existing data that are stored in relational databases must be converted to objects in memory when used by an object-oriented application.

An organization's lack of experience with object-oriented technology presents another set of problems. The staff must be trained to understand and employ object-oriented development and infrastructure. Because they are using new design methods and programming languages, staff members will make mistakes on their first projects, regardless of how much training they receive.

This lack of experience also pervades project management. Project leaders who are unversed in the new technology often cannot detect architectural flaws until very late in the development process. In addition, because most estimation models rely on previous data, managers have a difficult time with estimation and planning.

Given these costs, why adopt object technology at all? Many organizations take the leap to object technology for non-technical reasons, such as:

- *The fear factor*: "All of our competitors are doing it. So, if we don't do it, we'll fall behind."

- *The bandwagon effect*: "Everyone else is doing it. It must be right."

- *The seduction of new technology*: "This new object-oriented stuff is way cooler than the old stuff we use."

Although non-technical reasons may provide sufficient incentive for some to make the transition to object technology, other organizations want more tangible benefits to justify the switch. The possible technical benefits include the following:

- *Object-oriented systems can be more flexible.* Object-oriented programming languages offer features whose application promotes the extensibility and reuse of the resulting program.

- *Object-oriented development is a relatively seamless process.* Analysis and design are a continuous process with a continuous representation.

- *Class-based models closely mimic the real world.* Classes model real-world abstractions and, therefore, define a language of the problem domain. This analog with the real world makes object-oriented representations especially useful for modeling a business.

- *Object-oriented technology provides various ways of dealing with complexity.* You can decompose a system in different ways, and you can hide implementation complexity behind well-defined interfaces.

- *Object-oriented systems are relatively easy to prototype.* Reusable components and encapsulated implementations support prototyping.

The remainder of this section elaborates on those benefits.

Greater Flexibility

We in the software community cannot build enough software systems to satisfy the world's needs. The demand for software continues to explode. As a result, universities cannot produce enough software engineers and programmers to meet the industry's needs. The traditional approach to this problem has been to strive to build systems faster. A goal of research has been to find and develop a "silver bullet"—technology that will increase the productivity of software developers by an order of magnitude (or two).

Although better tools and practices contribute to higher productivity rates, awaiting a silver bullet is a forlorn hope. Given that many organizations build the same kinds of software systems again and again, a more realistic goal is to avoid building every new system from scratch, aiming instead to build systems that can be extended to incorporate new capabilities, and that can be (at least partially) reused in other, similar contexts.

Object-oriented technology is based on several concepts that, when applied to a design or program, can make the resulting product easier to extend and reuse. Five such features are abstraction, encapsulation, specialization, type promotion, and polymorphism.

In general, *abstraction* is the process of focusing only on the essential characteristics of an entity. A class provides a powerful abstraction mechanism for object-oriented design and programming. A class defines an abstraction in the problem or solution domain. In an order processing application, for example, an Order class defines the basic properties of each order instance. In particular, it defines both the state (data) and behavior (algorithms) that its instances have. Because it defines *both* state and behavior, a class provides a more powerful abstraction mechanism than a procedure or a data record does.

A class also defines both an interface and an underlying implementation. That implementation is invisible to external clients of the class (or of its instances). Defining such properties as private to the class is an example of *encapsulation*. In other words, a class encapsulates its state and behavior. Encapsulation is a mechanism to achieve *information hiding*. A major advantage of information hiding is that if the information is invisible to the client, you can modify its implementation without affecting the client in any way.

Object-oriented programming languages also support *class specialization*, or the *is-a-kind-of* relationship between classes. The Automobile class is a specialization of the Vehicle class (or, Automobile is a kind of Vehicle), the Router class specializes the Device class, and the Service Order class is a specialization of the Order class. The operational result of the specialization relationship is *inheritance*—the specialization (or subclass) inherits all of the state and behavior of the generalization (or superclass). The Automobile class, for example, inherits all of the properties of the Vehicle class.

Class specialization allows you to define the properties common to all vehicles in the Vehicle class and then to inherit those properties in the Vehicle specializations (such as Automobile, Truck, and so forth). Therefore, a major selling point of specialization is that you can define those common properties once and inherit them where necessary. Hence, you have a single copy of those properties. With multiple copies of a piece of code, any corrections to the code must be introduced in each copy. With class specialization, however, any changes in the superclass properties are propagated to the subclasses through inheritance.

Type promotion allows you to treat a specific type of object as a more general type. For example, you can refer to an Automobile instance either as an Automobile or as a more generic Vehicle. (Recall that Automobile is a kind of Vehicle.) This principle is also called *substitution*. When a client expects to be given a reference to a generic Vehicle, you can substitute any more specific reference (such as a reference to an Automobile).

Type promotion allows you to write client code that refers only to generic types such as Vehicle. This implies that the client code is unaware of the specific types. Therefore, when you introduce a new specialization of Vehicle, the client code is unaffected. Instances of that new class will be treated by the client code as generic Vehicles.

At this point, you may be thinking, "But I want an Automobile to behave like an Automobile, not like a generic Vehicle." The complement of type promotion is *polymorphism*. Polymorphism simply means that an object still acts like what it really is, regardless of how a client refers to it. When a client tells a Vehicle to do something, the Vehicle will respond appropriately based on what it really is (at execution time). If what the client is referencing is actually an Automobile, it will act like an Automobile. On the other hand, if it is a Truck, it will behave like a Truck.

The combination of type promotion and polymorphism allows you to write very generic client code that is de-coupled from the existence of particular specializations. As noted previously, your client code that references only generic Vehicles is unaffected by the addition or removal of specializations of Vehicle. Nonetheless, when that code acts on a Vehicle, you still see the correct behavior based on the actual type of the Vehicle. Furthermore, the same generic code can act on *any* type of Vehicle.

The use of such features to achieve design flexibility is a major point of emphasis in this book. Chapter 2, "Class Diagramming Notation," addresses these principles and their benefits in more detail.

A Relatively Seamless Process

The object-oriented development *process* itself is an attraction for many organizations. Compared to many alternative development approaches, which suffer points of discontinuity during the process, object-oriented development is a relatively seamless process.

As an example of a development process with a seam, consider *Structured Analysis and Structured Design (SA/SD)*. During analysis, you create data flow diagrams that describe how data is transformed by the system. When your analysis is complete and you turn your attention to design, you draw structure charts that indicate what subroutines will exist in your implementation and how those subroutines interact. In other words, you draw one type of diagram during analysis and an entirely different type of diagram during design.

These two different representations form a discontinuity in the SA/SD process. The fact that the two models are largely unrelated further exacerbates the problem. Except in a few rare cases, you cannot transform a data flow diagram into a beginning set of structure charts. When you start the design phase, you essentially start anew.

In contrast, object-oriented development enjoys what I call *representational continuity*. As you proceed through analysis and design, you continue to draw the same kinds of diagrams. During high-level analysis, you draw a class diagram, a use case diagram, and perhaps a set of interaction diagrams. Many weeks later, during low-level design, you are still drawing these same diagrams (and perhaps a few others).

The fact that the analysis and design representations are the same provides one form of continuity. A second form is the continuity of the model itself; the design is an elaboration of the analysis. That is, the classes and use cases that exist in the initial analysis also appear in the final design. The analysis of an order processing application will include Order, Line Item, and Customer classes. Those classes will continue to appear in the refined analysis and design models. In fact, they will exist in the ultimate implementation! These two forms of representational continuity provide you with a more coherent development process.

Mimicking the Real World

For some organizations, a major advantage of object technology is the fact that classes model real-world abstractions in an intuitive way. A class can also model both the state and the behavior of its instances. For example, an Order class in an order processing application defines the state that an order has (such as an order number and a set of line items), as well as the actions one could perform on an order (such as canceling or committing it).

A class diagram can, therefore, serve as a model of the business. Business analysts and software analysts can work together to develop an object-oriented analysis model. The result of that effort is a final business model to the businessperson, but it is viewed by the software professional as an initial model from which the final system will be derived.

This situation is far preferable to the more common situation in which business analysts build a business model that is ignored by the software developers, who in turn develop an analysis model that is eschewed by the business analysts. David Taylor (1995) devotes a book to this use of object technology, as do Ivar Jacobson, Maria Ericsson, and Agneta Jacobson (1994).

Dealing with Complexity

Object-oriented design notations and programming languages support the decomposition of a system along different dimensions, thus allowing developers to deal with complexity in various ways. The fundamental building block of an object-oriented system, a class, presents a public interface while encapsulating the details (and the complexity) of its implementation. A client of that class must understand only the interface of the class.

A system can be broken into components, each of which presents a well-defined interface while hiding its underlying implementation. To compose these components, you need to understand only those interfaces. In that sense, a component is essentially a class on steroids. The same principles of encapsulation are at play.

Classes can also be organized in different types of hierarchies. The hierarchy that receives the most press, of course, is the specialization hierarchy (often referred to simply as the class hierarchy). Classes are arranged according to the specialization (or is-a-kind-of) relationship. In the typical case, a specialization (or subclass) is also a subtype. So, the specialization hierarchy mimics the type hierarchy. A specialization inherits the properties of its generalization (or superclass). A subclass is simplified because it contains only the properties that distinguish it from its superclass.

In some cases, classes (and their instances) can be arranged in a composition hierarchy. Classes are organized based on whole-part relationships, meaning that the instances of one class are composed of the instances of others. For example, a document consists of paragraphs, which in turn consist of words. Requests can be delegated from a whole to its parts, providing a convenient and consistent way of dealing with certain types of complex structures.

Ease of Prototyping

Prototyping can entail anything from simply providing an interface mock-up to slapping together a crude proof-of-concept sample of the intended system. Although prototyping is never easy, object technology can make the job easier.

Perhaps the biggest advantage of prototyping is the existence of libraries of reusable classes. The classes in a class library provide standard versions of some of the prototype's potential components. For example, when building a graphical user interface (GUI) prototype, you can employ the GUI widgets such as frames, buttons, and check-boxes that come with your favorite GUI class library. You simply add whatever special processing is required by the prototype.

Encapsulation also assists the development of prototypes. Because objects are self-contained, they can provide implementations of some operations while "stubbing out" others. This permits you to build a prototype incrementally. Although a class may provide a fairly rich interface, it need not implement any part of that interface not required by the current prototype.

What Is an Object-Oriented Design Method?

The successful prosecution of OOA and OOD requires an effective design *method*. To support the development of large-scale, flexible object-oriented systems, such a method should include at least three components:

- *A set of concepts and their notation*: The concepts provide the rudiments of the discipline. The notation permits you to capture the analysis model and design in a form that can be reviewed and implemented.

- *A set of approaches to transform a problem into an analysis model and a design*: How do you turn a problem into a set of classes, for example? How do you identify the required system behaviors and translate those to object behaviors?

- *A set of guidelines that lead you toward more flexible designs*: What makes one design preferable to another? When should you use inheritance, and when should you eschew it? What forms of coupling do you have in an object-oriented design, and how do you reduce them?

This book provides guidance in all three areas. It explains basic object-oriented concepts and describes the essential aspects of the UML notation. It outlines and illustrates a set of approaches for identifying system functions, classes, and object dynamics. It also offers guidelines for assessing the flexibility of a design.

What Is the Unified Modeling Language?

For its analysis and design notation, this book employs the Unified Modeling Language (UML). As its name suggests, UML is a *notation*. More specifically, it is an object-oriented analysis and design notation. As such, it includes features for everything from high-level analysis concepts (and even business process models) down to very detailed design elements. However, it is *only* a notation, and so UML is silent on the subject of design process or flexibility guidelines.

UML is a *unification* of the concepts of previous object-oriented design notations. It provides notation for the "garden-variety" features present in most existing object-oriented design methods. In addition, it adds concepts and notation missing from those methods. Some are large-scale additions, such as the inclusion of new types of diagrams from other disciplines (the activity diagram, for example). In other cases, it provides incremental yet important additions, such as its integration of concurrency features into interaction diagrams.

UML is a relative newcomer to the design notation field. The initial release occurred in January of 1997. Nevertheless, the following factors have led to UML's rapid and widespread acceptance in the object-oriented design community:

- *The language is based on experience.* The three primary developers of UML—Grady Booch, Ivar Jacobson, and James Rumbaugh—each had previously contributed to a method that had been in use for several years. They also incorporated good ideas from other methods and notations.

- *The language is expressive.* It offers notation for different views of the system, and the notation within each view is relatively rich. You can describe a system or application at any stage of development, from high-level analysis through low-level design. Furthermore, UML offers well-defined ways of extending the notation.

- *The language has been adopted as a standard by the Object Management Group (OMG), a consortium of companies in the object business.* As a result, numerous CASE tools support it.

The current version of UML is 1.1, 1.2, or 1.3, depending on whom you ask. Version 1.1 was the initial version accepted by the Object Management Group as its standard design language. That version was developed by Booch, Jacobson, and Rumbaugh at Rational Software Corporation and is maintained on the Rational Web page as *The Unified Modeling Language Notation Guide: Version 1.1* (1997) and *The Unified Modeling Language Semantics: Version 1.1* (1997). (These are available at www.rational.com.) The OMG subsequently released version 1.2 as an editorial cleansing of version 1.1 and is currently developing version 1.3. Those later versions are available from the OMG (1998). Finally, the authors of UML have published a pair of books that offer some additional refinements to the language, *The Unified Modeling Language* (1999) and *The Unified Modeling Language Reference Manual* (1999). For the most part, this book employs the version 1.1 notation.

UML is an extensive language that allows you to construct several views of a system through the use of its different diagrams. Some important views and their diagrams follow:

- *Functional view*: This view describes the basic functional requirements of the system. UML use case diagrams depict a *static* functional view in terms of functions and their static relationships, whereas activity diagrams can be used to depict a *dynamic* functional view.

- *Static structural view*: This view defines the static (that is, non-temporal) structure of the system. Class and object diagrams fulfill this view. A class diagram defines the legal configurations of the system; it specifies what objects and links you may have at any moment in time. An object diagram depicts a particular configuration in that it shows a set of objects and links at a specific moment in time during the execution of the system.

- *Behavioral (dynamic structural) view*: This view describes the temporal behavior of the system. UML interaction diagrams (in particular, collaboration and sequence diagrams) depict the specific sequences of interactions between objects in different scenarios. State transition diagrams show the state-based behavior of the instances of a class.

- *Architectural view*: This view outlines the logical and physical structure of the system's major building blocks. Component diagrams show the programming language source and binary unit architecture, whereas deployment diagrams show the physical hardware architecture. Logical collections of use cases (system functions) and classes (such as layers or subsystems) are represented in UML as packages. By *superimposing* concurrency onto interaction diagrams, you can also show the process and thread architecture.

This book covers all these views and diagrams.

What Constitutes a Flexible Design?

Although this book includes the Unified Modeling Language as part of its title, this is not just a book about UML. It is primarily a book about conducting object-oriented analysis and design for the purpose of developing flexible programs. A major goal of this book is to provide a set of guidelines for constructing more flexible designs.

A flexible design is one that is extensible or reusable. New features can be added to an extensible design relatively painlessly. Ideally, adding a new capability should affect as few classes as possible. A reusable design is one that can be used, either entirely or in part, in another system or application.

To increase its flexibility, an object-oriented design should exhibit several properties:

- *High cohesion*: Cohesion is a measure of the degree to which an entity does just one kind of thing. The more cohesive it is, the more it limits itself to one area of interest. In an object-oriented design, your classes should be cohesive in that they should represent a single abstraction (or handle a related set of responsibilities). A class that is not cohesive is more difficult to understand and, in some cases, to extend. It can also require specialization along orthogonal dimensions, resulting in problems when those dimensions must be composed. Operations (methods, member functions) also should be cohesive in that each should handle a single responsibility.

- *Low coupling*: Coupling measures what an entity needs to know about the world around it. In an object-oriented design, coupling involves what a class or object knows about other classes or objects. You strive for low coupling, which means that you want your classes and objects to know as little as possible about other classes and objects. If one class is coupled to another and the public interface of that second class changes, the implementation of the first class may be affected. Reducing coupling can limit the scope of a change to the design. There are several forms of coupling in an object-oriented design; four of them are addressed in this book.

- *An even distribution of behavior*: A good object-oriented design is one that distributes behavior as evenly as possible. You strive to keep state and behavior together in an object and to have that object "do things for itself." In doing so, you avoid objects that control other objects.

- *Strong modularity*: This is the degree to which "like things" are grouped together. You strive to group objects into meaningful packages, subsystems, processes, and so forth.

This book covers all those topics. Be aware, however, that all these guidelines are just that—guidelines. No guideline is applied in every case; each has its exceptions. For example, you sometimes introduce controllers to achieve a degree of optimization. In fact, you typically face a trade-off between flexibility and simplicity and between flexibility and performance. A flexible design is typically more complicated and often sacrifices some performance for the sake of flexibility.

This book presents several flexibility guidelines and explains their implications. You will have to choose the degree of flexibility (at the price of complexity and perhaps performance) that you require.

Because most organizations face the task of continually maintaining and extending applications over time, this book's primary flexibility focus is on extensible applications. Nonetheless, the ability to reuse a design or program is an alternative measure of flexibility, and reuse is an important concern in many organizations. Therefore, the book also discusses four forms of reuse (class libraries, frameworks, components, and patterns), and it contrasts the application and scale of each.

Additional Pleasures

The most effective way to learn the design approaches and guidelines described in this book is to apply them to sample problems. Toward that end, Macmillan Technical Publishing has provided a Web site that hosts a set of problems and, for each problem, a discussion of one possible design. The URL for that site is http://www.macmillantech.com/richter/.

CHAPTER **1**

System Functional Models

The task of transforming a product description into a software implementation is part of most software development projects. The initial description may take several forms. It could be a very informal outline of the desired product, perhaps communicated by word of mouth from sales or marketing to the development organization. In some cases, it is a rigorous system specification written by an engineering or product-planning group. It could also be nothing more than an idea in a software engineer's imagination. Regardless of the description's precision and specificity, it provides the requirements for the eventual system.

The first step in a typical development effort is to analyze the description of the system and produce a model of the system's requirements. That model represents the project members' understanding of what the system must do. From that model, the project team will subsequently create a design and, from that design, an implementation. The requirements model, therefore, provides the primary baseline from which the ultimate implementation will be derived. System requirements come in several varieties:

- *Functional requirement*: This describes a required behavior of the system from an external point of view. (On the other hand, the way that the system behaves internally to achieve that external effect is part of the design.)

- *Performance requirement*: This states, for example, that a particular function must be executed within a given time interval.

- *Minimum robustness of the system*: This can be, for example, an indication of what errors are handled and how.

Some systems must also satisfy other kinds of requirements, such as the need for interfaces to conform to a particular standard, or a requirement that a component be reusable in another system.

While a system may have performance and robustness requirements, all systems have functional requirements. Modeling the functional requirements entails enumerating the functions the system will provide (again, from an external point of view). A complete functional model also specifies the external entities, such as human users and legacy systems that engage in those functions. UML provides two notational conventions for defining a system functional model:

- *Use case diagram*: Depicts a *static* view of system functions and their static relationships both with external entities and with one another.

- *Activity diagram*: Imparts a *dynamic* view of those functions. In particular, it can specify the temporal sequencing of the functions relative to one another, or the temporal ordering of the steps required to carry out an individual function.

This chapter explains the concepts and notation for both use case diagrams and activity diagrams, and then it uses those diagrams to develop a functional model for an order processing system, as follows:

- *A first functional model*: You are led through the creation of a model of DryGoods.com, a fictional catalog order company, that shows how system functional modeling is used in the real world. Its various functions—from order taking to fulfillment—are modeled with UML. A use case diagram that models basic business functions is developed that depicts the business from the point of view of a customer of DryGoods.com.

- *Activity diagrams*: You are shown how to define the workflow view of each use case as an activity diagram.

- *A system-oriented use case diagram*: The use case diagram is refined to present a more design-oriented view of the system's functions. The updated diagram incorporates the external systems with which the system must interact.

- *The dangers of going too far*: You are cautioned against employing use case and activity diagrams to undertake a functional decomposition of the system. Refining use cases below the level of system functions can result in a structured (rather than object-oriented) design.

1.1 A First Functional Model

To illustrate the application of UML to system functional modeling, this chapter presents a functional model for an order processing system to be developed for a fictional catalog order company, DryGoods.com. The company mails catalogs to customers who then place orders for items listed in the catalog. Despite the name of the company (which was selected to boost sales of the company's stock), customers can place orders only by telephone. To be more specific, customers interact with the company by calling Telephone Agents who, in turn, interact with the system.

Problem: Creating a Catalog Ordering System

Customers can place orders for goods and perform various transactions, as follows:

- A single order can be for multiple line items. (For example, with a single order a customer can purchase a sweater, a pair of boots, and an umbrella.)

- Customers can cancel both entire orders and individual items in orders. Canceling an order entails canceling all items in the order.

- An item can be canceled if it has not already been shipped or previously canceled.

- Customers can also return items they do not want.

A customer may have any number of orders pending at any time. The DryGoods.com system must generate a unique order number for each order. This number serves as a key the customer can use to identify the order.

DryGoods.com maintains an inventory of goods. Order items are allocated from that inventory. When its inventory is exhausted, an item will be back-ordered from a supplier.

Customer orders are funded from credit or debit cards. Hence, each order must include a credit or debit card number. DryGoods.com obtains funds from that card when the order is placed.

DryGoods.com ships only complete orders. If one or more items in an order are currently unavailable, the shipment of the other parts of the order will be delayed until those items become available.

The order processing system must also interact with legacy software. DryGoods.com has a product warehouse legacy system that handles inventory management (including ordering goods from suppliers). It also has a legacy shipping system that handles shipping (including tracking the progress of the shipment).

The functional model should provide at least three pieces of information by answering the following questions:

- What functions does the system offer?

- What external agents interact with the system?

- In what functions are those external agents involved?

From the first two items, you can determine the boundary of the system. (The term *system* is used loosely. It could be a subsystem, an application, or a component.) Note that the preceding list is not exhaustive; a functional model sometimes includes additional information, such as assumptions made during requirements analysis. Such information typically appears in a separate document, although it can be introduced into a UML diagram in the form of a note.

In some cases, the initial functional model is a *model of the business*. Such a model describes the business (or system) from the point of view of the ultimate user or customer. The business functions are those visible to that ultimate user. A business view or business model is sometimes called an *analysis model* or a *domain model*. Any classes defined in this view become part of a *business object model* (or analysis-level class diagram).

In other cases, you may be interested in a more *system-oriented* view of the system you must build. That is, you want to take into account the actual devices, legacy systems, and so forth, with which the system must interact, as well as the exact nature of the interactions. The example in the next section is a high-level business model of the functionality of the catalog order processing system. That model is subsequently refined into a more system-oriented model.

1.1.1   Actors in the Business View

An *actor* in UML is anything outside the boundary of the system that interacts with the system in some way. Actors come in many forms, including

- A role played by a human user, such as a customer or sales manager

- An external system, legacy system, client application, or component

- An external device, such as a light sensor or a fault monitor

Modeling actors enables you to see exactly what interacts with the system and how. In the business view of the catalog order processing system, your actors are the ultimate users of the system. In the DryGoods.com system, you have just one such actor: the Catalog Customer. The Catalog Customer is someone who orders goods from the DryGoods.com product catalog. (Other, more system-oriented actors, such as the Telephone Agents who take calls from customers, are introduced in Section 1.3, "A System-Oriented Use Case Diagram.")

1.1.2   Use Cases in the Business View

To model system functions, UML offers the *use case*. Jacobson adopted this term because a use case describes how an actor uses the system (Jacobson et al. 1992, 129). Therefore, a use case represents a function that would "make sense" to an actor.

Use cases can be identified in any of several ways. Jacobson recommends that you consider how each actor interacts with the system (Jacobson et al. 1992, 155). That is, ask yourself two questions:

- What interactions with the system does the actor initiate?

- What interactions with the actor does the system initiate?

Each such interaction is a use case (or a part of a use case). In the business functional model for DryGoods.com, a Catalog Customer participates in at least five functions and initiates all five:

- The placing of an order

- The canceling of an order

- The canceling of an order item

- The returning of an order item

- Various queries about orders

In the interest of brevity, ignore the queries here (although in a real development setting, you would have to model them). As noted above, each of these interactions becomes a use case in the functional model.

You can write a paragraph (or more) of text to describe each use case. This is called a *specification* in UML: a description that appears not in a UML diagram, but in a separate, non-UML document. The following are textual specifications of the four use cases:

- *Place Order*: The customer places an order for one or more catalog items. The order is entered in the system after it is funded (for example, by a credit card). Each order item is allocated from available inventory, or from back-ordered inventory if no available inventory exists.

- *Cancel Order*: The customer asks that an order be canceled. Each item in the order that has not already been shipped is canceled and returned to available inventory.

- *Cancel Order Item*: The customer asks that an individual item in an order be canceled. The item may be canceled only if it has not been shipped; in which case, the item is returned to inventory.

- *Return Order Item*: The customer returns an item that was shipped. The item must be returned to inventory, and the customer must be credited for the return.

You can describe use cases in other ways. This topic is addressed in Chapter 6, "Developing Dynamic Diagrams."

1.1.3   A Use Case Diagram of the Business View

Now that the system's actors and use cases have been identified, you can combine this information in a use case diagram. This diagram contains three basic components:

- *System*: The system is depicted as a rectangle (possibly with the name of the system inside).

- *Actor*: Each actor is shown as a stick figure.

- *Use case*: Each use case is shown as a solid-bordered oval labeled with the name of the use case.

The use cases appear within the rectangle of the system providing that function. Actors, on the other hand, are external to the system and, therefore, always appear outside the rectangle.

A use case diagram also depicts participation relationships between actors and use cases. The diagram has an association—a solid line—between an actor and each use case in which the actor participates. (Note that the actor does not need to *initiate* the use case; the association shows only that the actor is involved in some way.)

The business functional model, which is cast as a use case diagram, is shown in Figure 1.1.

Ure cases (within rectangle)

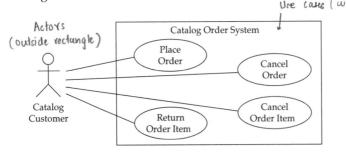

Actors (outside rectangle)

FIGURE 1.1   *A use case diagram of the business.*

static model (static Relationships)
NOT Dynamic relationships (Activity Diagrams)

1.1.4   Use Case Relationships

Use case diagrams can include relationships between actors and use cases, as illustrated by Figure 1.1. In addition, they can depict relationships between the use cases themselves. Because a use case represents a system function, these relationships indicate corresponding relationships between those system functions.

A use case diagram is a static model of functionality. The relationships in it, including relationships between use cases, are static relationships. Put another way, these relationships do not connote any temporal sequencing. The basic static relationship between two system functions (or use cases) is the notion that one includes the behavior of another. This primary form, in turn, comes in two secondary forms: One use case *always* includes another's behavior, or it *sometimes* includes another's behavior.

Note that dynamic relationships, such as the temporal sequencing of use cases (that is, one use case is followed by another), are not included in use case diagrams. They can be represented in activity diagrams, and those diagrams can be traced back to use cases, as discussed in Section 1.2, "Activity Diagrams."

The Uses Relationship

The careful reader may have observed that two of the use cases in Figure 1.1 are related: When a Catalog Customer cancels an order, the order items in that order will also be canceled. In other words, the behavior of Cancel Order always includes the behavior of Cancel Order Item.

This relationship is modeled in UML as a *uses* relationship between the two use cases. The UML Notation Guide describes this relationship as follows:

> A uses relation from use case A to use case B indicates that an instance of the use case A will also include the behavior as specified by [use case] B (78).

The notation is a closed-headed arrow annotated with the stereotype name *uses*. Stereotypes are discussed in Chapter 2, "Class Diagramming Notation"; for now, it suffices simply to point out that the stereotype name is placed within *guillemets* (which are similar to double angle brackets) and appears next to the shaft of the arrow. Figure 1.2 shows this relationship between Cancel Order and Cancel Order Item.

FIGURE 1.2 *An example of a uses relationship.*

Such relationships are added to the use case diagrams. Figure 1.3 contains the updated use case diagram with the relationship between the two use cases.

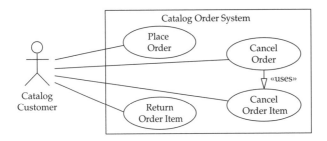

FIGURE 1.3 *An expanded use case diagram of the business.*

The Extends Relationship

A uses relationship describes the situation in which one use case *always* includes the behavior of another. What if one use case *conditionally* includes the behavior of another? Suppose, for example, that an Add Customer use case describes adding a new customer to the DryGoods.com customer database. This use case would be invoked when a Catalog Customer makes his or her initial order. In other words, *sometimes* while placing an order, the customer is added. This occurrence is based on an internal system condition in the Place Order use case—whether there is already a record of the customer or not.

UML defines this concept as an *extends* relationship between use cases. The UML Notation Guide states:

> An extends relationship from use case A to use case B indicates that an instance of use case B may include (subject to specific conditions specified in the extension) the behavior specified by [use case] A (78).

The notation is the enclosed-headed arrow directed away from the extension (that is, toward the use case that is being extended) with the «extends» stereotype annotation. Figure 1.4 illustrates the extension example.

FIGURE 1.4 *An example of an extends relationship.*

An extending use case defines exceptional behavior for the use case it extends. Add Customer is exceptional behavior for the Place Order use case. Your goal is the Place Order functionality; Add Customer occurs as a "side effect" to that behavior.

Uses Versus Extends

Consider the two use case relationships shown in Figure 1.5. One way to view these two relationships is in terms of invoking behavior. *A uses B* means that A always invokes B, whereas *B extends A* means that A sometimes invokes B. This interpretation leads to confusion, however, because *one of the arrows goes the wrong way.*

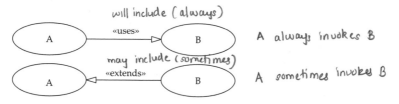

FIGURE 1.5 *The two use case relationships.*

An alternative way to think of these two relationships is as *inheritance* (subsumption) of behavior. (Each relationship is a stereotype of the specialization, or inheritance, relationship between classes.) When A uses B, the behavior of A includes the behavior of B. That is, you can do B by itself, but the behavior of A always includes B. On the other hand, when B extends A, the behavior of B includes the behavior of A. You can do A by itself, but the behavior of B includes (that is, is an extension of) the behavior of A.

Of course, there are some variations of the *extends* relationship. The most common is when one use case includes exactly one of several others. That is, the other use cases extend the first one, but exactly one of them will occur. Furthermore, the selection of the extending use case will be based on some condition in the extended use case. This relationship has no syntax in UML use case diagrams. It is probably better represented in an activity diagram (in which it does have notation that includes the condition itself) and is discussed in the next section.

1.2   Activity Diagrams

A use case diagram presents a static view of system functionality. It defines the actors, use cases, and relationships between them, but it contains no information about the dynamics of these functions:

- Consider when one use case *uses* several others. You do not see in what order those other use cases are used.

- Consider when one use case *extends* another. You do not see under what conditions or at what point the extension occurs.

- Consider use cases that must be temporally ordered in a particular way. You do not see the required sequencing among them.

Activity diagrams provide one solution to these deficiencies. An activity diagram depicts a *workflow view* of activities. You can refine a use case into an activity diagram that "flowcharts" the steps in the use case. When the use case uses several other use cases, the diagram depicts the order in which they are used. When the use case is extended by another use case, the diagram shows when and why the extension occurs.

You can also draw a system-level activity diagram in which each use case is modeled as an activity. That activity diagram specifies the temporal sequencing (if any) of the use cases.

1.2.1   Activity Diagram Notation

An activity diagram shows the workflow of activities (or *action states*). An activity can correspond to any of several kinds of tasks, such as the following:

- When modeling business processes, it can correspond to a human task, such as approving a document.

- When specifying temporal constraints among use cases, it can correspond to a system function (that is, to a use case).

- When "flowcharting" a use case, it can correspond to one step in that use case.

An activity is modeled as a *capsule* (that is, as a rectangle with rounded corners) with the activity name enclosed.

The simplest relationship between two activities occurs when one must follow the other. Figure 1.6 illustrates the notation used to indicate that activity Y must follow activity X.

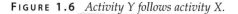

FIGURE 1.6   *Activity Y follows activity X.*

You can also indicate that one activity *conditionally* follows another. Figure 1.7 shows the two forms for specifying that Y follows X if, at the end of activity X, i is equal to 0. The diamond in the upper half of Figure 1.7 is the good old-fashioned *choice point* (or *decision point*) from flowchart notation. Each outgoing edge is labeled with a guard enclosed within square brackets. In general, any boolean-valued guard can appear as a condition, provided that all guards for a decision point are mutually exclusive. UML does not prescribe any syntax for the guard. (C-style syntax is employed in the figure.) The *bull's eye* in the diagram indicates the end of this workflow.

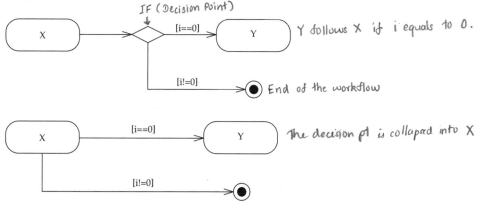

FIGURE 1.7   *Activity Y conditionally follows activity X.*

The upper and lower halves of Figure 1.7 have identical semantics. In the lower half, the decision point is *collapsed* into activity X. Decisions can also be nested, as shown in Figure 1.8. The first decision point in that figure could also be col-lapsed into activity X.

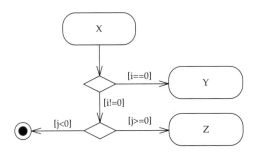

FIGURE 1.8 *Nested decision points.*

In some cases, you might want to specify that activity X is followed by many possible *instantiations* (or *invocations*) of activity Y. Although it is not an official part of the UML, the *star* notation shown in Figure 1.9 is a common syntactic extension. (One motivation for this notation is the collaboration diagram, which uses the star to indicate iteration.) You may also add a note stating the bounds of the iteration, as shown in Figure 1.9.

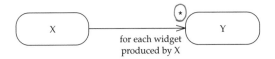

FIGURE 1.9 *Activity X is followed by multiple activity Y's.*

Until now, the activity diagrams have looked a lot like flowcharts. Unlike a flowchart, however, a UML activity diagram may specify parallelism (or, more generally, non-linear temporal orderings). In the top half of Figure 1.10, for example, activity X is followed by activities Y1 and Y2. Y1 and Y2 may happen in either order (or in parallel). Once Y1 and Y2 have both finished, then Z occurs. The dark bars in Figure 1.10 are *synchronization bars*:

- When multiple activities immediately follow a synchronization bar (as Y1 and Y2 follow the leftmost bar in the top half of Figure 1.10), those activities may occur in parallel.

- When multiple activities immediately precede a synchronization bar (as Y1 and Y2 precede the rightmost bar), they must all be completed before execution continues beyond that bar.

In some cases, only a subset of activities leading into a synchronization bar must finish before execution proceeds. To specify the minimum condition required for execution to pass the synchronization bar, you can add a guard to the bar (as shown in the bottom half of Figure 1.10). Z can occur after Y1 and either Y2 or Y3 have completed.

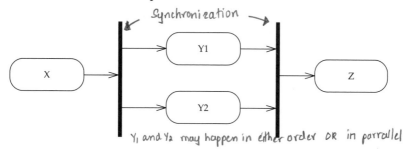

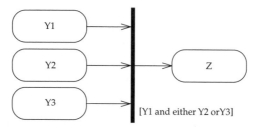

FIGURE 1.10 *Parallel activities.*

You can also show the states of objects between activities. The instance of the Thing class depicted in Figure 1.11, for example, is in the *completed* state after activity X finishes. The solid rectangle indicates either a class or an instance. The underlining in the rectangle indicates an instance (rather than a class). Following the colon is the name of the class of which this is an instance. (This syntax is covered in Chapter 2, "Class Diagramming Notation.") The object is attached to a transition between activities using a dependency (the dashed "stick arrow," also described in Chapter 2). The state of the object is listed within square brackets.

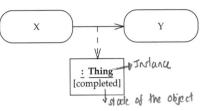

FIGURE 1.11 *Thing's state is completed after activity X.*

In some cases, you may want to represent communication between objects. Because activity diagrams are being used here to model requirements, communication at this level would typically be between the system and actor instances. (The communication among objects within the system is determined during design. It will be described by interaction diagrams, which are explained in Chapter 5, "Dynamic Diagramming Notation.")

In an activity diagram, communication between objects is modeled as events. The sender generates an event that is delivered to the receiver. This may represent the sending of an asynchronous event (or message or signal), meaning that the sender emits the message and continues executing, while the receiver at some point accepts and processes the message. Alternatively, it may model a synchronous procedure invocation, in which the sender (or caller) suspends its execution while the receiver (or callee) handles the event.

Events that are sent to and received from objects can be included in activity diagrams, as shown in Figure 1.12. The concave and convex pentagons indicate the receiving and sending of events, respectively. The pentagon is labeled with the event name being received or sent. In Figure 1.12, the *create havoc* event is being sent; then, the *havoc created* event is received. Note that the actual receipt of the event allows the transition to a concave pentagon. (If the event is received before that transition, it will be *posted* for subsequent receipt. If it has not yet been received when the transition is reached, the transition will not occur until the event is received.)

The object receiving a sent event or sending a received event can also be included, as shown in Figure 1.12. The *Create Havoc* event is being received by a Thing instance; that same instance is generating the *Havoc Created* event. As previously noted, when an activity diagram is used to model functional requirements, the objects that generate or receive events are typically actor objects.

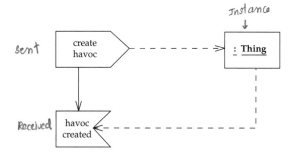

FIGURE 1.12 *Sending and receiving events.*

1.2.2   An Activity Diagram for Placing an Order

Recall the business use case diagram from Figure 1.3. That diagram contains four business use cases: Place Order, Cancel Order, Cancel Order Item, and Return Order Item. You can now introduce an activity diagram to describe the dynamics of each.

First consider placing an order. This use case consists of at least four distinct activities:

1. Entering the order, which involves taking information about the order and the payment method from the customer

2. Authorizing the purchase, which requires verification that the required funds can be obtained from the customer using the specified payment method

3. Allocating the order items from inventory

4. Shipping the order

Figure 1.13 depicts the resulting activity diagram. When placing an order, you must first enter the order. The solid dot points to the initial activity. That activity concludes in one of two ways: either the customer provides all of the required information and then tells the telephone agent to commit the order, or the customer decides to abort the order entry activity. In the former case, you must then attempt to authorize funds for the purchase; in the latter case, the use case (and, hence, the activity diagram) is completed.

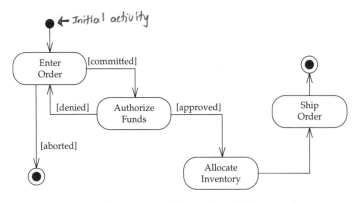

FIGURE 1.13 *A first activity diagram for placing an order.*

The activity for authorizing funds can finish with one of two results:

- *Denied*: If the authorization request is denied, you re-enter the Enter Order activity and give the customer a chance to alter the order. (The customer may remove items from the order, provide a different payment source, or simply abort the activity.)

- *Approved*: If the request for funds is approved, you proceed to the Allocate Inventory activity. This is where inventory for each order item is allocated. Once that activity is complete, the order is shipped.

Observe that one implication of the activity diagram in Figure 1.13 is that only complete orders are shipped. In other words, DryGoods.com will not ship partial orders.

Note

While activity diagrams bear similarities to state transition diagrams, they are somewhat different both in intent and semantics. In the state transition diagrams used in object-oriented design, for example, a transition from one state to another is enabled either by a specific condition arising, or by the receipt of a specific event. On the other hand, a transition between activities occurs when an activity finishes. What indicates that an activity has finished is not always precisely specified.

Furthermore, in object-oriented design, a state transition diagram depicts the states through which an object passes, and so entering a state implies that a specific pre-condition on that object holds. Conversely, an activity can be entered in different ways under different conditions.

In the activity diagram for placing an order, the Enter Order activity may either be entered when the customer first calls on the phone, in which case a new order is initiated, or when a credit authorization fails, in which case an existing order must be modified (or thrown away). If you were modeling the placement of an order using state machines, you would separate these two cases into two different states, because they have different entry conditions (meaning that the order is in different states). When using an activity diagram, however, you may elect to lump the two into a single activity, as in Figure 1.13. The description of that activity would then outline the different cases.

The activity diagram in Figure 1.13 describes what occurs during the Place Order use case in Figure 1.3. In other words, the activity diagram is a *refinement* of the use case. This kind of refinement is a relationship between a construct and a more detailed description of that same construct. The activity diagram in Figure 1.13 is a more detailed description of the Place Order use case in Figure 1.3.

You may want to make refinement relationships explicit in your UML diagrams. Refinements are represented in UML using a *directed dependency*. (As shown in Figure 1.11, the notation for a dependency is the dashed stick arrow.) The dependency is directed from the more refined to the less refined item and is stereotyped to indicate the specific type of refinement. UML defines the following refinement stereotypes:

- «trace» indicates a design (or development) refinement. During the development process, detail has been added to something. The two features represent the same concept at differing levels of detail.

- «refine» indicates any other kind of refinement, such as the refinement of an obvious design into a less obvious, but more efficient, one.

The refinement of the Place Order use case into an activity diagram is shown in Figure 1.14. Note that this particular refinement relationship is a *hyperlink* across two different diagrams (from an activity diagram to an element in a use case diagram). The inclusion of that refinement relationship makes that relationship explicit to reviewers of the model. It likewise allows those reviewers to trace from specific activity diagrams back to the use cases (and, hence, the functional requirements) that spawned them. In general, using these relationships throughout the development process allows reviewers to trace low-level design constructs back to features in the high-level design and from there back to analysis components.

What is the activity diagram for the Cancel Order Item use case? Canceling an item in an order requires the following steps:

1. Update that order item (or line item). This entails checking to see that the item is still pending and, if it is, changing its status to *canceled*. (If the item has been shipped or previously canceled, nothing more can be done.)

2. Credit the customer's account for that item. During the funds authorization phase when the order was entered, DryGoods.com either debited the customer's account or placed a hold on funds. That operation must now be negated.

3. Release the inventory request for that item.

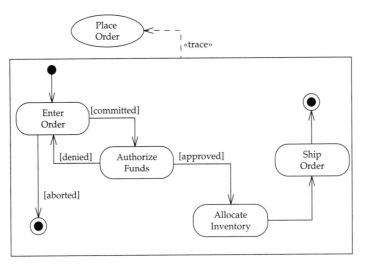

FIGURE 1.14 *The explicit representation of a design refinement.*

Furthermore, although step 1 must occur first, steps 2 and 3 can happen in either order (or in parallel). Figure 1.15 contains the activity diagram for the Cancel Order Item use case.

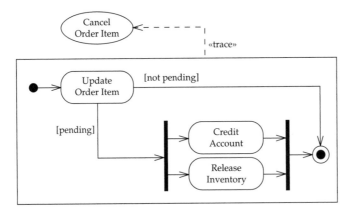

FIGURE 1.15 *The activity diagram for Cancel Order Item.*

Recall that there is a uses relationship between the Cancel Order and Cancel Order Item use cases (refer to Figure 1.3). This means that the Cancel Order use case subsumes the behavior of Cancel Order Item. Furthermore, when canceling an order, each of its items must be canceled. Therefore, the activity diagram for Cancel Order is the one shown in Figure 1.16. The Cancel Order activity in that diagram sets the order's status to *canceled*. Upon completion of that activity, each order item in the order is subsequently canceled.

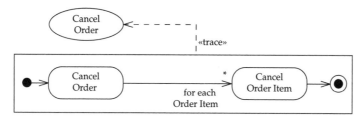

FIGURE 1.16   *The activity diagram for Cancel Order.*

Observe that the Cancel Order Item activity in Figure 1.16 refers to the *entire* process of canceling an order item, which is described by the activity diagram in Figure 1.15. You can again depict this as a refinement relationship; this time, however, a single activity is being expanded into a separate activity diagram, as shown in Figure 1.17. This illustration also depicts an explicit trace relationship from the Cancel Order Item activity to the Cancel Order Item use case. Therefore, the presence of an activity that corresponds to the Cancel Order Item use case represents the fact that the Cancel Order use case uses the Cancel Order Item use case.

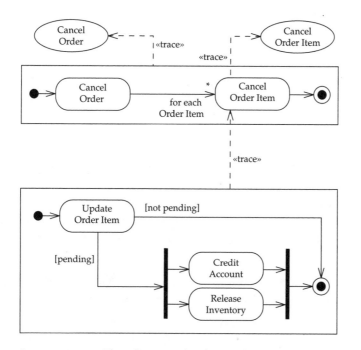

FIGURE 1.17   *The refinement of an activity by an activity diagram.*

The activity diagram for Return Order Item, the final use case in Figure 1.3, is given in Figure 1.18. Note that it is essentially the same as the diagram for Cancel Order Item in Figure 1.15 (except that the specific details of the Update Order Item activity are a little different, because it must alter the state of the item to returned rather than canceled).

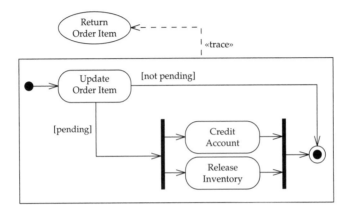

FIGURE 1.18 *The activity diagram for Return Order Item.*

At this point, you have an initial business functional model. The use case diagram in Figure 1.3 together with the refinements of those use cases as activity diagrams in Figures 1.14, 1.15, 1.17, and 1.18 form that model. You might choose to write textual descriptions of the activities in those activity diagrams at some point.

1.3 A System-Oriented Use Case Diagram

The use case diagram in Figure 1.3 is a business-oriented view, because it considers the system from the point of view of the ultimate user: the Catalog Customer. In some cases, however, you may choose to develop a more *system-oriented* (or architecture-oriented) use case diagram. Working with the environment for the DryGoods.com system, for example, results in the following actors:

- *Telephone Agents*: This class is implemented as a graphical user interface, which is used by the Telephone Agents when entering orders.

- *Credit Authorization Agencies*: These agencies are systems outside the company that it must contact to obtain funds from (and credit funds to) a customer's account.

- *A Product Warehouse System*: This is a legacy system within the company that handles inventory control (including obtaining items from suppliers).

- *A Shipping System*: This legacy system handles the packaging and shipping of orders to customers.

In the system-oriented use case diagram, each of these will be an actor. Furthermore, the Catalog Customer actor from Figure 1.3 is no longer required, because that actor communicates only with the Telephone Agent and Shipping System actors (by telephone and through the mail, respectively) and, therefore, is invisible to the system.

Once again use cases can be obtained by considering the interactions between the actors and the system. The interactions involving a Telephone Agent are

- *Enter Order:* Agents tell the system to enter a catalog order.

- *Cancel Order*: Agents tell the system to cancel an order.

- *Cancel Order Item*: Agents tell the system to cancel an order item (that is, a line item in an order).

- *Queries*: Agents may submit various queries that will be ignored here for the sake of brevity. (You would include these in a real development project.)

The Credit Authorization Agencies' interactions are

- *Authorize Purchase*: The system asks a credit agency to authorize a purchase against a credit or debit card.

- *Credit Account*: The system asks a credit agency to credit an account (when an item is returned or any part of an order is canceled).

The interactions with a Product Warehouse are

- *Request Inventory*: The system asks the warehouse to allocate an item (in an order) from inventory.

- *Cancel Inventory Request*: The system asks the warehouse to cancel a pending allocation request.

- *Return Inventory*: The system tells the warehouse to return items to inventory.

- *Query Product Availability*: The system asks the warehouse about product availability (which will be ignored here).

- *Receive Inventory*: The warehouse tells the system when a requested allocation is available.

The interactions with the Shipping System are

- *Ship Order*: The system asks the Shipping System to ship an order to the customer.

- *Return Order Item*: The Shipping System informs the system that an item in an order has been returned by the customer.

These actors and use cases produce the more system-oriented use case diagram shown in Figure 1.19.

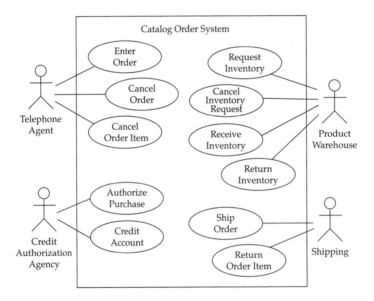

FIGURE 1.19 *A refined use case diagram.*

Many of the use cases in Figure 1.19 are very similar in name and behavior to activities in the earlier activity diagrams. This is hardly surprising, because the activity diagrams and the system-oriented use case diagram are refinements of the original business-level use case diagram. In other words, you can refine a use case diagram in either of two distinct ways:

- You can produce activity diagrams for each of its use case diagrams.

- You can develop a more detailed use case diagram. (Mostly used)

Which approach is better? Many projects employ the latter approach. That is, they first identify some course-grained use cases, and then they attempt to refine each into a set of smaller constituent use cases. Nonetheless, activity diagrams are often preferable vehicles of refinement for a combination of at least two reasons:

- You can depict the refinement explicitly (using a «trace» dependency).

- You can show the temporal sequencing of steps in the use case.

To illustrate these advantages, suppose you want to show the relationship between the business-level Place Order use case and the system-level use cases to which it was refined: Enter Order, Authorize Purchase, Request Inventory, Receive Inventory, and Ship Order. You could employ «uses» relationships, as shown in Figure 1.20. Place Order uses each of the five system-level use cases. There are at least three problems with this approach:

- The «uses» relationship is misused, because this is refinement rather than a «uses» relationship.

- The fact that this is refinement is not apparent.

- The temporal sequencing of the five system-level use cases is not specified.

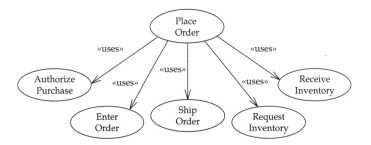

FIGURE 1.20 *Depicting use case refinement with «uses».*

Note that introducing a special aggregation relationship among use cases (whereby Place Order is the *whole* whose parts are the five system-level use cases) has the same three disadvantages.

You can solve the first two problems by replacing the «uses» relationship with a «trace» relationship, as shown in Figure 1.21. Unfortunately, the third problem still exists, because you have not depicted the temporal order of the five system-level use cases.

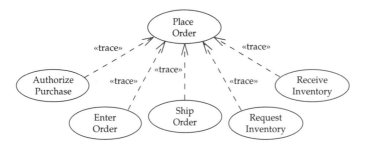

FIGURE 1.21 *Depicting use case refinement with «trace».*

Employing activity diagrams as refinements of use cases (as outlined in the preceding section, "An Activity Diagram for Placing an Order") addresses all three problems. For example, you might expand the business-level use case diagram to include the system-oriented actors, as shown in Figure 1.22. You can then refine each use case into activity diagrams.

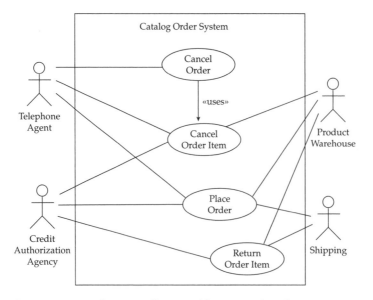

FIGURE 1.22 *A use case diagram with system-oriented actors.*

You can also extend your activity diagrams to show exactly how the actors interact with the system. To do this, you depict the generation and receipt of events to and from actor instances. In Figure 1.23, for example, the Allocate Inventory activity is expanded into its own activity diagram. The lower-level diagram depicts the events received by Request Inventory and Receive Inventory from the Product Warehouse legacy system. Note that these events are *logical* events that can be implemented in various ways.

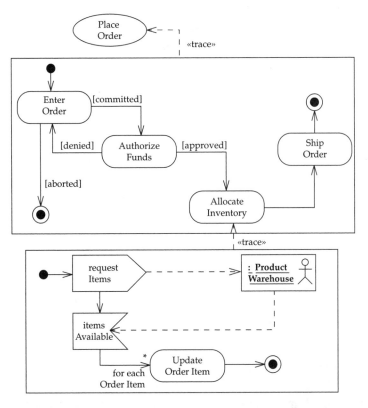

FIGURE 1.23 *Asking the Product Warehouse actor to allocate inventory.*

You can extend the activity diagrams to show exactly who carries out what activities. In Figure 1.24, for example, the activity diagram for Place Order is divided into *swimlanes* (delineated by the lighter lines). Each swimlane corresponds to a subsystem, and each activity in a swimlane is handled by the subsystem whose name appears in that swimlane (e.g., Finance).

> **Note**
>
> When you use an activity diagram to model the dynamics of each use case, you create several small activity diagrams that, considered together, describe the overall behavior of the system. If you choose to employ only a use case diagram instead (in which you break up the original use cases into smaller use cases), you have one large, complicated diagram. A model with many small activity diagrams (rather than one huge use case diagram) is probably easier to understand.
>
> Creating and maintaining so many diagrams, however, may seem daunting to the typical developer. Some CASE tools assist with this process. (For example, if you rename something, many CASE tools modify the name everywhere.) If you don't use a CASE tool, you must take care to carefully organize your diagrams so that you minimize redundancy.

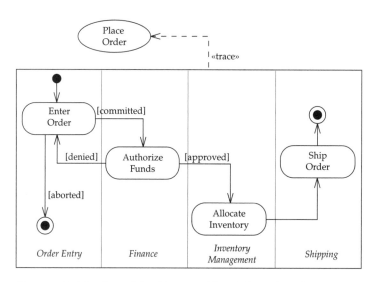

FIGURE 1.24 *An activity diagram with swimlanes for subsystems.*

1.4   The Dangers of Going Too Far

An objection to use cases is that they force you into a functional decomposition (rather than an object-oriented decomposition) of a problem. The alternative—responsibility-driven design—concentrates first on classes and their responsibilities, and then works upward, using scenarios to validate the class model.

However, for large, complex systems, developing a thorough understanding of the functional requirements is imperative. Proceeding from individual object responsibilities can lead to a situation in which no one can really explain what the system is supposed to do. (For other development efforts, such as designing a class library or a small system, starting with object responsibilities may be the preferred approach.)

Use case diagrams and activity diagrams provide the notation for a static and dynamic view of functional requirements. The danger, of course, is that you may go too far in your functional decomposition. As Figure 1.23 illustrates, you can take any activity in an activity diagram and refine it into a separate activity diagram. You could, therefore, continue this refinement process until you have a *structured* design centered on procedures rather than objects.

Use case diagrams and activity diagrams are employed in this chapter only to model basic functional requirements. Recall that a use case defines how an actor uses the system; it therefore should always model a function that makes sense to an actor. (If it doesn't, then the use case is too fine-grained, describing a function internal to the system.)

Likewise, an activity diagram should be used to describe general dynamic properties of a use case (or of an activity in another activity diagram) and *not* to describe invocations of subroutines (or related decompositions). Furthermore, a use case or activity should *not* map to a class in your class diagram. (If it does, then you have classes that describe functions rather than objects.)

When an activity diagram depicts the dynamics of a use case, it can also be used to identify the scenarios and interaction diagrams for that use case. The intuition is that each path through the activity diagram constitutes one scenario. This topic is addressed in Chapter 6.

CHAPTER 2

Class Diagramming Notation

Whereas Chapter 1, "System Functional Models," describes how to model functional requirements using use case diagrams and activity diagrams, this chapter focuses on class diagrams. Chapter 3, "Developing Class Diagrams," continues the discussion by concentrating on approaches for devising a class diagram.

A class diagram is a static model that defines the system's legal object configurations. Any objects that exist during the system's execution must be instances of classes in the class diagram, and any relationships between those objects must be instances of associations between those objects' classes. A class diagram, therefore, is a key component of an object-oriented design.

UML offers a very rich class-diagramming notation. It provides notation for basic constructs, such as classes and class relationships, and for a few more esoteric features. This chapter describes the concepts and accompanying UML notation for the basic and uncommon features, as follows:

- *Basic class concepts and notation*: The concepts and notation for class, object, attribute, and method are defined.

- *Links and associations*: The concepts of object links and class associations are explained. The notation for links, associations, and association cardinality constraints is presented. The differences between attributes and associations are examined.

- *Uncommon association notation*: Some UML association notation, not often included in other methods, is explained. This includes notation for role names, qualifiers, and association classes.

- *Aggregation*: The aggregation notation is presented. Possible semantics for aggregation are explained. The notation and semantics of composition are defined.

- *Class specialization*: The concepts of class specialization, inheritance, type promotion, and polymorphism are explained. The class specialization notation is presented.

- *Dependencies*: The concept and uses of a dependency are explained. Both the dependency notation and examples of some UML dependency stereotypes are presented.

- *Notes*: The notation for a note is illustrated.

- *Extension mechanisms*: The mechanisms for extending the UML notation—properties, constraints, and stereotypes—are explained. Examples of each are presented.

- *A class diagram for order processing*: A partial class diagram for the DryGoods.com system is offered.

When it is possible, the examples in this chapter are drawn from the DryGoods.com example that first appeared in Chapter 1. In some cases, UML examples are augmented with fragments of implementation, all of which are in Java. (A detailed discussion of Java is beyond the scope of this book. For more information, see *The Java Programming Language* by Ken Arnold and James Gosling.)

Note

Some of the notation in this chapter also applies to other diagrams. Dependencies, notes, and extension mechanisms can be introduced in any UML diagram. An example is trace relationships, which are dependencies that employ an extension mechanism (stereotyping). They were used in use case and activity diagrams in Chapter 1.

2.1 Basic Class Concepts and Notation

The most fundamental concepts of object-oriented design and programming are classes and objects. The classes in a class diagram define what objects may exist as a system executes. Each class defines the state (or data) and behavior (or functions) its instances will have. Class definitions exist in the implementation source code. So, in that sense, a class diagram defines the overall static structure of a system.

An object is an instance of a class and serves as a node in an object diagram. Objects in a program are created as the program executes. Therefore, a UML object diagram depicts a set of objects at some specific moment in time. Whereas a class diagram defines all legal system configurations, an object diagram describes one particular configuration.

2.1.1 Classes and Objects

The basic nodes in class and object diagrams are the class and object, respectively:

- A *class* defines a collection of similar instances. It exists at compilation time and serves as a type. It defines the interface and implementation of its instances.

- An *object* is a particular instance of a class. Each object represents a particular instance of something in the problem or solution domain and is created as needed.

In the DryGoods.com system, for example, the Order class defines the features that all orders have, whereas an Order object describes a specific order, such as the order placed by John Smith at 2:03 p.m. last Tuesday.

Note

Some writers and developers use the term object to describe both classes and instances. The standard UML definition of object is used in this book: The UML Notation Guide states, "An object represents a particular instance of a class" (46).

An object can represent several kinds of concepts. It might represent a tangible (physical) entity, such as an automobile or a credit card scanner. It might represent a role being played, such as John Smith in the role of a customer (that is, as an instance of a Customer class). An object might also represent an organization unit, an interaction, and so forth.

Some objects represent events. Events are typically treated as operations, but sometimes an event must be an object because it must be remembered. Sometimes an event describing a request, for instance, must remain pending until the required resources are available to fulfill the request. A pick-up request in an elevator control system is one example. Alternatively, it may be an event about which a *permanent* record must be maintained, such as a deposit to a bank account.

Generally an object must have three properties:

- *Identity*: The object has some (perhaps implicit) notion of identity. Imagine holding a *handle* to the object. The handle allows you to distinguish this object from all others. (An explicit identity is sometimes introduced in the form of a *key* for the object.)

- *State*: An object should maintain data about itself beyond just its identity.

- *Behavior*: An object should be able to perform actions. That is, an object responds to requests or acts independently in some way.

Sometimes, you may choose to relax these guidelines. In some cases, for instance, you may want to model an algorithm as a class, which requires that you relax the state (and perhaps the identity) rule. One such case is when you may have different implementations of an algorithm that have different time and space trade-offs. You might choose to define each implementation as a class. Modeling algorithms as classes is the basic idea behind the Strategy design pattern (Gamma et al. 1995, 315–323).

Note

A design pattern is a way of solving a small problem. The problem and the pattern that solves it are independent of any particular problem domain. So, a design pattern strives to reuse general knowledge rather than domain-specific code.

The Strategy pattern, for example, is a solution to situations with varying implementations of an algorithm. Design patterns are discussed in Chapter 9, "Reuse: Libraries, Frameworks, Components, and Patterns."

A class represents an abstraction in the problem or solution domain. For DryGoods.com, the Order class defines the intuitive notion of a catalog order, a particular concept in the DryGoods.com problem domain. It defines that abstraction in terms of the state and behavior each catalog order would have. An example of a catalog order's state and behavior are its order number and the cancellation semantics, respectively.

A class defines the "look" of its instances. Technically, it defines both a public interface and an underlying implementation for those instances. It therefore defines both a *type* (in terms of a public interface) and an *implementation of that type*. The Order class defines a public interface for *cancel* and *commit* operations. This interface is a type in the sense that it describes what a client can do with an Order instance.

> **Note**
>
> A class need not provide an implementation of its type. You can define a class that contains only abstract methods. Such a method defines an interface but no implementation. Section 2.5.4, "Abstract Methods and Classes," addresses this subject.

Figure 2.1 depicts this dichotomy between an object's public interface (the outer "onion skin" visible to other objects) and its *hidden middle* (the part of the object that is not visible to the outside world and contains the implementation of the object's state and behavior). Although this type of object depiction is not part of UML, it is occasionally employed in this book to illustrate fundamental concepts.

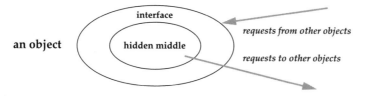

FIGURE 2.1 *The interface versus the implementation of an object.*

The UML notation for class and object are shown in Figure 2.2 and Figure 2.3. Both are represented as rectangles. A class rectangle includes the class name. An object may include the object name, the class name (following a colon), or both; the underlining indicates that the rectangle represents an object (rather than a class).

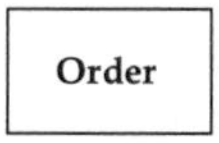

Order

FIGURE 2.2 *UML notation for an Order class.*

FIGURE 2.3 *UML notation for Order objects.*

2.1.2 Attributes and Methods

The state of an object includes its attribute values. An *attribute* is an instance variable with *value semantics* (rather than *reference semantics*).

A precise characterization of value semantics is given later in this chapter, during the discussion of associations (see Section 2.2.5, "Value Versus Reference Semantics"). For now, suffice it to say that an attribute's value is either a *primitive* type (such as a character or an integer) or a reference to an object that behaves as if it were a primitive type

An example in the DryGoods.com system is an Order's order number and total price. A value for total price is just a floating-point number (for example, 104.79), whereas an order number is an integer (for example, 537466). Each Order instance will have places to store the two values.

An attribute appears in the second compartment of a class, as shown in Figure 2.4. The type and/or the default value may also appear; the syntax is

```
<attribute-name> : <type> = <default-value>
```

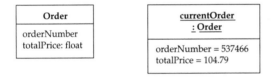

FIGURE 2.4 *UML notation for attributes.*

An instance in an object diagram may specify the values for some or all of its attributes, as also shown in Figure 2.4.

Attributes typically are implemented as *instance variables* in classes. For example, the Java implementation of the Order class in Figure 2.4 is

```
class Order {
   private int orderNumber;
   private float totalPrice;
   }
```

The `orderNumber` and `totalPrice` attributes are called *fields* in Java, *data members* in C++, and *instance variables* in Smalltalk. (These fields are declared with private access, which will be explained in Section 2.1.3, "Encapsulation.") Each Order instance has values for these fields, as depicted in Figure 2.5.

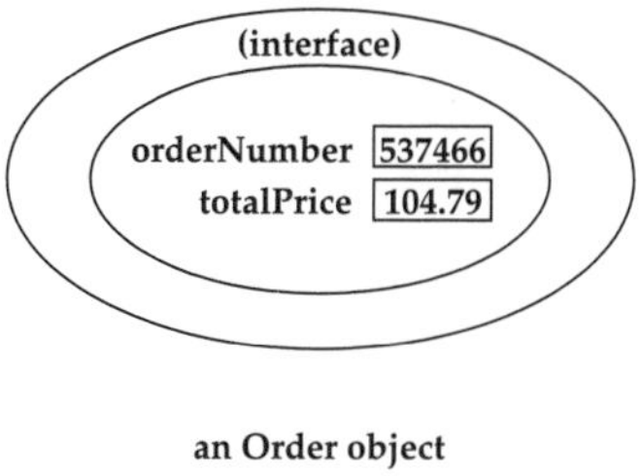

an Order object

FIGURE 2.5   *Attribute values in an Order object.*

An Order instance may also perform operations, such as `cancel`, `commit`, and `removeLineItem`. In other words, an *operation* (*method* in Java, *member function* in C++) is something you can ask an instance to do.

Operations are listed in the third compartment of the class, as shown in Figure 2.6. You may also specify the parameter types within the parentheses following the method name, as well as the return type following a colon (after the parentheses), as illustrated by the declaration of `removeLineItem`. The `removeLineItem` method takes an `int`-valued `itemNumber` (the item number of the line item to be removed) and returns a `boolean` (`true` if the item was deleted successfully, `false` otherwise).

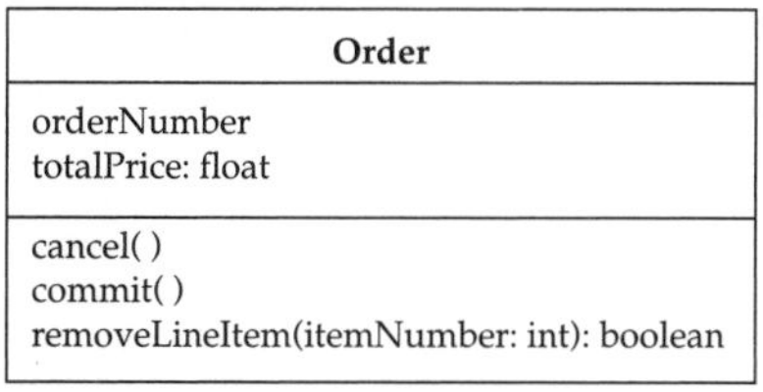

FIGURE 2.6   *UML notation for operations.*

Specifying `in`, `out`, or `inout` (before the parameter name) indicates a parameter's *direction*. (The default is `in`.)

The expanded Java definition of the Order class is

```
class Order {
   private int orderNumber;
   private float totalPrice;
   public void cancel() {
    /* implementation omitted here */
   }
   public void commit() {
    /* implementation omitted here */
   }
 }
```

Note that early in the analysis and design process, you may elect to postpone decisions about the types of attributes and the parameter types and return types of methods. These can all be omitted in your initial class diagrams and then added later in the development process.

2.1.3   Encapsulation

Observe that the fields in the preceding Java code are defined as private, whereas the methods have public access. A private field or method in Java (and in C++), is visible only within that class, whereas a public field or method is visible to everyone. (Other access options are explained in a list later in this section.) Assigning private access to fields is an example of *encapsulation*, which in turn is a mechanism to achieve *information hiding*. Information hiding entails the hiding of data or code from external view. To encapsulate something is to build a wall around it and hide it.

In the Order example, only the method interfaces are publicly visible. Both the method and attribute *implementations* are hidden, as shown in Figure 2.7. The shaded area in the figure is the *hidden middle* discussed in Section 2.1.1, "Classes and Objects."

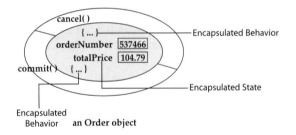

FIGURE 2.7 *Encapsulated state and behavior.*

Encapsulation offers several important benefits, including the following:

- *You can modify the internal details of a class without affecting other classes.* Obviously, changing the hidden middle doesn't affect clients of the object, and these internal details typically change more frequently than the external protocols. For example, changing an Order so that it computes its total price from its Line Items (rather *storing* its total price in a field) affects nothing outside the Order class. (Note that in C++, however, the clients of a class must be recompiled if the class header file changes in any way—even if the public interface of that class doesn't change.)

- *You can use and reuse an abstraction without regard to its implementation.* A client can use the Order's interface without inspecting its implementation. For example, you don't need to understand the internal cancellation details to cancel an Order; you only need to know to call *cancel*.

- *You can prevent "accidental" updates.* Because encapsulated data is hidden, a client must access that data through a function interface. If you don't provide such an interface, the client can't alter the data at all. If you offer an interface, you can implement the function so that it guarantees that the fields aren't changed at the wrong time.

On the other hand, data that is encapsulated must be accessed through a method call; therefore, you incur a performance penalty. This is an example of the trade-off between flexibility and performance.

UML provides special graphical notation to indicate the intended access of attributes and operations. A leading plus sign (+), minus sign (–), or pound sign (#) indicates public, private, or protected access, respectively. A description of the different levels of access follows:

- *Public access*: The item is accessible anywhere. This definition is true for both Java and C++.

- *Private access*: Members in C++ are accessible by the class and its *friends*. (One class can declare another as its friend.) Java has no friend relationship among classes; so, a private member is accessible only in the class.

- *Protected access*: Members in C++ are accessible by the class and its subclasses. In Java, they are accessible by classes in the same package and by subclasses everywhere. (A package is a grouping of classes.) Subclasses are described in Section 2.5, "Class Specialization."

- *Package access*: In Java, an item is accessible only from classes in the same package. C++ has no analogous access permission, and UML provides no special notation for package access.

Figure 2.8 contains an example. You can also specify the access as a textual property, as also depicted in Figure 2.8.

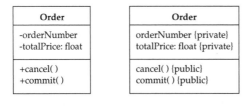

FIGURE 2.8 *UML notation for access control.*

To avoid adding explicit graphical symbols or textual properties to define the access permissions on every attribute and method, *reasonable assumptions* are often used as the defaults. Because attributes are typically private, you can normally assume that all attributes are private unless otherwise noted. Likewise, because most methods are public you can assume methods are public unless otherwise indicated.

2.1.4 Class Attributes and Methods

So far in this chapter, the attributes and methods described have been *instance* properties. For example, each Order object has its own order number and total price. Likewise, when you want to invoke the `cancel` or `commit` method, you must invoke it on an Order instance. (In other words, you *tell an Order to cancel or commit itself*.) Sometimes, however, you must define attributes and methods of a *class* rather than of its individual instances.

Suppose you must generate a unique order number for each Order. A simple solution is to keep a running count of the number of orders that have been created and to use that count as an Order's order number. (Hence, the first Order instance created is assigned order number 1, the second is given order number 2, and so on.)

Where do you define the attribute that keeps a count of the Order instances already created? The logical location is the Order class. This is not a property of Order instances, however, because it is not convenient to store this count in each individual instance. This is a property of the Order *class*, where you want to define a single *class* variable.

Likewise, suppose you define a method that returns the number of Orders that have been created. This method is a *class* method, in that you would like to be able to invoke it on the class, regardless of whether any instances of the class exist. A class attribute or method is underlined, as shown in Figure 2.9.

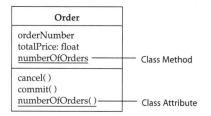

FIGURE 2.9 *UML notation for class attributes and methods.*

Class members are implemented in Java and C++ as static members. The following Java code implements the class members in Figure 2.9:

```
class Order {
   private static int numberOfOrders;
   // ...
   public static int numberOfOrders() {
    return numberOfOrders;
   }
   // ...
   }
```

This means that there will be a *single* copy of the numberOfOrders field that is shared by all Order instances. This field belongs to the Order class and will exist before any Order instances are created. Likewise, the numberOfOrders method belongs to the class and can be invoked even if no Order instances exist.

2.1.5 Notation for Method Categories and Class Compartments

Some designers like to specify if a method changes the state of the instance where it is invoked. For example, the following are four categories based on the general effect of the method:

- *Constructor*: Initializes the instance. (It is invoked only when an instance is created.)

- *Query*: Returns a value but does not change the state of the instance.

- *Update*: Carries out some action that may change the state of the instance.

- *Destructor*: Handles any cleanup required by the deletion of an instance. (It is invoked only when an instance is deleted.)

Each method can be categorized by using either a property or a stereotyped list as shown in Figure 2.10. (Properties and stereotypes are explained in detail in Section 2.8, "Extension Mechanisms.") Note that these category names are not specified by UML; designers can use any categorization and any category names.

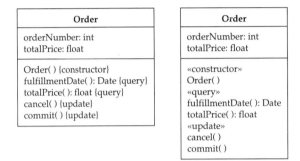

F IGURE 2.10 *Depicting the purpose of a method.*

UML permits the introduction of user-defined class compartments. The first three compartments are always the class name, attributes, and methods (in that order). Designers may introduce additional compartments to describe other properties of the class (such as its requirements, its basic responsibilities, and so forth). The only stipulation is that the compartment be headed by an explanation of its purpose. Figure 2.11 contains an example.

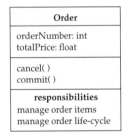

F IGURE 2.11 *Defining additional class compartments.*

2.1.6   Actors as Classes

As noted in Chapter 1, external agents are called *actors* in UML. They interact with the system, but are not a part of the system itself. In that sense, they are *black boxes* to the system because their interactions with the system are important, but their internal implementations are irrelevant. Such actors include human users, client programs, external systems, and external devices. They are included in the class diagram so the way that they interact with the objects in the system can be modeled.

UML treats actors as special *stereotyped* classes. A stereotype of a class is like a normal class, but it has special semantics. (See Section 2.8.5, "Stereotypes," later in this chapter.) Like a normal class, an actor class can have instances (specific instances of client programs, devices, and so forth); its instances can communicate with objects in the system. Unlike a normal class, however, an actor class is a black box because you don't have to implement it or understand its internal details.

The normal notation for a stereotype is to place the name of the stereotype within guillemets (which are similar to double angle brackets). In the case of the actor class stereotype, however, UML provides a special graphical adornment: the stick figure. This adornment takes the place of the «actor» string in the class. Both forms are illustrated in Figure 2.12 for the Telephone Agent actor in DryGoods.com. (This particular actor will be implemented as the user interface used by the human telephone agents.)

FIGURE 2.12 *The Telephone Agent actor class.*

Note

UML permits CASE tools, individual designers, and development organizations to define additional graphical symbols for different types of actors. Such a user-defined symbol is an adornment, which is described in Section 2.8.2, "Adornments." Some CASE tools offer additional actor adornments. Furthermore, in UML Extensions for Business Modeling, UML includes a set of other actor symbols for business process modeling (4).

2.2 Links and Associations

Elements in class and object diagrams are not "islands." They can be related to one another. An object diagram describes a system configuration at one point in time. At that temporal moment, each object may be linked to other objects, which means that the object refers to and perhaps communicates with those other objects. Such links in an object diagram, therefore, depict the momentary connectivity among instances.

A class in a class diagram can likewise be related to other classes in the class diagram. Such an association between classes represents a structural property among the classes where the instances of one class may be linked to the instances of another. An association between the Order and Customer classes, for example, indicates that an Order instance and a Customer instance may be linked.

An association may have an intuitive meaning in the problem domain. The association between Order and Customer, for instance, might suggest the notion of a Customer placing or owning an Order. An association also has an effect on the design and implementation of a system, because it defines which objects must be visible to other objects.

2.2.1   Links Between Objects

An object's state information includes its attribute values (refer to Section 2.1.2, "Attributes and Methods") and its links to other objects. In the DryGoods.com system, for example, an Order's state information includes a link to its Customer object. The UML depiction of that link is illustrated by Figure 2.13. The link is an undirected edge between the two objects. It has an optional name, places, but that name has no semantic content. (That is, the link would mean the same thing and would be implemented in the same way if the name were omitted.) It also has an optional "scroll bar" arrow that indicates which way to read the name (*John Smith places current order*, rather than vice versa). Therefore, like the name, the arrow has no semantic value.

FIGURE 2.13 *A link between an Order and its Customer.*

The link from an Order object to its Customer instance allows the Order to "talk to" its Customer by invoking methods in the Customer object's interface. This link is implemented as an object *reference* or *pointer*, as shown in Figure 2.14. The Order object will hold a pointer (or reference) to its Customer object in either a local variable or instance variable within the Order object. The Order object can then invoke methods on the object indicated by that pointer.

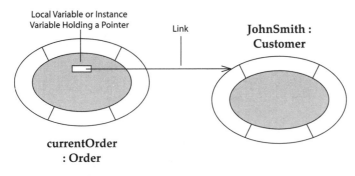

FIGURE 2.14   *Another view of a link between an Order and its Customer.*

An object's links to other objects may change at execution time. For example, a Customer object adds a link to its Order instance when that instance is created. Furthermore, one object, X, can obtain a link (that is, a reference or pointer) to another object, Y, in several ways:

- X may store Y's reference in a field (instance variable) inside X.

- X may look up Y's reference in a global variable (or in a public class variable of some class).

- X may call a method in another object, Z, and receive Y's reference as a return value.

- Object Z may call a method in X and pass Y's reference as a parameter.

These are all links from X to Y in an object diagram (and would require an association from X's class to Y's class, which is described in the following section).

2.2.2   Associations Between Classes

An association is a relationship between classes in a class diagram. Figure 2.15 illustrates an association between the Order and Customer classes. A business analyst might view an association as a logical relationship between classes (or entities), whereas a software designer uses an association to define the dependencies between classes (or types) in the implementation.

A link between objects is an instance of an association between classes. Therefore, any link in an object diagram must be derived from an association in the class diagram. The link in Figure 2.13 is an instance of the association in Figure 2.15. The diagrammatic conventions for links and associations are the same, except that the name of a link is underlined (because it is an instance), and an association includes cardinality constraints on its ends (e.g., the asterisk [*] in Figure 2.15, which indicates that a Customer may have any number of Orders).

FIGURE 2.15 *An association between the Order and Customer classes.*

Following are the UML conventions for cardinality constraints:

- If the end of an association is unadorned, the cardinality is unspecified.

- A non-negative integer (for example, *1*) indicates that specific value.

- An asterisk (*) means many.

- A range is denoted using two ellipsis points (..). Hence, *1..* indicates *one or more*.

- An asterisk (*) alone is shorthand for *0..* (that is, zero or more).

- Commas separate discrete values. For example, *3, 6* means 3 or 6.

Note

The earliest versions of UML used an unstated cardinality constraint as shorthand for a cardinality constraint of 1 (rather than indicating that the cardinality is unspecified). Some projects and books still use this convention (Harmon and Watson 1988, 170). If you intend for an unstated constraint to be interpreted as a specific value, such as 1, be careful to document this assumption explicitly.

Figure 2.15 contains an example of a one-to-many association. An Order is related to one Customer, whereas a Customer may be related to any number of Orders. Figure 2.16 contains an example of a one-to-one relationship between a Catalog Item (a listing in a catalog) and a Product (the commodity behind that listing). It also illustrates one possible object diagram for that association. The model fragment in Figure 2.17 shows a one-to-optional association and a corresponding object diagram. A Credit Authorization object is tied to one Order, but an Order may or may not have a Credit Authorization, depending on whether it has been funded. (Assume the Customer is using one credit or debit card per Order.)

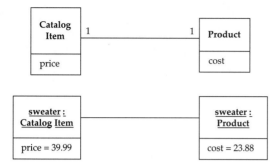

FIGURE 2.16 *A one-to-one association and one of its links.*

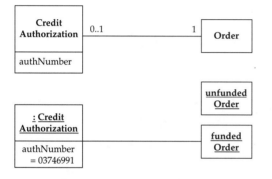

FIGURE 2.17 *An optional-to-one association and one of its links.*

The association examples up to this point have been undirected edges. Recall that an association defines the dependencies among classes. Figure 2.16 is unclear about whether a Catalog Item holds a reference to its Product (meaning that Catalog Item depends on Product), a Product holds a reference to its Catalog Item, or both. You can show the direction of visibility of an association explicitly by adding a *stick arrow* to either or both ends. In Figure 2.18, for example, the Catalog Item class can *see* the Product class but not vice versa. This implies that the links of that association are also so directed, as shown in the lower half of the figure.

Implementing an association in one direction only is preferred when possible (rather than also having a Product object hold a reference to its Catalog Item, for example). One reason for this is that maintaining consistency is a problem: creating a link in one direction may also require creating one in the opposite direction. A bigger reason is the goal of reducing *coupling*. Consider Figure 2.18 again. If the public interface of the Product class changes, you may have to modify code in the Catalog Item class (specifically, the code that calls methods in Product). If the public interface of the Catalog Item class changes, however, you know that the Product class will not be affected. The Product class is unaware of the existence of Catalog Items.

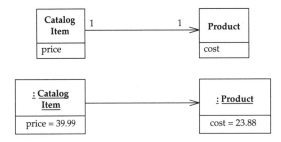

FIGURE 2.18 *Adding the direction of visibility to an association and its links.*

Suppose you have to implement the association between Catalog Item and Product in both directions. You want the relationship to be symmetric (at the instance level); if a Catalog Item object refers to a Product instance, then that Product instance refers to that same Catalog Item instance. (That is, the instances point to each other.) You can specify this using a constraint, as shown in the upper half of Figure 2.19. The constraint (in curly braces) specifies that the two associations are symmetric. (See Section 2.8.4, "Constraints," for more information.) A popular stylistic convention, however, is to use a double-headed association to indicate symmetry; by that convention, the upper and lower halves of Figure 2.19 have equivalent semantics.

What are the visibility assumptions for an undirected association, such as the one in Figure 2.16? UML permits the designer to apply either of two meanings to such an association: Either the visibility indications are deferred (and will be added later in the development process), or the association is shorthand for the double-headed arrow shown in the lower half of Figure 2.19. The former meaning is employed in this book. This permits the specification of associations without being certain in what directions those associations must be implemented. (In fact, this sort of approach—starting with a simple model and adding detail as necessary—is often an effective way to develop all aspects of a class diagram.)

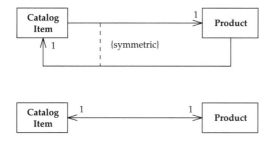

FIGURE 2.19 *Two ways of indicating symmetry.*

2.2.3   Association Implementations

Suppose the association between Order and Customer described in Figure 2.15 must be implemented in both directions. An Order instance holds a reference to a single Customer instance. A standard implementation of this is to define an instance variable in the Order class that will hold that reference. The Java code for this is

```
class Order {
   private Customer recipient;
   // ...
   }
```

The recipient field is of Customer type, meaning that you can store a reference to a Customer instance in that field. Figure 2.20 depicts an Order instance with such a reference. You can access that Customer instance using the contents of that field. For example, suppose the Customer class defines a name method that returns the customer's name as a String. The implementation of a customerName method in the Order class (to return the name of the customer who placed this order) might be

```
class Order {
   private Customer recipient;
   // ...
   public String customerName() {
     return recipient.name();
   }
   // ...
   }
```

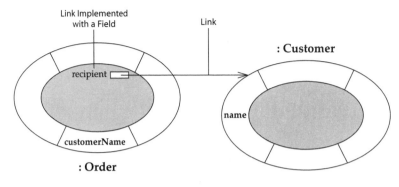

FIGURE 2.20 *Implementing a link with a field.*

The customerName method returns the result of calling the name method in this Order's Customer object. It accesses that object using the reference stored in the recipient field. Specifically, the call uses the *dot notation* where the items before and after the dot are who and what, respectively. The *who* in this case is the Customer object whose reference is stored in the recipient field (and the *what* is that object's name method).

What about a Customer's references to Orders? In general, a Customer may have many Orders. The standard in-memory idiom for this is a *container*, such as a linked list. A Customer object holds a reference to some kind of linked list object. That list object encapsulates a list of pointers (or references) to the Customer's Order instances. Figure 2.21 depicts a possible object diagram. Note that the list in Figure 2.21 is an object and, therefore, will have behavior. In particular, the list provides methods for adding and removing an Order instance to and from the list.

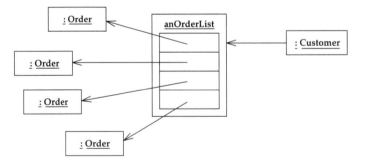

FIGURE 2.21 *An implementation of Customer's references to its Orders.*

While an Order's link to its Customer is probably permanent (meaning that an Order will always hold a reference to its Customer object), such permanence is not required. In some cases, one object may hold a reference to another temporarily, such as when that object receives that reference as a parameter or holds it in a local variable.

2.2.4 Ternary and Reflexive Associations

The degree of all of the associations described until now is two, meaning that each relates two classes. UML permits the specification of associations of any degree, however. The notation for associations of degree three or greater is a diamond with "legs" to all classes that participate in the association, as depicted in Figure 2.22.

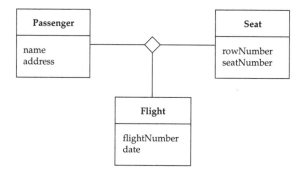

FIGURE 2.22 *An example of a ternary association.*

While ternary (and larger) associations are permitted in UML, you should normally try to avoid them during design. One reason is based on human cognition: Such associations are not intuitive and are somewhat difficult to describe. In a ternary association, for instance, there are six cardinality constraints. What is the best means to specify those constraints?

Another problem with ternary associations is that they have no standard implementation idioms. Binary associations have idioms, such as the containers (lists) described above, but how would you implement the association in Figure 2.22? If the association is implemented as a class (where each instance of the class is a link), why not simply introduce that class in the design? In Figure 2.23, for example, the ternary association in Figure 2.22 has been transformed into the Seat Assignment class. An instance of this class represents a ternary link between a Passenger, Seat, and Flight instance.

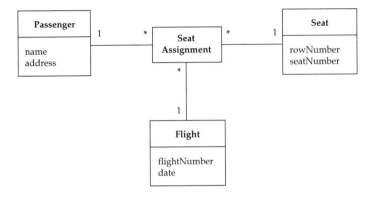

FIGURE 2.23 *Using a class to implement a ternary association.*

UML also allows *reflexive* (or *recursive*) associations in which a class has an association with itself. In such a case, one instance of the class is linked to another. An example of such an association appears in Figure 2.24.

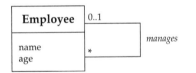

FIGURE 2.24 *An example of a reflexive association.*

2.2.5 Value Versus Reference Semantics

Consider the class diagram in the upper half of Figure 2.25. According to this diagram, each Customer instance will have a name (String) and a link to an Account instance. If String is a class (as it is in Java, Smalltalk, and many C++ class libraries, including the C++ Standard Library), both the attribute and the association will be implemented as object references, as shown in the lower half of Figure 2.25. Why, then, is one modeled as an attribute and the other as an association?

The difference between the two is that name has value semantics, whereas the Account link (in the acct field) has reference semantics. Fowler and Scott offer a clear and concise characterization of the specific differences (Fowler and Scott 1997, 88–89). In summary, the differences are as follows:

- *Identity*: When comparing two Customer names (that is, two Strings) for equality, the identity of the String objects is irrelevant. That is, it doesn't matter whether it is the same String object; what matters is whether the *contents* (the actual String values) are equal.

When checking to see if two Customers have the same Account, on the other hand, the identity of an Account is important. Two Customers have the same Account if they refer to the same Account instance. (There are exceptions, of course. In some cases, you might compare two separate Account instances for equality by comparing their account numbers.)

- *Sharing*: An attribute value is not shared among instances. Each Customer object has its own name String. So, changing one Customer's name will not affect another. On the other hand, a referenced object may be shared. Two Customers can refer to the same Account (and if one Customer changes that Account, those changes are seen by the other Customer).

- *Cardinality of values*: An attribute is single valued (although this guideline is sometimes relaxed for arrays of primitive types). For example, a Customer can have only one value for its name. In contrast, the cardinality of an association may indicate the possibility of multiple object references; a Customer might have multiple references to Accounts.

- *Direction of navigation*: For an attribute, navigation is always *to* the value. A Customer accesses its name String, for example, but that String is unaware of its owning Customer. As you have seen, navigation across an association can be in either one, or both directions. A Customer can access its Account, an Account can access its Customer, or both.

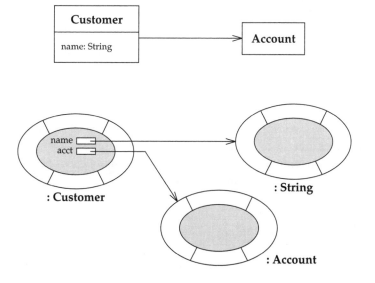

FIGURE 2.25 *A name attribute versus an Account association.*

These distinctions between an attribute and an association provide information about a property's semantics and, therefore, about its required implementation.

2.2.6 Role Names

A class inherently plays a role in an association in which it participates. Consider again the association between Order and Customer (see Figure 2.15). From the Order's point of view, the Customer is playing the role of a recipient—that is, the Customer is the one who receives the contents of the Order. Role names can be added to the ends of associations, as shown in Figure 2.26.

FIGURE 2.26 *Specifying the Customer's role in the association.*

One benefit of role names is that they can indicate (or be mapped to) instance variable names. An Order object's reference to its Customer instance can be stored in a field in the Order, as discussed previously and illustrated by Figure 2.20. The Java code for this (which is given in Section 2.2.3, "Association Implementations," and repeated here) is as follows:

```
class Order {
    private Customer recipient;
    // ...
}
```

Observe that the field name is `recipient`, which is the role the Customer plays in its relationship with an Order.

Role names are also useful in reflexive associations where the two cardinality constraints differ. Consider Figure 2.24 again. Does the company have one supervisor for many subordinates, or many supervisors for one subordinate? Figure 2.24 is ambiguous as to whether the company is a top-heavy organization or one that is conventionally aligned. The role names in Figure 2.27, however, specify that a supervisor has many subordinates.

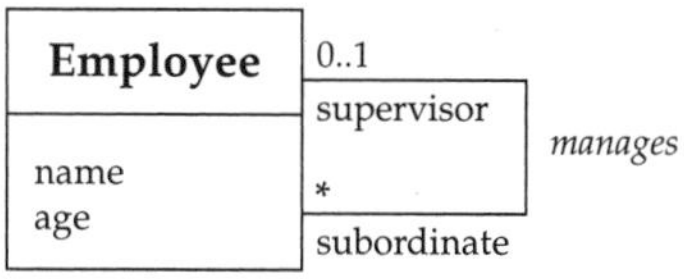

FIGURE 2.27   *A reflexive association with role names.*

2.3   Uncommon Association Notation

The concepts discussed so far—classes, objects, associations, and links—have graphical representations in almost every object-oriented design notation. UML augments these basic forms with some less common ones—representations often omitted from other object-oriented design systems. Two examples of unusual notation for associations are the *qualified association* and the *association class*.

In a one-to-many or many-to-many association, an instance of one class can hold references to several instances of another class. In the standard interpretation of such an association, one instance would access those many references simply by iterating its list of references. In some cases, however, that single object might also need to select a subset of those instances based on the value of a key. A qualified association is used to depict such a case.

You may encounter situations in which you want to design an association as a class. An instance of that class represents an instance of the association (that is, a link). UML provides a special notation, the association class, for that purpose.

2.3.1   Qualified Associations

Consider the model fragment in Figure 2.28. A Product Catalog lists the items DryGoods.com sells; therefore, it has links to many Catalog Item instances. Suppose, however, that a Product Catalog uses an item number to select a particular Catalog Item instance. In other words, an item number is a key by which a Product Catalog can select a Catalog Item.

A *qualified association* is an association in which an object on one end can employ a key to select either one, or a subset of the instances on the other end. The qualified association in Figure 2.29 indicates that a Product Catalog is linked to many Catalog Item instances, but it also indicates that a Catalog can use an item number to select one Catalog Item from among the many.

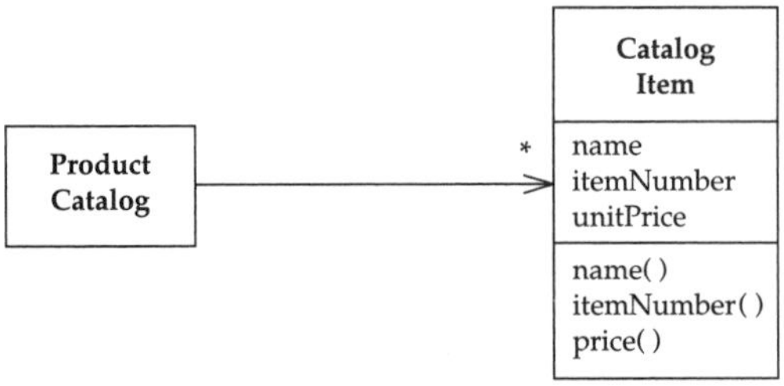

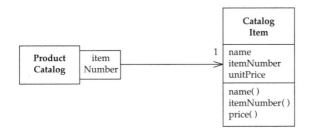

FIGURE 2.28 *An association from Product Catalog to Catalog Item.*

The small rectangle adjacent to the Product Catalog class in Figure 2.29 is a qualifier. The qualifier serves as a key and always lies adjacent to the class doing the selecting (*not* the class whose instances are being selected). The implicit cardinality opposite the qualifier is always many. (If it weren't many, you wouldn't require a qualifier for selection.) The *explicit* cardinality specifies how many are selected using the qualifier as a key. Because that cardinality is 1 in Figure 2.29, a single Catalog Item is selected by using an item number as a key.

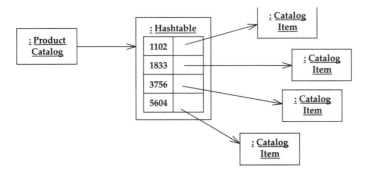

FIGURE 2.29 *A qualified association from Product Catalog to Catalog Item.*

The standard in-memory implementation idiom for a qualified association is a *keyed list* (a hash table, dictionary, indexed list, map, and so forth), where the key is the qualifier. Figure 2.30 illustrates an example.

FIGURE 2.30 *The implementation of a qualified association.*

A qualifier may be used to select a set (rather than a single item), as illustrated by Figure 2.31. In that figure, a Product Catalog uses a product type to select a set of Catalog Items (of that type). This form of selection can be implemented with what is sometimes called a *multimap*.

A multiple-valued qualifier can be specified in UML simply by separating the different qualifier components by commas. For example, a Customer Catalog might select a Customer using the combination of name and phone number as a key.

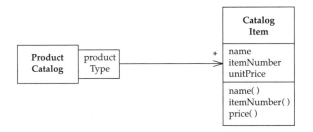

FIGURE 2.31   *Another qualified association from Product Catalog to Catalog Item.*

The same basic syntax is employed to show qualifier values in an object diagram, as illustrated in Figure 2.32. The name of the qualifier may be included when multiple qualifiers exist; for example, the contents of the qualifier rectangle in Figure 2.32 would be `itemNumber = 1102` when a Product Catalog uses multiple qualifiers to select an instance.

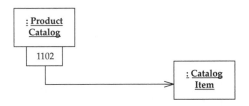

FIGURE 2.32   *A qualifier in an Object diagram.*

2.3.2   Association Classes

An association can be modeled as a class, as shown in Figure 2.33. Each instance of the class represents a link between objects. Therefore, the lifetime of an instance is the lifetime of the link it represents.

Figure 2.33 uses the Item Source class to model the association between a Supplier and a Catalog Item: A Supplier may supply many different Catalog Items, and a Catalog Item may be supplied by multiple Suppliers. For each link between a Supplier and a Catalog Item, there is an Item Source instance in which the cost and lead time is retained for that Item from that Supplier.

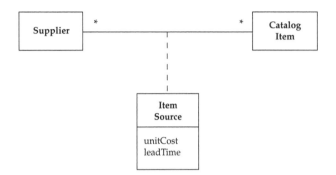

FIGURE 2.33 *An association class.*

An association class is like any other class except that its instances represent links. It can have independent behaviors, for example, and it can be associated with other classes.

2.4 Aggregation

The *aggregation* relationship is a special form of association used to model the *whole-part* or *part-of* relationship. It is drawn with all of the diagrammatic conventions of associations except that a diamond symbol appears next to the *whole* element. Figure 2.34 indicates that an Order is a whole with any number of Line Items as parts.

FIGURE 2.34 *An aggregation relationship.*

In a case where a whole has multiple types of parts, a special *shared target* (or *branching*) notation can be applied, as illustrated in the top half of Figure 2.35. The two halves of Figure 2.35 mean the same thing. Note that the shared target notation does *not* indicate that the parts can talk to one another.

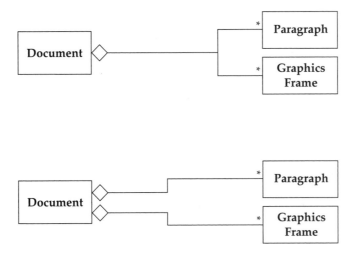

FIGURE 2.35 *The shared target notation in aggregation.*

Although UML provides the aggregation notation, it defines no semantics for it (beyond the semantics for an association). You could simply use aggregation as a conceptual mechanism, employing it when your intuition suggests you have a whole-part relationship. In that case, the relationship might not have any special semantics; that is, you can implement it in the same way you would implement an association.

Suppose, however, that you want to assign some specific semantics to the aggregation relationship. Furthermore, suppose that you want these semantics to manifest themselves in the implementation of the relationship. That is, the semantics of aggregation should require something of the implementation of the relationship beyond what is required to implement an ordinary association.

Special semantics that can be applied to the aggregation relationship include the following:

- *Lifetime containment (or life-cycle management)*: In an aggregation relationship, the whole is responsible for the life-cycle management of its parts, which means (in the typical case) that the whole must create and destroy its parts. In an association, on the other hand, a peer has no inherent responsibility to create or destroy another peer.

- *Visibility containment*: A part in an aggregation relationship is visible only to its aggregate whole, whereas in an association, a peer may be visible to anyone. (Note that visibility containment normally implies lifetime containment.)

- *Deep copy*: When copying an aggregate whole, the parts must also be copied. When copying a peer who has an association with other peers, however, only the references to those other peers are copied.

- *Propagation of operations*: An aggregate propagates some of its operations to its parts by calling the same methods in its parts. When told to cancel or commit itself, for example, an Order invokes the `cancel` or `commit` method in each of its Line Item parts. In contrast, little such propagation occurs across an association relationship.

This list is certainly not exhaustive; you may want to assign alternative semantics. The key point to remember is that the normal UML aggregation relationship has no special meaning beyond that of an association.

In the UML Notation Guide, UML provides a second form of aggregation with very specific and strong semantics, which is the *composition relationship*. Filling in the diamond specifies it. (See Figure 2.36.) The composition relationship indicates "strong ownership and coincident lifetime of part with the whole" (62). The whole must therefore create the part when the whole is created, and it must delete the part as it is deleted (and not earlier). This also implies that a part can belong only to a single whole. One possible implementation of the relationship is what is called *by-value containment* in C++, although obviously by-value containment is not required.

FIGURE 2.36 *The composition relationship.*

2.5 Class Specialization

Association and aggregation describe relationships between instances. *Specialization*, on the other hand, is a relationship between *classes*. In particular, specialization is the *is-a-kind-of* relationship, in which the specialization is the *subclass*, or *subtype* (or *derived class* in C++) and the generalization is the *superclass*, or *supertype* (or *base class* in C++).

The notation for class specialization is depicted in Figure 2.37, where Vehicle and Customer are the superclasses. You can either draw a separate inheritance arrow from each subclass to the superclass, as in the left half of the figure, or use the shared target notation, as in the right half. The left half indicates, for example, that Automobile is a kind of vehicle.

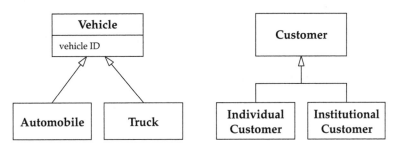

FIGURE 2.37   *The class specialization relationship.*

2.5.1   Inheritance

Inheritance is an operational result of specialization. A child (subclass) *inherits* all attributes, associations, and operations of its parent (superclass). In Figure 2.37, for example, the Automobile class inherits the vehicleID attribute from Vehicle. As a result, when you create an Automobile object, you get a *fat object* that has all the properties of both Vehicle and Automobile (as depicted by Figure 2.38). (The lines in the figure separate the Vehicle and Automobile portions of that object.)

Figure 2.38 also illustrates that specialization is *not* a special kind of association. If it were, an Automobile instance representing the subclass part would be linked to a separate Vehicle instance defining the superclass part.

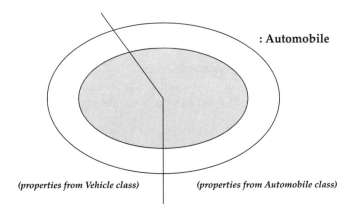

FIGURE 2.38   *A fat automobile object.*

Given that inheritance flows from superclass to subclass, why not draw the specialization arrow in the other direction? That is, why not define the arrow so that it points from the superclass to the subclass, thereby illustrating the flow of inheritance? The specialization arrow depicts the direction of visibility, not of inheritance. A subclass can "see" its superclass (and, therefore, access members in its superclass), but a superclass cannot see its subclasses. The reason for this is that an Automobile object always has a Vehicle part (as illustrated by Figure 2.38), but a Vehicle is not necessarily an Automobile and, therefore, may not always have an Automobile part.

You can also think of this relationship as "inherits from" or "specializes." The direction of the arrow, therefore, indicates how to read the relationship. The Automobile class *inherits from* and *specializes* the Vehicle class.

Some (but not all) languages permit multiple inheritance in which a subclass inherits from more than one immediate superclass. This is depicted in UML in an obvious way, as shown in Figure 2.39, where Amphibious Vehicle inherits from both Land Vehicle and Water Vehicle. Multiple inheritance of implementation can result in various problems, however, and is often discouraged.

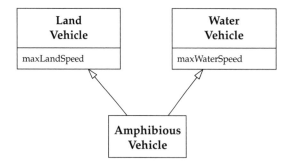

FIGURE 2.39 *An example of multiple inheritance.*

Different languages employ different syntaxes for class specialization. The Java syntax is

```
class Vehicle {
   private int vehicleId;
   // ...
   }

class Automobile extends Vehicle {
   // ...
   }
```

In particular, Java's extends keyword means *is a subclass of.*

A common confusion regarding class specialization is whether access directives affect what is inherited. Assume that private access indicates that a property is private to its class, as in Java and (ignoring friends of the class) C++. (UML defines the notation for these access directives but defers the exact definition to the target implementation language.) In particular, are private members of a superclass inherited by the subclasses?

Consider the model fragment in Figure 2.40. A private member is private to its class. Is the private vehicleId field in the Vehicle class inherited by the Automobile class? The answer is that Automobile inherits the field but cannot see it. Because it is private, the field is in the hidden middle of the Vehicle portion of a fat Automobile object. This is illustrated by Figure 2.41. It is therefore included in an Automobile instance, but it cannot be referenced by code in the Automobile part of the object (that is, by code in the Automobile class). In other words, the access directives dictate what is visible, *not* what is inherited.

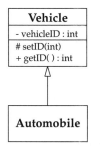

FIGURE 2.40 *The vehicle example expanded.*

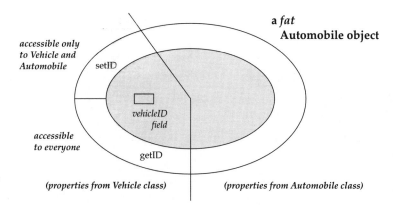

FIGURE 2.41 *A private superclass attribute in a subclass instance.*

If the methods in the `Automobile` class must access the `vehicleId` field, you could adopt one of two approaches. You could declare the field to be protected (rather than private), meaning that it is accessible by subclasses of `Vehicle`. Alternatively, you could require that the `Automobile` code access the field through the `getId` and `setId` methods (which may be public or protected). From the point of view of flexibility, the latter solution is preferable. In general:

- *Public fields are not good.* The access may be fast, but changing the implementation of a public field requires an inspection of every client of the class to see whether that client accesses that field (and, if so, to alter the client).

- *Protected fields are somewhat better.* Changing the implementation of a protected field requires that you look only at the class and its subclasses. (External clients cannot access the field.)

- *Private fields are the best of all.* Changing the implementation of a private field requires that you look only at the class itself (and its friends in C++). Even subclasses cannot access the field directly.

Avoiding protected data is especially important when other groups or organizations will be deriving subclasses from your superclasses. In those situations, you may have no idea who is developing such subclasses; therefore, you are left with only two options when altering the implementation of protected fields in those superclasses:

- You can massively distribute a warning, informing everyone that the class will be altered in a way that may "break" the implementations of any subclasses of the class.

- You can simply make the change and handle the complaints as existing code fails to compile.

Because in many cases the recipients of the message in the first approach will ignore the warning, you often end up with broken code and irate email messages or telephone calls in any case.

Class specialization and inheritance provide several benefits, including the following:

- *Class hierarchies allow programming by difference.* That is, you can determine how a subclass differs from its superclass by looking only at the subclass. For example, an Automobile extends the properties of a Vehicle. (I am assuming only what C++ calls *public inheritance* here.)

- *Class hierarchies offer reuse choices.* Each class in the hierarchy represents a reusable abstraction. Classes higher in the hierarchy are more general, whereas those lower in the hierarchy are more specialized.

- *Class hierarchies enable easy modification of shared code.* Inheritance, rather than *copy and edit*, is used to share code. So, there is only one copy of the shared code. Furthermore, when that code is modified, the changes are propagated through inheritance to the subclasses.

The last benefit is particularly important as you strive for flexible designs. When using the copy-and-edit form of code reuse, you have multiple copies of an implementation. If that implementation must change (to correct an error in the code or to add an extension, for example), you must modify all of its copies. Inheritance obviates the need for multiple copies of an implementation.

2.5.2 Type Promotion

Type promotion (or *up-casting*) occurs when you treat a specific object as a more general type. Consider an Automobile object, for example. You can view that object either as an Automobile or as a generic Vehicle. In the latter case, you have a reference to an Automobile that you are *casting upward* to refer to a Vehicle. Put another way, you are *promoting the type* of the reference from Automobile to Vehicle.

Recall from Section 2.1.1, "Classes and Objects," that a class defines both a type (in terms of a public interface) and an implementation. A subclass inherits both the type and implementation of its superclass. From a client's point of view, an Automobile can do at least as much as a Vehicle can do (and perhaps more). In other words, an Automobile has at least as much interface as a Vehicle has. In Figure 2.42, for example, Vehicle has a *run* interface, whereas Automobile has both *run* and *race* interfaces. (The *run* interface and implementation are inherited from Vehicle.)

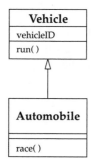

FIGURE 2.42 *Automobile as a subtype of Vehicle.*

Consider the following fragment of Java code:

```java
class X {
   public static void f(Vehicle v) {
     v.run();
   }
 }
```

Suppose a piece of client code creates an Automobile instance and calls X.f, passing a reference to that instance. Such an invocation of X.f is an example of type promotion. Whereas X.f expects to be passed from a reference to a Vehicle, the client is substituting a more specific reference (to an Automobile). Put another way, the client's reference to an Automobile is being promoted by X.f to that of a Vehicle reference. X.f is actually talking to an Automobile object but only knows it as a Vehicle. Such type promotion is always safe because, as noted earlier in this section, an Automobile is always a Vehicle too (and, therefore, an Automobile has all the properties of a Vehicle).

The use of type promotion allows you to write code that deals with generic types, such as Vehicle, rather than with specific types, such as Automobile. Your code is therefore ignorant of the existence of specific subclasses and need not change either when new subclasses are added, or when old ones are removed. This advantage is explained in greater detail in Section 2.5.3, "Method Overriding and Polymorphism."

On the other hand, the following Java code will not compile:

```java
class X {
   public static void f(Vehicle v) {
     v.race();
   }
 }
```

Note that X.f is attempting to call v's race method, but v is of type Vehicle, and the Vehicle class does not define such a method. Such a reference is illegal because X.f knows only that it is receiving a reference to a Vehicle, not (necessarily) to an Automobile. Therefore, X.f is permitted to call only methods that any Vehicle is guaranteed to have, and those are the methods either defined in Vehicle, or inherited by Vehicle from its superclasses. Hence, in strongly typed languages, the compile-time type of the reference (or pointer) determines *what* you can access.

The opposite of type promotion is *down-casting*. This is the notion of taking a general reference and casting it down in the type hierarchy to be of a more specific type. Consider the following Java fragment:

```
class Y {
   public static void g(Vehicle v) {
    Automobile a = v;
    a.race();
   }
}
```

The assignment of v to a is an example of down-casting, because it is converting a general Vehicle reference into a more specific Automobile reference. Unfortunately, this code will not compile. The down-casting operation is not necessarily safe, because a Vehicle may not be an Automobile. Java and C++ compilers do not permit potentially unsafe conversions without specific instructions from the programmer. The following code, on the other hand, will compile:

```
class Y {
   public static void g(Vehicle v) {
    Automobile a = (Automobile) v;
    a.race();
   }
}
```

The right side of the assignment statement is *explicitly* casting v (a Vehicle reference) to be a reference to an Automobile. (Then, the right side places that reference in a.) This code will compile but may throw an exception during its execution. Suppose Y.g is called and passed a reference to a Truck (which is another subclass of Vehicle). In such a case, v refers to a Truck instance, which the code is attempting to treat as an Automobile. The execution of that program will throw an exception (in Java) at the point at which v is cast to be of type Automobile.

Because you must sometimes down-cast a reference, object-oriented programming languages offer mechanisms to safely perform that cast. The following Java code provides the intended effect. The instanceof operation evaluates to true if, and only if, v refers to something that can be cast to be of type Automobile. (C++ has a slightly different mechanism to achieve the same end.)

```
class Y {
   public static void g(Vehicle v) {
    if (v instanceof Automobile) {
     Automobile a = (Automobile) v;
     a.race();
    }
   }
}
```

In summary, type promotion (or up-casting) is always safe, because *the subclass is a kind of the superclass*. Down-casting, on the other hand, is not necessarily safe and requires a test to guarantee safety.

Note

Be aware that although down-casting can be done in a safe way, it is generally discouraged. It often indicates that you have a design flaw, because you have not adequately generalized (in the super-class) the interfaces of the subclasses.

2.5.3   Method Overriding and Polymorphism

Consider the example in Figure 2.43. A run method has been introduced in the Automobile class. Note also that a run method is defined in Vehicle, the super-class of Automobile. The Automobile class is *overriding* the run implementation it inherits from Vehicle, which means that it is replacing the inherited run behav-ior with its own variant. The run implementation in Automobile may either call the run implementation inherited from Vehicle (in which case it extends, rather than replaces, the behavior), or it may ignore the inherited implementation altogether.

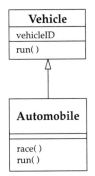

FIGURE 2.43 *Overriding a method.*

Consider the Java code fragment for method X.f (repeated from Section 2.5.2, "Type Promotion"):

```
class X {
    public static void f(Vehicle v) {
      v.run();
    }
}
```

Suppose that you call X.f, passing a reference to an Automobile. Which run implementation will be invoked? The compile-time type of the reference in X.f is Vehicle, which means that if the decision is made at compilation (or link) time, the run method in Vehicle will be called. On the other hand, the execution-time class of the object to which v refers in this example is Automobile; therefore, if the binding is deferred until execution time, Automobile's run method could be invoked.

In the typical case, the binding is delayed until execution time; so, the run method for Automobile will be called. (There are ways to force binding at compilation time, but that is beyond the scope of this book.) This means that, even though an Automobile object is being referenced as a Vehicle, it still acts like what it really is—an Automobile. This is referred to as *run-time* (or *execution-time*) *binding, polymorphism,* or *single dispatching.* (The "dispatching" part of the last term refers to the selection of a method implementation, whereas the "single" portion indicates that the selection is based on the type of a single object. In the example, the correct implementation of run is selected based on the type of the object on which run is invoked.)

Note

Polymorphism *means many forms; therefore, the mere overriding of a method technically would qualify as polymorphism, regardless of when the binding occurs. The customary use of the term, however, includes execution-time binding.*

What are the advantages of type promotion and polymorphism? Consider this scenario of a system that has text and binary files. You occasionally must print files, but text and binary files employ different print implementations. If you were to write C-style code to print files, you would do something like the following:

```
class Client {
  public void handleFile (File f) {
    switch (f.getType()) {
      case TEXT:  // print text file
      case BINARY: // print binary file
    }
  }
}
```

In other words, each time you must print a file, you introduce conditional code that is based on the type of the file . You originally intended to write this conditional code only once, but over time, the code is duplicated in several places. When confronted with your colleagues' comments about the proliferation of conditional code, you offer that there shouldn't be any additional types of files. After all, other than text and binary files, what types of files could possibly exist?

Over time, of course, you encounter several new file types, each printed in a different way. Postscript™ files, for example, require the invocation of a Postscript driver. Image files require some rendering of the image. In each case, you must find every occurrence of the conditional printing code and add a new condition with the code to print the new type of file.

The alternative to the preceding conditional code is to employ type promotion and polymorphism. A File superclass defines the print method. Each different type of file is represented by a subclass of File that implements the print method appropriately for that type of file. An initial hierarchy with Text File and Binary File is depicted in Figure 2.44.

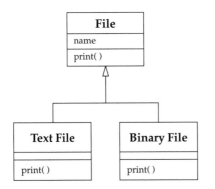

FIGURE 2.44 *The initial File class hierarchy.*

A client that prints files is passed a reference to a specific type of file, but the client receives it as a reference to a generic File. The client code for printing files is as follows:

```
class Client {
    public void doIt (File f) {
        f.print(); // polymorphic print call
    }
}
```

Note that this client code is completely ignorant of the specific (sub)types of files. In some part of your application, of course, you must create the specific types of files. You should strive to restrict the code that is aware of the File subclasses to a small part of your application. After creating instances of specific File subclasses, promote those references to be of type File (and deal only with Files in the rest of the application).

Adding a new type of file requires adding a new subclass. Figure 2.45 illustrates the addition of an Image File. The preceding client code does not change, because it deals only with generic File references.

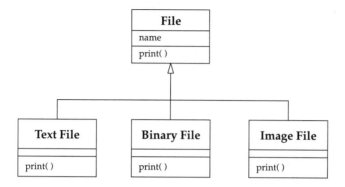

FIGURE 2.45 *Introducing an Image File class.*

Following is a list of the benefits of type promotion and polymorphism:

- *They allow clients to be unaware of specific subclasses.* The client is given a reference to the more abstract superclass type (avoiding a form of coupling called *subclass coupling* or *subtype coupling*).

- *They shield the client from changes in the subclasses.* Adding or removing subclasses does not affect the client. Changing existing subclasses does not affect the client (as long as the interface of the superclass does not change).

- *In some languages, they can lessen the need for recompilation.* As long as the public interface of the superclass is unchanged, the client need not be recompiled. This is a major issue in large systems (Lakos 1996, 327–471).

A client should therefore refer to the most general type possible.

2.5.4 Abstract Methods and Classes

Consider Figures 2.44 and 2.45 again. Each of the subclasses provides its particular implementation of the print method. The File superclass, nonetheless, must define a print method so that a client holding a File reference can call that method. It would be preferable, however, to define only an interface in the File class; there is no need to define an implementation given that each subclass implements the method.

The following is the Java code to define such an interface:

```java
class File {
    // ...
    public abstract void print();
    // ...
}
```

Note the `abstract` keyword and the absence of a method implementation. An *abstract method* (or *pure virtual function* in C++) is one that defines an interface but no implementation. (This is not strictly true in C++, where a pure virtual function can also have an implementation.) Each subclass *must* provide its own implementation of that method (or, it must declare the method to be abstract).

The UML notation for an abstract method is shown in Figure 2.46. Either the method name is italicized, or the `abstract` property appears after the method declaration.

File
name
print( )

File
name
print( ) {abstract}

FIGURE 2.46 *The notational conventions for abstract methods.*

The preceding Java code fragment will not compile as is. Once an abstract method is declared in a class, the class itself must be abstract. An *abstract class* is one for which instances cannot be created. (It can still be used as a type, however, and subclass references can be promoted to be of that type.) Any class with an abstract method must be abstract. Otherwise, what would happen if you created a File instance and invoked its `print` method? Your program would fail, because File has no implementation of that method.

The notation for an abstract class is essentially that of an abstract method. You can either italicize the class name, or add the `abstract` property after the name. Both variants are illustrated by Figure 2.47.

Observe that while a class with an abstract method must be abstract itself, an abstract class does not need to have an abstract method. You may have classes whose interfaces are fully implemented, but you do not want to create instances of them. For example, consider a library that loans books and videos. Suppose you introduce a `Lendable` superclass, of which `Book` and `Video` are subclasses, as shown in Figure 2.48. The `Lendable` superclass defines all the common properties of `Book` and `Video`. Even if `Lendable` has no abstract methods, the class should still be abstract, because you want to create only `Book` and `Video` instances.

File
name
print

File {abstract}
name
print

FIGURE 2.47   *The notational conventions for abstract classes.*

Note

A Java class with an abstract method must be declared abstract. A C++ class with a pure virtual function is automatically abstract. On the other hand, when a class has no abstract methods or pure virtual functions, how do you make the class abstract?

In Java, any class can be declared as abstract, regardless of whether it contains an abstract method. In both Java and C++, a constructor must always be called when an instance of the class is created. Therefore, in both languages, a class is abstract when it contains only private constructors (or protected constructors if you want to allow subclasses of the class, because a subclass constructor must call a superclass constructor). In addition, in C++, you can make a class abstract by declaring an abstract destructor in it.

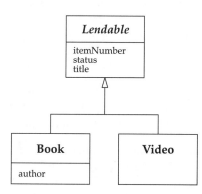

FIGURE 2.48   *An abstract class with no abstract methods.*

2.5.5   Types of Class Specialization

What does *class specialization* really mean? What are its forms? A subclass can specialize its superclass in two general ways:

- It can extend the superclass by adding a property.

- It can restrict the superclass by removing or restricting a property.

Some languages, such as C++, permit both forms. Private inheritance is an example of *restriction* because the interface of the superclass is being restricted in the subclass. Other languages, such as Java, permit only extension. A subclass extends its superclass by

- Adding state information in the form of an attribute

- Adding state information in the form of an association

- Adding behavior by introducing a new method or by implementing a method that is abstract in the superclass

- Replacing behavior by overriding a method defined in the superclass

Extension follows the "the subclass is everything the superclass is" principle, thereby permitting type promotion and polymorphism. With restriction, however, the subclass is *less* than the superclass; as a result, it may be unsafe to employ type promotion and polymorphism (depending upon the type of restriction). An example is C++ private inheritance, in which public methods in the superclass become private in the subclass. As a result, the subclass has "less interface" than the superclass. Whereas normal inheritance (or what C++ calls *public inheritance*) means "is a kind of," private inheritance means something closer to, "is implemented in terms of."

2.6 Dependencies

A *dependency* is a "catch all" relationship in UML. It can appear in any UML diagram and is used to model any of three different kinds of relationships:

- A refinement, such as the `trace` design refinement in Chapter 1. (Recall that such a refinement was used to trace an activity diagram to the use case or activity it describes.)

- A programming language relationship that isn't an association, such as the relationship of a C++ class to the template from which the class was instantiated.

- A refinement of an association to specify the nature of the association, such as specifying that instances of one class create instances of another.

A dependency is drawn as a dashed line and is often stereotyped to show the specific type of dependency. It may also be directed (with a stick arrow) when the dependency is directional (as in the case of a `trace` relationship, which always points to the higher-level construct).

Figure 2.49 illustrates the use of a dependency to depict a programming language relationship: *template instantiation*. Template (or generic) classes exist in some languages, such as C++, and not in others, such as Java. UML provides the bind stereotyped dependency to indicate template instantiation. Linked List is a template class that defines a linked list of items of a generic type. Line Item List is an instantiation of that template where Line Item is bound to the generic type.

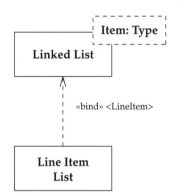

FIGURE 2.49 *Template instantiation.*

Figure 2.50 shows another example of a stereotyped dependency: a design trace. The trace shown is from the Line Item List class to the aggregation relationship between Order and Line Item. It indicates that a Line Item List instance (a linked list of Line Items from Figure 2.49) will be used to implement the one-to-many relationship from an Order object to its Line Item instances.

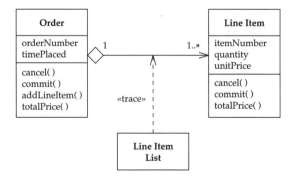

FIGURE 2.50 *Design refinement.*

The fragment in Figure 2.51 illustrates the use of a dependency to add semantics to an association. The figure specifies that the association from Order Factory to Order is employed for the purpose of creating Order instances. Put another way, an Order Factory knows about Orders but only for the purpose of creating them. (The Orders are then handed to some other object.) Other examples of dependencies appear throughout the book.

FIGURE 2.51 *The refinement of an association.*

2.7 Notes

A note is a comment about another item in a UML diagram. It appears in the same diagram and is physically attached to the item. This distinguishes a note from an "off the diagram" description of an item; a note is a first-class element of a diagram.

A note, like a dependency, may appear in any UML diagram. It is depicted as a dog-eared box with the textual note inside. The note is always attached by a dependency to the item it describes. Figure 2.52 contains an example of a note about the commit method in the Order class. The note indicates that an Order must call the commit method in its Line Items as a part of the implementation of that method.

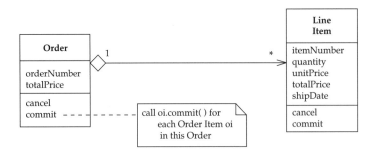

FIGURE 2.52 *A note.*

2.8   Extension Mechanisms

Different programming languages offer different sets of features. For example, Java has the Class metaclass, and Smalltalk implements the full metaclass protocol, but many other languages have no explicit metaclasses. Java also has interfaces, whereas Smalltalk and C++ have no analogous construct; C++ has an explicit *friend* relationship not present in other languages. How is it possible for a notational system to accommodate all of these variations?

Furthermore, you may want to model concepts that don't lend themselves to graphical depiction. One example is a constraint, which is simply a rule that the implementation cannot violate. How could you hope to formulate a graphical language that permits all the various forms of constraints?

To address these needs, UML includes a set of *mechanisms* that allow the addition of new things to the UML notation. The mechanisms come in two general forms:

- *Annotation mechanisms*: These are annotations of existing items in a UML diagram. The two annotation mechanisms are *specifications* and *adornments*.

- *Extension mechanisms*: These allow the introduction of new properties, constraints, stereotypes, etc.

2.8.1   Specifications

A specification is an "off the page" description of a model component. In other words, it is a description that appears in another document rather than in the diagram itself. Either the description may be textual, such as documenting each use case with a paragraph of text (as was done in Chapter 1), or it may be graphical, such as employing a type of diagram not offered by UML. For example, you could describe the implementation of a method using a data flow diagram. (Data flow diagrams are not a part of UML.)

UML does not specify any particular means of relating a specification to the UML item it describes. You could use hyperlinks or some form of naming or numbering scheme.

2.8.2 Adornments

An *adornment* is a graphical element that represents something that otherwise would have to be described in text. UML provides several adornments, including the stick figure in a class (to take the place of the «actor» stereotype name in text), and the plus sign (+), minus sign (–), and number sign (#) for access control (rather than specifying public, private, and protected as properties). Designers may also define additional adornments.

2.8.3 Properties

A *property* is used to assign to a model component some characteristic that is not otherwise defined in the UML syntax. Syntactically, a property is a tag-value pair that defines the characteristic. The property always appears within braces in or after the component to which it is applied. In Figure 2.53, a property has been introduced to a class to indicate who designed the class. (The tag and value are `author` and `John Smith`, respectively.)

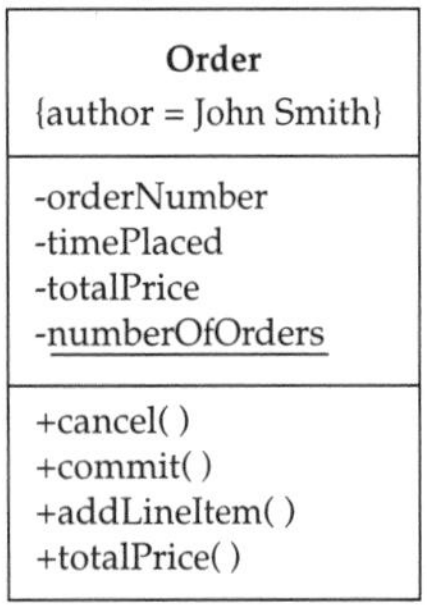

Order
{author = John Smith}
-orderNumber -timePlaced -totalPrice -numberOfOrders
+cancel( ) +commit( ) +addLineItem( ) +totalPrice( )

FIGURE 2.53 *The author of a class as a property.*

In some cases, the tag or value may be implied (but not explicitly stated). Suppose the `private` property is added to an attribute (rather than using the minus sign (–) adornment). In this case, the tag (`access`) is not included. Alternatively, suppose that an attribute is optional, meaning that it may not always have a value. The attribute's `optional` property is a tag with an implied value of `true`.

2.8.4 Constraints

A constraint is an *invariant*: a rule that cannot be violated. Like properties, constraints are placed in curly braces. They appear in or near the component being constrained. UML does not prescribe any particular syntax for the specification of the constraint. One possible syntax, the Object Constraint Language, (which is described in *The Object Constraint Language: Precise Modeling with UML* by Jos

Warmer and Anneke Kleppe) is included with UML, but its use is not mandated by UML. Some designers write constraints in the syntax of the target implementation language.

One example of a constraint is the cardinality of a class, as shown in Figure 2.54. The constraint indicates that only a single instance of the Order Factory class will be created.

FIGURE 2.54 *Constraining the cardinality of a class.*

Figure 2.55 illustrates another use of a constraint (in this case, to limit the values that attributes can assume). One constraint in the figure requires that the total price of a Line Item be equal to the product of its quantity and unit price, while the other constrains the total price of an Order to be the sum of the total prices of its Line Items.

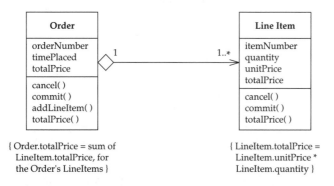

FIGURE 2.55 *Constraining attribute values.*

The constraint in Figure 2.56 requires that a Customer's links to Orders be sequenced by the Order's timePlaced attribute. In other words, if a Customer iterates through its list of Orders, the Customer will see the Orders in the sequence in which they were placed (from earliest to latest). Without the constraint, the links to Orders could be sequenced in any way (including randomly).

FIGURE 2.56 *Constraining the order of an object's links.*

Sometimes a constraint places requirements on the *relationship* between two things. In those cases, the constraint may be tied to a dependency between the two things. The upper half of Figure 2.19, for example, includes a constraint that specifies that two associations must be symmetric. Figure 2.57 illustrates the use of a constraint for an *either-or* relationship between associations. Here, an Order instance has a link to a Corporate Account or to a Customer, but not to both. The dependency between two things is directed when the constraint is directional, such as to specify that one association is a subset of another.

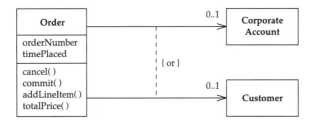

FIGURE 2.57 *Constraining a pair of associations to be either-or.*

2.8.5   Stereotypes

A stereotype defines a construct that is similar to some other construct, but has special semantics. Any notational construct can be stereotyped. The name of the stereotype appears in guillemets (or double angle brackets if guillemets are unavailable). As discussed in Section 2.1.6, "Actors as Classes," for example, actors are normally modeled in a class diagram as stereotyped classes, where the name of the stereotype is <<actor>>.

Actor classes are like normal classes in that they have instances, can be associated with other classes, and can have a public interface. They differ from regular classes, however, in that you don't implement them. (They are black boxes to your design.) The notation for them is shown in Figure 2.12.

Any UML construct can be stereotyped. In Chapter 1, you saw the stereotyping of the specialization relationship for the uses and extends relationships between use cases. Figure 2.49 includes a stereotyped dependency (binds) for template instantiation. Figure 2.58 contains a model fragment with a stereotyped class and stereotyped dependencies. The Order Not Pending Exception class is special, because its instances are exceptions. Furthermore, Order instances throw those exceptions, which are caught by Telephone Agent instances.

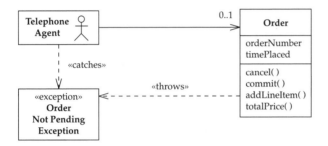

FIGURE 2.58 *A stereotyped class and stereotyped dependencies.*

2.9 A Class Diagram for Order Processing

This chapter describes much of the UML notation for class diagrams. Figure 2.59 contains part of a class diagram for DryGoods.com.

This class diagram describes the application layer of the system. The Telephone Agent actor class will be implemented as a graphical user interface (GUI). The GUI uses an Order Registry and Customer Catalog to obtain access to an Order and a Customer, respectively.

The Order Registry uses an order number as a qualifier to select a particular Order instance. A Customer Catalog employs a customer name and phone number as a two-valued qualifier to identify a Customer instance.

The attributes of an Order are the order number and the time it was placed. The Order also has a list of references to its Line Items. This relationship is modeled as aggregation, because an Order creates and deletes its Line Items. (This definition, *lifetime containment*, is one of the possible semantics for aggregation outlined in Section 2.4, "Aggregation.") It is not modeled as composition because an Order creates its Line Items as they are required, which is as the customer on the phone adds line items to the order. Composition requires *coincident lifetime*; that is, the whole object must create its parts when the whole is created. A Telephone Agent adds a Line Item to an Order by calling the Order's `addLineItem` method.

A Line Item has an item number, a quantity, and a unit price. It also has a reference to a Catalog Item that represents a listing in the product catalog. When it is created, a Line Item employs a Product Catalog to locate its Catalog Item (using an item number as a key).

When an Order is canceled or committed, it cancels or commits each of its Line Items. When an Order's `totalPrice` method is invoked, the Order calls the `totalPrice` method of each of its Line Items and returns the sum. A Line Item computes its total price by multiplying its quantity by its unit price.

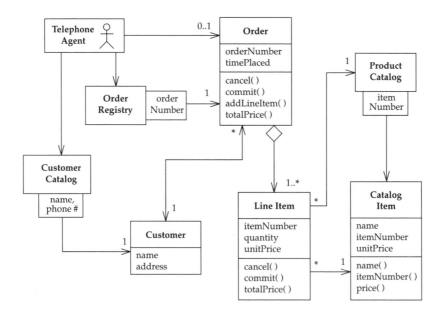

FIGURE 2.59 *A class diagram for order processing.*

Although this example illustrates the class-diagramming notation, it does nothing to explain how the classes and class properties were identified. Chapter 3, "Developing Class Diagrams," addresses the process of creating class diagrams.

Developing Class Diagrams

A set of concepts and their accompanying notation are important ingredients of an analysis or design method. What are the basic concepts, and how are those concepts depicted? Chapter 2, "Class Diagramming Notation," describes some of the concepts and UML notation for class diagrams. Using that notation, you can create a *shared model* of the static structure of your application.

Another required ingredient is a process or approach that leads you from a problem to a model. This chapter addresses how to turn a description or concept of an application into a class diagram of that same application.

Several class identification approaches have been proposed in the past. Unfortunately, no single approach works best in all situations. The choice of an approach depends on several factors, including the type of system, the domain expertise of the staff, and the form of the requirements documentation (if such documentation exists). This chapter, therefore, describes three different approaches and illustrates each with an example. It then compares and contrasts the three approaches, citing the advantages and disadvantages of each.

In many cases, employing a combination of approaches can result in a more complete model. Toward that end, this chapter describes how to employ the three approaches in different combinations:

- *Developing a class diagram from noun phrases*: One approach for developing a class diagram is to use the noun phrases in a problem description (or system specification) as an initital set of potential classes. This approach is explained and applied to a small library system.

- *Developing a class diagram using abstraction*: Developers who are problem-domain experts can sometimes "abstract" a class diagram from their knowledge of the domain. This method is illustrated through its application to a small stock trading system.

- *Developing a class diagram from use cases*: In some cases, you may want to identify use cases and then, by stepping through the use cases, generate a class diagram based on the required behaviors of the system. This approach is outlined and applied to a small factory control system.

- *Comparing and combining approaches*: Different ways of combining the three approaches are explained.

- *Enhancing a model with specifications*: Forms of valuable information beyond the normal class diagram are outlined.

Because a DryGoods.com class diagram was presented at the conclusion of Chapter 2, this chapter employs three new examples to illustrate the three class diagramming approaches.

3.1 Developing a Class Diagram from Noun Phrases

One approach for identifying classes is to use the syntactic elements of a problem statement or system specification. The reasoning behind this approach is that abstractions that represent classes are the kinds of things that would appear as noun phrases in a written description or specification of the system. Following are some examples of such abstractions:

- *Physical objects*: Credit card scanners, factory machines, and automobiles.

- *Roles*: Customer, patient, and doctor.

- *Concepts*: Review processes, telephone calls, and tax tables.

This approach is driven directly by a problem specification. The noun phrases are isolated (underlined, for example) to provide an initial set of classes, after which any spurious classes are eliminated. The resulting list of noun phrases provides a first approximation of the classes in the application. (Then, you "flesh out" the model by identifying the attributes, associations, and methods for each class.)

One method that prescribes this approach is the Object Modeling Technique (OMT) (Rumbaugh et al. 1991, 152–56). The approach is illustrated by its application to the following problem, "Developing a Library Checkout System."

Developing a Library Checkout System

You must develop code to handle checkout duties at a library. Library members may check out books and videos from the library. The system must keep track of which books and videos each member currently has checked out.

Each book and video has a unique item number that is used by the system to index that book or video. A clerk may check the status of a book or video (in the library, checked out, checked out and overdue) by supplying the item number. A clerk may also check either on a book by supplying the title and author, or on a video by supplying only the title.

Each library member has a library card that includes their membership number. When a member checks out a book or video, a clerk enters the membership number and the item number of the book or video. If the borrower has fewer than ten borrowed books or videos (in total), and if the borrower has no overdue books or videos, the book or video is loaned to the borrower. The conditions of the loan include a due date (two weeks for books and three days for videotapes).

Note

Given its use as an example in this book, the description of the library checkout system is concise and to the point. Real problem specifications often tend to ramble. Obviously, a more concise description increases the speed and sometimes the effectiveness of this approach.

3.1.1 Identifying Noun Phrases

Isolating the noun phrases in "Developing a Library Checkout System" produces the following candidate classes (organized by the paragraph in which each first appears):

> You, code, checkout duties, library, library member, book, video, system, member
>
> Item number, clerk, book status, video status, title, author
>
> Library card, membership number, borrower, borrowed book, borrowed video, overdue book, overdue video, loan condition, due date

Some of these noun phrases, such as "book" and "video," seem like classes. Others, such as "you" and "code," clearly are not classes because they are neither a part of the system itself nor actors that interact with the system.

Therefore, you need a set of elimination criteria that you can use to eliminate the spurious classes. The OMT method provides such a set, which follows. Note that you may (and perhaps should) use these criteria regardless of how you obtain the initial set of classes.

- *A candidate class is redundant*: That is, two classes represent the same abstraction. In such a case, keep the most descriptive one. (In some cases, this could indicate the presence of class specialization. This topic is addressed in Chapter 4, "Flexibility Guidelines for Class Diagrams.")

- *A candidate class is irrelevant*: That is, the class has nothing to do with problem to be solved. Unless you want a more expansive model that describes the context in which the system operates, eliminate the class.

- *The candidate class is vague*: The class is too broad or is poorly defined. You should either refine the class, or eliminate it. (This could occur if the class is a generalization. Chapter 4 discusses the introduction of generalizations.)

- *The candidate class is an attribute*: Attributes typically appear as noun phrases. You distinguish the noun phrase as an attribute (rather than a class) because it has *value semantics*. (See Section 2.2.5, "Value Versus Reference Semantics," in Chapter 2. You can eliminate the class, but you might choose to note it for later use as an attribute. (After all, your class diagram includes attributes, too.)

- *The candidate class is an operation*: That is, the class name describes either an operation of another class, or of the system (that is, a use case). An example in the library specification is *checkout duties*. In such a case, you eliminate the class, but you may choose to note it for inclusion as an operation of a class, an object, or the system.

- *The candidate class describes a role*: That is, the class name is actually a role name (describing the role one class plays in an association with another). An example is the noun *source* (or *source account*) in a banking application. The term *source* defines the role an account plays in a relationship with a transaction (that is, it is the source from which the transaction extracts money). Eliminate the class, but ensure that the class playing the role exists. (You may also choose to note the role name and the suggested association.)

- *The candidate class represents an implementation construct*: You typically don't clutter your initial class diagram with such classes as Set, String, and Linked List.

Applying these criteria to the candidate classes for the library system eliminates 18 of the 24 candidate classes. The following classes are eliminated because they are redundant:

System: An instance of this would represent the entire system. This is, therefore, the same as Library.

Member: This is an abbreviated form of Library Member.

The following classes are irrelevant:

You: This pronoun represents those asked to develop this software.

Code: This describes the desired form of the library system. (Alternatively, you might think of this as being redundant with System and Library.)

Library Card: The only state information a Library Card has is a membership number, which serves as a key for the Card or, alternatively, for the Library Member. Likewise, it has no apparent behavior and, therefore, is irrelevant in this design.

If you think a Library Card might have state and behavior in future versions of the system, you might include it here to allow subsequent extensions of the system. In that case, separating Library Card from Library Member, even though the two are in a one-to-one relationship, makes the two classes more cohesive than a single Library Member class that combines both concepts would be. (Cohesion is discussed in more detail in Chapter 4.

The following are the classes that, in fact, represent attributes:

Item Number: This is just an integer-valued identification number. A particular value indicates a particular physical copy of a book or video.

Book Status: This is a simple value that indicates whether a physical copy of a book is either in the library, or checked out. It, therefore, is an attribute of Book (an instance which represents a physical copy of a book).

Video Status: This is essentially the same as Book Status above, except that it applies to a physical copy of a video (rather than a book) and, therefore, is an attribute of Video.

Title: This is a string that holds the title of a book or video. A string has value semantics (as discussed in Section 2.2.5, "Value Versus Reference Semantics") and, therefore, is modeled as an attribute (of Book and of Video).

Author: This indicates the author of a book. For now, assume that this is just a name and, therefore, a string. (If you decide later that you need additional information about an author, you might introduce an Author class.) Because this is a string, it is an attribute of Book.

Membership Number: This is an integer-valued number assigned to a library member. This, therefore, is an attribute of Library Member.

Due Date: This is a date that indicates when a book or video is due. Dates have value semantics and, therefore, are modeled as attributes. Because only a book or video that is checked out will have a due date, this seems like an attribute of a checkout transaction.

One candidate class is, in fact, an operation:

Checkout Duties: This suggests a use case or perhaps a collection of use cases (Checkout Book, Checkout Video, and so forth).

The following classes describe roles (or perhaps states):

Borrower: This is a role that a Library Member plays in a relationship with a Book or Video. If a Library Member has a Book or Video checked out, then from the point of view of that Book or Video, the Library Member plays the role of a borrower.

Borrowed Book and Borrowed Video: This indicates a possible state of a physical copy of a book or video, namely that the copy is currently borrowed. It suggests one value for the *status* attribute (which was previously discussed) of the Book and Video classes. (That attribute, therefore, has another possible value that indicates the book or video is available in the library.)

Overdue Book and Overdue Video: This suggests another possible state, but in this case, it sounds more like a possible state of a checkout transaction:

- *Borrowed*: The item is borrowed but not overdue.

- *Overdue*: The item is borrowed and overdue.

- *Returned*: The item has been returned.

No classes are eliminated because they are vague or because they describe implementation constructs.

Following are the remaining eight classes:

Library: The single instance of this class is a facade for your application layer. A *facade* is a top-level class through which the outside world obtains access to a layer, subsystem, or component (Gamma et al. 1995, 185–93).

Library Member: An instance of this class represents a particular member.

Book and Video: An instance of one of these two classes represents a physical copy of a book or video.

Clerk: This is your actor class (and will be implemented as a presentation interface).

Checkout Transaction: This originally appeared as *Loan Condition* (but this name is more descriptive). An instance of this class describes the checking out of a physical book or video.

Observe that an instance of the Book or Video class represents a physical copy of a book or video, respectively. At some point in the analysis, you would recognize the need to introduce a separate class that represents a *title*. For example, the library owns four copies of the videocassette of *The Milagro Beanfield War*. An instance of the Title class would describe that video (such as its title, director, running time, and reviews), whereas each Video instance linked to that Title would describe a physical copy of that video (such as its item number, and whether it is currently checked out).

Several attributes have also been identified during this process:

Attributes of Book: Item Number, Status (inLibrary, checkedOut), Title, Author

Attributes of Video: Item Number, Status (inLibrary, checkedOut), Title

Attributes of Library Member: Membership Number

Attributes of Checkout Transaction: Status (borrowed, returned, overdue), Due Date

Observe that, if a Book or Video that is checked out is linked to its Checkout Transaction (which seems likely), the *status* attribute defined for Book and Video is redundant.

3.1.2 Creating the Class Diagram with Noun Phrases

At this point, you can create an initial class diagram. That diagram includes the classes and attributes that have been identified, as shown in Figure 3.1. Observe that the Clerk has been denoted as an Actor class; this will be implemented as some form of user interface. The diagram also specifies that the cardinality of the Library class is 1, meaning that only a single instance of that class will be created.

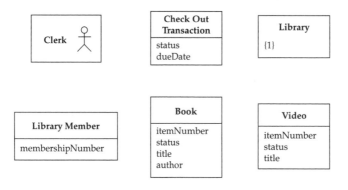

FIGURE 3.1 *An initial class diagram for the library system.*

Note

The class diagram in Figure 3.1 contains no associations or attributes. You might "flesh out" the model using abstraction, which is discussed in the next section. OMT, on the other hand, recommends using verb phrases as candidate associations. The reasoning is that because an association is a relationship between classes and because a class equates to a noun phrase, you are looking for relationships between noun phrases.

In my experience, however, I have not found verb phrases to be particularly suggestive of associations. (On the other hand, you can often use verb phrases to identify use cases or even the methods of a class. An illustration of the former is provided in Chapter 6, "Developing Dynamic Diagrams.")

To obtain associations for the class diagram in Figure 3.1, you might employ abstraction, described in the following section. That is, you might use your problem domain expertise (perhaps together with the verb phrases in the problem description) to determine what state information each type of object requires. You might also use verb phrases to obtain the methods for each class (Wirfs-Brock, Wilkerson, and Wiener 1990, 62–63). Alternatively, you might postpone the consideration of associations until you undertake dynamic modeling, which is a subject that is addressed in Chapter 6.

3.2 Developing a Class Diagram Using Abstraction

A second approach for building a class diagram is to *abstract* from your problem domain expertise. The basic idea is that you employ your knowledge of the domain to drive the generation of a model. This is an especially efficient method if you are a domain expert, as you are "hacking" a model directly from what you know. On the other hand, you must understand the domain extremely well to apply this approach successfully because you are not using any "crutches" (such as noun phrases or use cases) to aid the process.

Several methods adopt this technique, including the methods described in *Object-Oriented Analysis* (Coad and Yourdon 1991, 52–78), *Object-Oriented Systems Analysis: Modeling the World in Data* (Shlaer and Mellor 1998, 14–25), and *Object-Oriented Development: The Fusion Method* (Coleman et al. 1994, 38–39). Each method provides a set of *identification keys* to help you identify the major abstractions. For example, in *Object-Oriented Analysis*, Coad and Yourdon recommend the following set:

Are there any *kind-of* or *part-of* relations? If so, list the relationships and the classes involved in them.

With what other systems will this system interact? At a minimum, an external system is an actor class.

With what devices will the system interact? Again, an external device is an actor class. You may also require a regular (non-actor) class to track the state of instances of the device.

What things or events must be remembered?

What roles are played? These may be actor classes, or they may represent individuals about whom you must retain information.

What operational procedures exist in the system? You typically don't treat an algorithm or procedure as a class, although in some cases you may. For an example, see the Strategy pattern in *Design Patterns* (Gamma et al. 1995, 315–323).

What physical sites and organizational units exist?

In *Object-Oriented Systems Analysis: Modeling the World in Data*, Shlaer and Mellor offer a much shorter list of identification keys. Following are the major four:

What tangible things exist?

What roles are played?

What events must be remembered?

What interactions must be carried out?

Finally, in *Object-Oriented Development: The Fusion Method*, the authors recommend the following keys:

> What physical objects exist? (These are what Shlaer and Mellor call tangible things.)
>
> What people and organizations are involved?
>
> What abstractions are there?

3.2.1 Determining Classes Using Abstraction

Once you obtain a set of abstractions, then you determine whether each is truly a class and, if it is, what state information is required. To illustrate this approach, consider a second problem, "Developing a Stock-Trading System," which follows.

Developing a Stock-Trading System

You are to develop a small stock-trading system. Customers place buy and sell orders and securities transfers with service representatives; then, the service representatives enter those orders into the system. The system is closed, meaning that all buy orders are matched with sell orders within the system. (This system does not use orders placed with any other system.)

A security transfer moves stock or cash into or out of the system. Each transfer includes the customer's account number and either the amount of cash, or stock name and number of shares that is being transferred. A service representative also creates accounts at customers' requests.

Each order includes the customer's account number, the name of the stock and the number of shares to be bought or sold, whether the order is a buy or sell, and the price the customer is willing to pay or receive. (Orders must include a price because this system does not employ market prices.) Optionally, an order may include an expiration time indicating the date and time after which the order is no longer valid. When an order is entered in the system, the service representative is given a unique order number for that order.

Orders have a status. When they are placed, buy and sell orders are registered as *open*. When a buy order is matched with one or more sell orders, the involved buy and sell orders are registered as *executed*. An order that expires without being exercised is registered as *expired*. An order that is canceled is registered as *canceled*. By supplying an order number, a service representative may request the status of an order and any relevant information about the order.

This system does not employ settlement periods or short sales. To execute a buy or sell order, the customer's account must have sufficient funds or stock to cover the trade.

You may match any number of buy orders to any number of sell orders. The only requirements are that in any match: the total number of buy order shares equals the total number of sell order shares (that is, you do not match partial orders), and the asking price of any sell order is no higher than the offering price of any buy order. (When the two prices do not match, the final price may be anything between the asking and offering prices.)

Obviously, this description applies several simplifying restrictions (in comparison to a real stock-trading system).

Suppose you employ the set of identification keys from Shlaer and Mellor. Following are the abstractions that you identify for this problem:

> *Tangible things*: Account, Stock, Order
>
> *Roles*: Customer, Service Representative
>
> *Events*: Stock Transfer, Cash Transfer
>
> *Interactions*: Match (of orders)

Next, you consider each abstraction to ascertain whether it is a class and, if so, what attributes and associations it has. An Account, for example, is obviously a class because you must retain information about each customer's account. Its state information is as follows:

- An account number

- A cash portfolio

- A stock portfolio

- A customer

The account number is an integer value and, therefore, is an attribute. Because the cash portfolio is simply a holding of United States dollars, it is a simple floating-point value and, therefore, is an attribute. (If an account could contain different types of cash assets, such as holdings of different currencies, you would define a separate Cash Asset class. Then, an Account would be associated with zero or more Cash Asset instances, each representing a different type of holding.)

The stock portfolio of an Account is a list of pairs, where each pair consists of the name of the stock and the number of shares of that stock being held by the Account. You therefore define a separate class, Stock Holding, which has as attributes a stock name and a number of shares. An Account has zero or more

Stock Holding instances. (Note that this system is not maintaining information about when particular shares are purchased and for how much.)

How do you represent an Account's customer information, such as the customer's name and address? You could place this information in the Account itself, but the resulting class is not cohesive in that it represents more than a single abstraction. In particular, the Account class represents both an account (account number, cash balance, and so forth) and a customer (customer name, customer address, and so on). You obtain a more cohesive design if you separate the two abstractions into two distinct classes. The Customer class has as attributes: the name, address, and social security number of the customer. An Account has one or more customers, whereas a Customer has zero or more Accounts.

Note that Customer was on your list of candidate classes, and so this analysis has taken care of two items on the list (Account and Customer). The resulting classes are shown in Figure 3.2. You might also have modeled the association from Account to Stock Holding as aggregation (rather than association), given that an Account creates and deletes its Stock Holdings.

FIGURE 3.2 *Accounts, Stock Holdings, and Customers.*

The next item on your list is Stock. An instance of this class represents a particular security. (That is, you would have an instance for each publicly traded company.) The only obvious state information for this class is a stock symbol, as shown in Figure 3.3. (Recall that this system does not employ market prices and therefore has no notion of price changes or P/E ratios. Furthermore, assume that trading volume and company press releases are not retained by this system.) Is such a class really necessary? A Stock instance clearly has identity (in fact, it has an explicit key, a stock symbol), but does it have state and behavior? This discussion takes place later in this section.

Note

When you encounter a part of the model that is murky, such as the question about including the Stock class, it is often better to defer decisions about that portion of the model and move on. Later, as other parts of the model are fleshed out, you can turn your attention back to those questions. This increases the chance that you will make meaningful progress somewhere.

Furthermore, if you're lucky, developing the other parts of the model may help you resolve the pending issues. This sounds like a trivial point, but I've seen several projects become bogged down because of worries about a few minor rat holes.

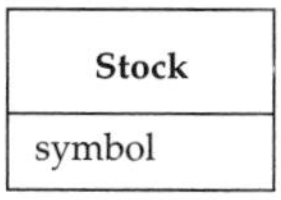

Stock
symbol

FIGURE 3.3 *Our initial Stock class.*

The next abstraction is that of an Order. An Order class is required because Orders have state and behavior. At a minimum, Orders have the following state information:

- An order number (an integer)

- A type (either buy or sell)

- A status (either open, executed, canceled, or expired)

- A stock name (a string holding the name of the stock being bought or sold)

- A number of shares (an integer)

- A requested price (a floating-point dollar amount)

- An optional expiration time (a timestamp)

- A reference to the Account on which the order is placed

An Order, therefore, is defined as shown in Figure 3.4. Note that you might want to replace the `type` attribute with two Order subclasses: Buy Order and Sell Order. This topic is addressed in Chapter 4.

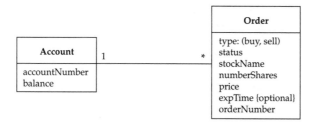

FIGURE 3.4 *The Order class.*

The next candidate class is Customer. You have already dealt with Customer as a software class. Is a Customer actor class also required? For this system, customers are not actors, as they do not interact directly with the system. (Customers talk with service agents, who then enter the customer's requests into the system.)

Service Representative, on the other hand, is obviously an actor class, as service representatives interact with the system. This class will be implemented as a graphical user interface (GUI). How does this GUI tie into the underlying application class structure? The Service Representative deals with Accounts, Customers, Orders, and Stocks. Therefore, it appears that the GUI must interact with instances of all of those classes. This is unfortunate, of course, as the GUI will be coupled to specific application classes. As a result, changes in the public interfaces of those application classes will require changes in the GUI.

As an alternative, the Facade design pattern is applied (Gamma et al. 1995, 185–93). Recall that a facade provides the outside world with a single point of contact to the underlying application code. A Trading System facade class is introduced into the design, as shown in Figure 3.5. A Trading System instance receives requests from the Service Representatives and dispatches those messages to the appropriate application instances. The Trading System, therefore, must select Customers by social security number, Accounts by account number, Orders by order number, and Stocks by stock symbol. The Service Representative and Trading System classes are shown in Figure 3.5.

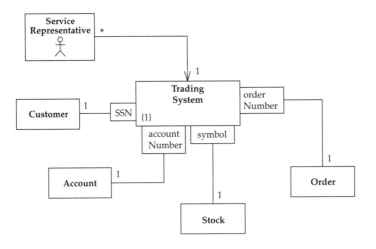

FIGURE 3.5 *The Service Representative and Trading System classes.*

Under the *events* heading are the Cash Transfer and Stock Transfer transactions. The most typical reason you would treat an event as a class is that the application must remember the event. The event may need to be remembered either temporarily because it is pending until the resources required to carry it out are available, or permanently because the application must retain a persistent record of the event.

A Cash or Stock Transfer is never pending because the transaction can always be executed immediately. (The transaction may fail, such as in an attempt to withdraw more cash or stock from an account than the account currently holds, but the transaction can execute immediately in any case.) In a real stock trading system, you would treat those transactions as classes in order to maintain permanent records of them. To illustrate a point, however, suppose that you have no requirement to maintain such records. In such a case, you could treat transfers as normal operations. Therefore, Cash Transfer and Stock Transfer are events that need not be remembered. As a result, they are not classes in the stock-trading model.

The final abstraction on the list is Match. You might treat this as a class if you had a requirement to retain records of which buy orders were matched against which sell orders. A Match instance would hold a list of references to the buy and sell Orders that were matched to one another. It would also have as attributes the final price and perhaps the time and date of the match. This small system has no requirement to record such information, however, and so it does not include this class. (Observe that, by eliminating this class, you must add attributes in each executed Order to indicate the final price and, if you need it, the time and date of the match. Those attributes are not present in the final solution.)

We still have the unresolved matter of whether Stock is a required class. As mentioned above, an instance of this class would represent a particular security. Do you need a Stock class? As discussed in Section 2.1.1, "Classes and Objects," in Chapter 2, "Class Diagramming Notation," one justification for a class is that its instances have state and behavior. What behavior might a Stock instance have? In other words, what must the application do on a security-by-security basis?

One required behavior of a particular security is the application of a stock split. This behavior is therefore assigned to the Stock class. When a stock splits, a Service Representative would call an `applyStockSplit` method in the Trading System instance, passing a stock name (or symbol) and a factor (for example, 2, indicating that one share becomes two). The Trading System, using the stock name, would look up the appropriate Stock instance and call its `applySplit` method, passing the factor. The Stock would then apply that split to its Stock Holdings and its open Orders.

A second behavior you might assign to Stock instances is that of matching Orders. As an object-oriented designer, your first inclination might be to place the matching behavior in the Orders themselves, thereby "pushing the behavior down" to the objects involved. In this case, however, such decentralization results in serious performance problems because each buy Order would have to consider all sell Orders as potential matches. Furthermore, matching, for example, three buy Orders of 200 shares each to two sell Orders of 300 shares each would be very difficult. The key insight here is that when trying to match the buy Orders of a particular security, you need to consider only sell Orders for that same security. It therefore makes sense for a Stock instance to maintain a list of its buy and sell Orders and to mediate the matching of those orders.

A Stock instance has behavior, and to carry out that behavior, it must communicate with its open Orders and with its Stock Holdings, as shown in Figure 3.6. Note that you might choose instead to "hide" Stock Holdings inside of their Accounts and to have a Stock communicate with Accounts when applying a split. (Then, each Account would call a method in the appropriate Stock Holding to apply the split.)

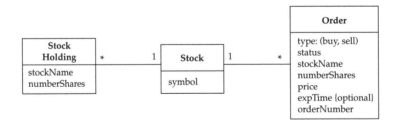

FIGURE 3.6 *The Stock class and its associations.*

3.2.2 Completing the Class Diagram with Abstraction

The final class diagram, developed using abstraction, is shown in Figure 3.7. Note that I have intentionally constructed a class diagram specific to the problem at hand, rather than a more general class diagram that permits additional types of assets. (In a more general solution, both Account and Stock would be subclasses of an Asset class, and an Order would simply be an attempt to exchange one Asset for another.)

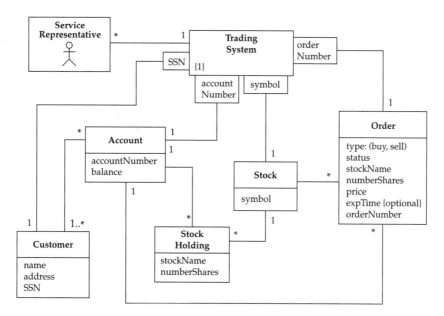

FIGURE 3.7 *The class diagram for the Stock-Trading System.*

3.3   Developing a Class Diagram from Use Cases

The previous two approaches, using noun phrases and applying abstraction, may seem very different in that one is a very tedious, almost mechanical approach, whereas the other is a somewhat unstructured, unfettered approach. The two approaches are similar, however, in that both are "information-oriented." In both cases, an *information model* was built with little regard for the required behaviors of the system. (In particular, the use cases supported by the library system and the stock trading system have not been identified.)

A third approach to building a class diagram employs use cases to guide the generation of the diagram. That is, you first identify the system's use cases, and then you "step through" each use case, adding enough to the class diagram to support the use case. The development of a class diagram for the following problem, "Tracking the States of Machines," illustrates that approach.

Tracking the States of Machines

You are to develop software to track the states of machines in a factory consisting of several machines. Each machine is in one of several states: running, idle, waiting, down for unscheduled maintenance, down for scheduled maintenance, or off. A running machine is currently processing an order. An idle machine is available for processing but is currently without an order to process. Waiting machines are

continues

discussed below. A machine that is down for either scheduled or unscheduled maintenance cannot process any orders; however, it has an estimated time at which it will be available for processing again.

Machine A may be dependent upon machine B, meaning that A receives material directly from B and hence cannot process an order unless B is also processing that order. In such a case, if machine B stops running, machine A must enter the waiting state; A must continue waiting either until B is processing again or until A is assigned a different order. Furthermore, waiting is propagated; any machine that depends upon A must also enter the waiting state.

Each machine has a maintenance schedule. Such a schedule has the date of the last scheduled maintenance and the period from that date until the next scheduled maintenance. When the date for the next maintenance arrives, the operator must be informed that the machine should enter the scheduled maintenance phase. However, scheduled maintenance need not occur immediately; the operator determines when scheduled maintenance occurs.

Unscheduled maintenance is conducted when a machine breaks while in operation. Each machine is connected to a failure monitor, which is an external device that senses hardware failures in the machine. When the monitor senses a failure, it informs the machine; then, the machine changes state to the unscheduled maintenance state and informs the operator of the state change. A running machine that either enters unscheduled or scheduled maintenance or is turned off also informs any machines that depend upon it that it is not running.

A machine operator issues commands that change the machine's state. When the machine's state is altered by an internal action, however, the machine must inform the operator that a state change occurred. The cases where the machine's state is altered internally are as follows:

- A machine senses its failure and enters unscheduled maintenance.

- The machine enters the waiting state.

- A machine leaves the waiting state because all of the machines that it depends on are running again.

All changes of machine states must be entered in a log. Each entry in the log includes the date and time of the state change, which machine changed state, and the states from and to which the machine changed.

(Note: You do not need to worry about how orders are entered into the machine or about how machine dependencies are established. A separate part of the system will handle that problem.)

As with the previous problems, some simplifying assumptions are made here, and some limitations are applied to the problem of factory control. For example, when a successor of a machine quits running, that machine is allowed to continue producing material for that successor. This may be unrealistic and also causes a problem when the machine quits running, causing that successor to wait when material is still available.

3.3.1   Determining Use Cases

You must first identify a set of use cases. One way to identify use cases is to identify the actors in the system and then consider how those actors interact with the system. (Other approaches for use case identification are described in Chapter 6.) This problem has two types of actors:

Operator: Implemented as a user interface

Failure Monitor: A sensor device on each factory machine

How does a Failure Monitor interact with the system? The Failure Monitor initiates the only interaction between a Failure Monitor and the system:

Machine Failed: This use case is initiated when a Failure Monitor detects a machine failure.

The system does not initiate any interactions with a Failure Monitor. (For example, it need not reset the Failure Monitor after unscheduled maintenance has been completed.)

An operator initiates one use case with the system:

`Change Machine's State`: This use case is initiated when an Operator wants to change a machine's state.

This use case also has a conditional extension; this extension occurs when an Operator changes a machine's state to scheduled maintenance:

Restart Maintenance Timer: This use case restarts the scheduled maintenance timer on a machine.

The requirements of this system are that a machine's maintenance timer be started when the machine *enters* scheduled maintenance. This implies that if scheduled maintenance on a machine starts on Wednesday and finishes on Thursday, for example, the date of last maintenance for that machine is Wednesday. The Restart Maintenance Timer use case is, therefore, a conditional extension of the Change Machine's State use case because it is a "side-effect" of an Operator changing a machine's state to scheduled maintenance.

The system initiates four interactions with an Operator:

Machine In Unscheduled Maintenance: The system informs the operator that a machine's state is now unscheduled maintenance (because that machine has failed).

Machine Now Waiting: The system informs the Operator that a machine's state is now waiting (because some other machine on which this machine depends is no longer running).

Machine Now Running: The system informs the Operator that a machine's state is now running (because all other machines on which this machine depends are now running).

Scheduled Maintenance Due: The system informs the Operator that scheduled maintenance is due on a machine. That is, the date that scheduled maintenance was last performed on this machine, plus the maintenance period, is now.

3.3.2   Developing the Use Case and Class Diagrams

You can depict these use cases with a use case diagram, as shown in Figure 3.8. Observe that you have several use case relationships: Restart Maintenance Timer is an extension of Change Machine's State; Machine Now Waiting and Machine Now Running are also extensions of Change Machine's State; and the former is also an extension of Machine Failed. Note that when Change Machine's State (or Machine Failed) is carried out on one machine, it may cause Machine Now Waiting or Machine Now Running to be executed against a *different* (dependent) machine.

In this particular case, you can increase the clarity of the use case diagram by including the *directions* of the relationships between actors and the use cases in which they are involved. That is, you might elect to add arrows to the ends of the associations in the use case diagram to indicate whether the actor or the system initiates the interaction. A use case diagram with directional arrows is shown in Figure 3.9.

A class diagram must now be developed from the use cases. To accomplish this, you "step through" each use case, adding enough to the class diagram to support each step. Therefore, you must describe the use case in sufficient detail so that you can identify its steps.

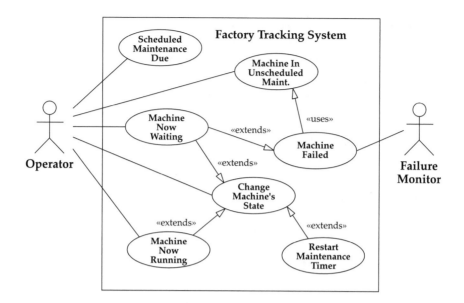

FIGURE 3.8 *The use case diagram for the Factory Tracking System.*

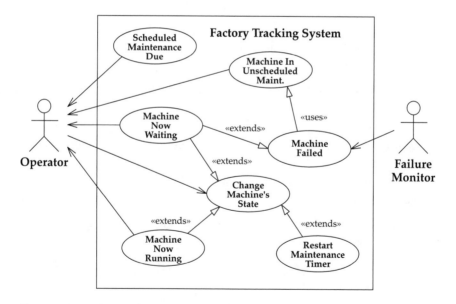

FIGURE 3.9 *A revised use case diagram.*

A use case description could take any of several forms; Chapter 5 outlines some of those forms. This example employs a textual description of each use case. Each description outlines (in text) the steps involved in the use case. Then, the classes and class properties required for each step can be identified.

Note

Getting from use cases to classes is not always straightforward. To bridge the gap, you might employ noun phrases or abstraction to help you identify the required classes. This topic is addressed in Section 3.4, "Comparing and Combining Approaches," at the end of this chapter.

A description of the first use case, Machine Failed, follows:

1. The Failure Monitor tells a software Machine instance that the corresponding factory machine has failed.

2. The Machine instance sets its state to unscheduled maintenance.

3. This use case «uses» the Machine In Unscheduled Maintenance use case. (The Machine informs the Operator (actor) that it has changed state.)

4. The Machine logs the state change with the Log.

5. The Log creates the appropriate Log Entry. (That entry must include the name of the machine, the old and new states, and the timestamp of the state change.)

6. The Machine tells any dependent Machine(s) that it is no longer running.

Note that Step 3 is the application of the Machine In Unscheduled Maintenance use case. (Because this use case is so simple, you could also simply merge it into the Machine Failed use case in the use case diagram.) At Step 6, the conditional extension, Machine Now Waiting, might be applied to a dependent machine, as follows: .

1. If it is in the running state, the dependent Machine changes its state to waiting.

2. The dependent Machine informs the Operator that it is now in the waiting state.

3. The dependent Machine logs the state change with the Log.

4. The Log creates the appropriate Log Entry.

5. The dependent Machine tells its dependent Machine(s) that it is no longer running.

This, in turn, may cause the Machine Now Waiting use case to be applied to yet another Machine.

The class diagram elements and properties required for these two use cases are shown in Figure 3.10. The numbers in circles annotate particular features in the class diagram. (They are not part of the UML notation and are used here for reference only.) A number on a feature indicates the step number in the preceding Machine Failed description that caused the addition of that feature to the class diagram. (The Machine Now Waiting use case did not require the addition of any features. The only feature required by the Machine Now Waiting use case is the reflexive *dependsOn* association from Machine to Machine.)

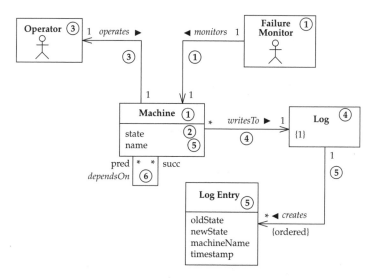

FIGURE 3.10 *A class diagram for the first two use cases.*

Recall that the "scroll bar" arrows next to association names tell you in what direction to read the name. One such arrow in Figure 3.10 indicates that an Operator operates a Machine (rather than vice versa). It does *not* indicate the direction of communication (or visibility). The open-headed arrow on the end of the association indicates that. (Hence, a Machine talks to its Operator.)

Unlike the other associations, the *dependsOn* association in Figure 3.10 (and subsequent figures) does not include arrowheads that indicate the direction of the association. The reason is that at this point in the design it is not clear how a Machine that is waiting will determine when it can run again. (This is the triggering condition for the Machine Now Running use case, outlined in the following paragraphs) For example, a waiting Machine could either poll its predecessors or the predecessors could inform that Machine of their changes from non-running to running (and vice versa). Until that decision is made, the dependency association remains undirected. (Recall from Section 2.2.2, "Associations between Classes," that this book adopts "the direction is unspecified" as its definition of undirected associations.)

While it is not done in this example, you could identify methods and develop interaction diagrams as you are constructing the class diagram. An interaction diagram shows the sequence of object interactions (for example, method calls) that occur during a particular scenario, and a scenario is one execution path through a use case. (These topics are discussed in Chapter 5, "Dynamic Diagramming Notation.") Because you are analyzing use cases to create a class diagram, it is often easy to generate interaction diagrams as a parallel activity.

The description of the Change Machine's State use case follows:

1. The Operator informs the Machine that its factory machine has changed state.

2. The Machine sets its state to the new state.

3. The Machine logs the state change with the Log.

4. The Log creates the appropriate Log Entry.

5. If the Machine was running and is now neither running nor idle, the Machine tells any dependent Machine(s) that it is no longer running.

The incremental additions to the class diagram for the Change Machine's State use case are depicted in Figure 3.11. The only required addition is the visibility on the association between Operator and Machine (to show that an Operator must talk to a Machine).

At Step 5, the conditional extension, Machine Now Waiting, which was described previously, might be applied. If the new state in Step 2 is scheduled maintenance, the maintenance timer must also be restarted by applying the Restart Maintenance Timer use case extension. The description of that use case follows:

1. The Machine tells its Maintenance Schedule to restart the maintenance cycle.

2. The Maintenance Schedule sets its date of last maintenance to now (thereby starting or restarting the timer).

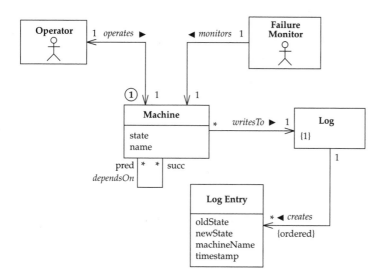

FIGURE 3.11   *Class diagram additions for Changing a Machine's State.*

The additions to the class diagram for this use case are shown in Figure 3.12.

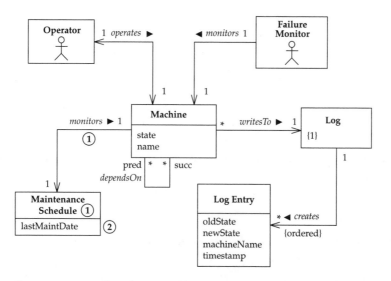

FIGURE 3.12   *Class diagram additions for Restart Maintenance Timer.*

If Step 2 of Change Machine's State causes a Machine to change its state from running to either off, or scheduled maintenance, you must also apply the Machine Now Waiting use case as described previously. If that step causes a Machine to change its state to running, however, you may have to apply the Machine Now Running use case extension that follows:

1. All of a Machine's predecessors are now running or idle. (This is the triggering condition.)

2. The Machine changes its state to running.

3. The Machine informs the Operator of the state change.

4. The Machine logs the state change with a Log.

5. The Log creates the appropriate Log Entry.

6. The Machine tells its dependent Machines that it is now running.

The Machine Now Waiting use case requires no additions to the evolving class diagram.

Note

It is important to work through the details of each use case. Even if you think it won't add anything new to the design, you can't be certain of that until you analyze the use case's behavior.

The final use case is Scheduled Maintenance Due, which follows:

1. A Maintenance Schedule's date of last maintenance plus its period is now. (This is the triggering condition.)

2. The Maintenance Schedule tells its Machine that scheduled maintenance is due.

3. The Machine informs its Operator that scheduled maintenance is due.

3.3.3 Completing the Use Case Class Diagram

Figure 3.13 contains the class diagram additions for this use case. This is your final class diagram for the problem as stated. Note that while a Maintenance Schedule runs a timer, no Timer class appears in Figure 3.13. The use of such a class is a low-level detail that will be added during detailed design (or perhaps during implementation).

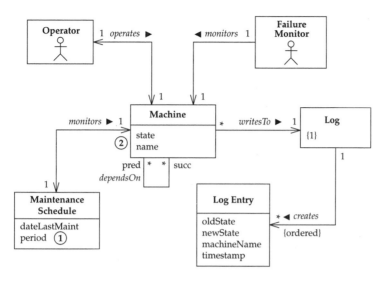

FIGURE 3.13 *Class diagram additions for Scheduled Maintenance Due.*

You might pose a question about this class diagram: Why introduce the Maintenance Schedule class? Why not just bury the date of last maintenance and maintenance period in the Machine? The simple answer is *class cohesion*. When introducing a class to the design, you should be able to offer a one-sentence characterization of the basic responsibility of the class. In this design, the basic responsibility of the Machine class is to respond to stimuli and make corresponding decisions about state changes, whereas the responsibility of the Maintenance Schedule is to produce a stimulus when maintenance is due.

By lumping the two abstractions (or responsibilities) into one class, you assume that the two are always in a one-to-one relationship. Suppose, however, that you must extend a Machine to include multiple maintenance schedules (one for oiling the machine, one for cleaning the wires, one for calibrating the gears, and so on). If you include the maintenance scheduling state and behavior in the Machine class, then that class becomes very messy when you introduce this extension because you must have a Machine running and responding to multiple timers. And what if some of the schedules use triggers other than timers?

Conversely, you might also encounter a situation in which one schedule applies to multiple Machines. Suppose, for example, that the only person who can perform maintenance on some of the factory machines comes from halfway around the world. Obviously, when that person visits the factory, he or she should perform maintenance on all of those machines. The simplest way to coordinate that effort is to have a single Maintenance Schedule object that applies to all of those Machine instances.

Once you introduce the Maintenance Schedule class, you might ask another question: Why doesn't the Maintenance Schedule inform the Operator directly? When maintenance is due, the Maintenance Schedule tells the Machine, which in turn informs the Operator. Why not expedite the process and have the Maintenance Schedule tell the Operator directly?

Recall the previous explanation of the basic responsibilities of the two classes. A Machine responds to external stimuli and decides about possible state changes, whereas a Maintenance Schedule produces a stimulus. If the Maintenance Schedule informs the Operator that maintenance is due, then the Maintenance Schedule is deciding what action to take when the stimulus is produced (in particular, to inform the Operator). This is a decision that should be made in a Machine, not in a Maintenance Schedule.

To illustrate the importance of this point, consider the following situation. After your system has been in the factory for several months, the factory manager asks you for a system extension. Some operators ignore the messages that scheduled maintenance is due and allow the machines to "burn up." Rather than have the system produce the maintenance message multiple times until the maintenance is undertaken, however, the factory manager wants you to distinguish between two types of machines:

- *Active maintenance machines*: These are machines for which the cost of correcting a catastrophic failure is very high. Therefore, you cannot allow an operator to overlook the need for maintenance on such a machine. From now on, each of these machines will be equipped with a switch. When maintenance on such a machine is due, your system should throw the switch (to *off*), change the machine's state to *scheduled maintenance*, log the state change, and inform the operator that the machine is now in scheduled maintenance.

- *Passive maintenance machines*: The cost of a catastrophic failure on these machines is not significantly greater than the cost of normal scheduled maintenance. Therefore, for these machines, your system should simply inform the operator that maintenance is due (as it has been doing for all machines).

Suppose that you adopted the expedient solution in which a Maintenance Schedule informs the Operator when maintenance is due. In the second version of the system, you will have to implement a type field in the Machine class to indicate whether the Machine is of the active or passive maintenance variety.

You will also have to implement the behavior in the active maintenance Machine that throws the switch and places the Machine in scheduled maintenance when maintenance is due.

In addition, however, you must alter the Maintenance Schedule class. When maintenance is due, a Maintenance Schedule first must ask its Machine for the Machine type (active or passive maintenance). Then, it must take the appropriate action based on that type (either informing the Operator of a passive maintenance Machine, or telling an active maintenance Machine to enter scheduled maintenance).

This solution is unattractive for two reasons. First, to introduce the required extension, it necessitates changes in both the Machine and the Maintenance Schedule classes. In addition, the Maintenance Schedule class now has code that is dependent upon the state information of a Machine (in particular, the Machine's type). Both of these disadvantages stem from the fact that a Maintenance Schedule is making a decision (about what to do when maintenance is due) that should be made in a Machine.

Note

Using different Machine classes and built-in run-time type identification, such as the `instanceof` *operator in Java, removes the Maintenance Schedule's dependence on specific state information of a Machine. Nonetheless, this approach does not eliminate a Maintenance Schedule's dependence on information about Machines. The Maintenance Schedule class still contains code to identify the type of machine, and that code is coupled to the existence of specific subclasses of Machine (for example, Passive Maintenance Machine and Active Maintenance Machine).*

Suppose, on the other hand, you adopt the design in which the Maintenance Schedule informs the Machine when maintenance is due (and the Machine subsequently informs the Operator). To introduce the requested extensions in the second version of the system, you need to introduce only the subclasses of Machine, as shown in Figure 3.14.

A Maintenance Schedule holds a reference to the base class, Machine. When maintenance is due, the Maintenance Schedule invokes its Machine's `scheduledMaintenanceDue` method. Each Machine subclass specializes that method as required. (Passive Maintenance Machines inform the Operator, whereas Active Maintenance Machines place themselves in scheduled maintenance.) Note that no changes to the Maintenance Schedule class are required for this extension. Through polymorphism, the correct implementation of `scheduled MaintenanceDue` will be called.

There is an important general principle at play in this example. No design can ever be completely flexible. Nonetheless, you can often anticipate some extensions your system may require and then develop a design that allows their subsequent addition. What if you have little idea of what new features will be required of your system in the future? You can still follow some basic guidelines, such as keeping classes cohesive, that will improve the chances that you can incorporate extensions into your design relatively easily. Several of these guidelines are discussed in Chapter 4, "Flexibility Guidelines for Class Diagrams," and Chapter 7, "Flexibility Guidelines for Dynamic Diagrams."

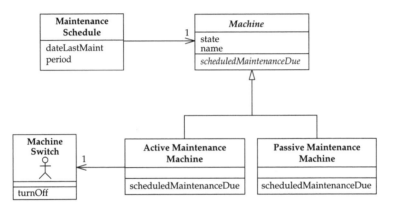

FIGURE 3.14 *Active and Passive Maintenance Machines.*

3.4 Comparing and Combining Approaches

This chapter outlines three different approaches for developing class diagrams, and indeed there are others (Booch 1994, 155–161). No approach is the correct one in every case. Each of these approaches has advantages and disadvantages, as described in the following sections.

3.4.1 The Benefits and Drawbacks of Noun Phrases

The first approach, using noun phrases as candidate classes, holds the following advantages:

- The process is almost mechanical and, hence, is appealing in situations where you're not certain how to start. (It is often appealing to object-oriented design novices for the same reason.)

- It requires little, if any, problem domain knowledge. Provided you have a written description of the system, you can "leap right in."

- There is a very clear stopping rule: You're finished identifying classes when you've looked at all noun phrases.

The disadvantages of proceeding from noun phrases are as follows:

- It is a very tedious process, and the written description of a large system could be hundreds of pages long.

- It requires a written description of the problem to be solved. Many development organizations are never provided such a description. (If the developers have to write the description, why not let them just build a model?)

- The quality of the model highly depends upon the quality of the problem statement, and many problem descriptions are not very good. (They have inconsistencies, holes, and so forth.)

3.4.2 The Benefits and Drawbacks of Abstraction

The advantages of developing a class diagram using abstraction are as follows:

- It is very efficient in terms of development time and effort because you do not underline nouns or describe use cases.

- It is therefore a good use of problem domain expertise.

The disadvantages of abstraction include the following:

- It requires extensive knowledge of the problem domain. Only a domain expert can use this approach effectively. Furthermore, the quality of the model is highly dependent on both the knowledge and skill of the domain expert.

- It can be difficult to trace design and implementation constructs back to requirements. If you employ use cases, you can trace classes to use cases and use cases to written requirements. If you isolate noun phrases from a problem statement, you can trace classes back to noun phrases. With abstraction, however, there is nothing available to which to trace classes.

- It can result in *analysis paralysis*: agonizing over details that aren't required in the model. (In "Tracking the States of Machines," which is described in Section 3.3, "Developing a Class Diagram from Use Cases," for example, you might invest a significant amount of time to consider classes that are not required by any functional requirement, such as Factory Orders.)

- How can you be certain that you've thought of everything? When to stop is not obvious.

3.4.3 The Benefits and Drawbacks of Use Case Diagrams

Consider developing a class diagram from use cases. Following are its advantages:

- The resulting model contains only features that are justified by behaviors. When developing a class diagram for the factory system, for instance, you didn't spend any time agonizing about factory orders or the estimated up time for down machines because no use cases required those features. In other words, you produced a minimal model.

- Use cases are good vehicles for eliciting, explaining, and validating requirements. Developers often have difficulty getting customers to identify and flesh out requirements. In addition, experts in object-oriented design, or even individuals with considerable domain expertise, sometimes struggle to write a requirements document. In these situations, working through use cases can be an effective first step.

- As described in Chapter 6, one way of identifying object interactions is to begin with use cases and "drill downward." With such an approach, you can reuse the use cases during dynamic modeling and design.

Developing a class diagram based on use cases also has some disadvantages, which follow:

- Some systems may involve tens or even hundreds of use cases. Therefore, the task of identifying and describing those use cases can be daunting.

- Writing use cases requires a good knowledge of the problem domain. As a result, this approach may not be suitable to designers who are not domain experts.

- Developing classes from use cases isn't always straightforward. For example, how do you go from the use cases in Figure 3.8 to the classes in Figure 3.13? (You may be able to minimize this disadvantage by combining this approach with noun phrase identification or abstraction, which is addressed later in this section.)

- How do you know that you've thought of everything? This chapter described a disciplined approach in which use cases are derived from actors, but what if you don't identify every use case? Overlooking a use case can result in an incomplete class diagram. (Chapter 6 outlines other approaches you can use to check the completeness of your list of use cases.)

3.4.4   Combining the Three Approaches

In many cases, you can maximize the advantages and minimize the disadvantages of these approaches by applying them in combination. For example, you can complement use cases with noun phrases. First, you might employ use cases to determine the required behaviors; after that you could use noun phrases to help identify possible classes.

In the development of the factory tracking system, for instance, you could have used the noun phrases in the written description of the system to identify Machine, Maintenance Schedule, and so forth as potential classes. Likewise, you might complement use cases with abstraction; for example, you could have looked for the tangible things, roles, events, and interactions in the machine tracking problem domain to bridge the gap from use cases to classes.

Another way you might combine approaches is to use abstraction complemented by use cases. That is, you use abstraction to come up with an initial model; after that, you write and step through use cases to help you validate and flesh out the model. Alternatively, you might complement abstraction with noun phrases. After using abstraction to develop an initial model, you could look at noun phrases in requirements or marketing information to check for completeness.

You can pair the approaches in any combination and order; you might even employ all three approaches together (again, in any order).

The approaches that you use and the order in which you use them are sometimes a function of the type of project and the information you have at hand. If you have a detailed system specification and little domain expertise, you might first isolate noun phrases. If you are working with business analysts who think in terms of "business objects," you might favor abstraction as an initial approach.

Likewise, if you are developing a library of reusable classes, you may prefer abstraction. (Identifying and specifying use cases for class libraries is often a tedious and unrewarding process.) If you must develop a functional requirements model and review that model with your customer, use cases may be the best place to start. In addition, control-oriented systems typically lend themselves well to use case analysis.

3.5   Enhancing a Model with Specifications

Up until now, the class diagram is the only static modeling product discussed. You may want to provide additional specifications for some model features. (Recall from Section 2.8.1, "Specifications," in Chapter 2 that UML permits off-the-page descriptions of anything.) Such descriptions may be useful for development reviews and system documentation.

For example, you may want to augment the class diagram with a *class dictionary* that includes a paragraph describing each class. That paragraph might summarize the abstraction that the class represents, the basic responsibility of the class, any assumptions about, or restrictions of, the class, and so forth. Likewise, you may choose to document each association with a paragraph that describes the relationship being modeled and any special restrictions on its implementation.

For some projects, you might even write a paragraph about each attribute and method. The description of an attribute might specify its initial (default) values as well as any restrictions on the values (such as how a value is computed). A method's description might include the signature of the method, a skeletal design of the method, and the time and space requirements of that design.

Many CASE tools support such descriptions within the tools themselves. A common approach is to allow the designer to select a model feature and open a dialog box that can then be used to describe that feature. (For a class, for example, it would allow you to define the class name, its cardinality, and so forth.) One field of the dialog box holds a short description of the feature. Such CASE tools often provide some means of generating a separate technical document that includes those descriptions.

CHAPTER 4

Flexibility Guidelines for Class Diagrams

Chapter 2, "Class Diagramming Notation," describes the concepts and notation for class diagrams, and Chapter 3, "Developing Class Diagrams," describes a set of approaches to turn a problem into a class diagram. Armed with the information in those two chapters, you can turn a problem into a static design of an application and represent that design in UML.

For many organizations, the lifetime of an application may be several years. A single application is extended many times to incorporate new features, or perhaps the core of the application is used in other related applications. For those organizations, merely developing a design and implementation that meets the requirements is insufficient. The design must be *flexible* enough to permit extension and reuse.

Assuming that there are two designs that meet the customer's requirements, how do you compare the designs for flexibility? This chapter describes a set of guidelines that, when followed, result in a more flexible design:

- *Cohesion and Coupling*: A diverse entity lacks cohesion. Entities should be as cohesive as possible. Rules for increasing cohesion are explained. A design's coupling, on the other hand, is a measure of the number and form of connections among its elements. The lower the coupling is, the more likely a change to the design will be local to one small area. Different forms of coupling and ways to reduce them are described.

- *Class generalization and specialization*: A superclass is a generalization of its subclasses (and, conversely, a subclass is a specialization of its superclass). The reasons for introducing a generalization or specialization are explained. The difficulties caused by creating subclasses based on the state of an object are outlined, and alternative design approaches are examined.

- *Specialization versus aggregation*: The use of class specialization can result in an inflexible design. In some cases, employing aggregation instead produces a superior solution. One such example is the specialization of a class along different (unrelated) dimensions. Another example is a property shared by some, but not all, subclasses. In some cases, multiple inheritance is used in situations that call for aggregation. These problems and their solutions are described.

- *Aggregation*: The advantages of hiding an aggregate's parts within the aggregate are outlined. Different approaches that allow an aggregate's parts to be reused in other applications are examined.

This chapter concludes with a section that summarizes the guidelines discussed throughout the chapter. Many of those guidelines are also discussed in Arthur Riel's excellent book, *Object-Oriented Design Heuristics*.

4.1   Cohesion and Coupling

Cohesion is a measure of the diversity of an entity's features. The less diverse its features are, the more cohesive the entity is. In other words, a highly cohesive entity represents a single concept (or engages in just one general type of activity). Because many simpler elements are generally preferable to a few complicated ones, each entity in a design should be as cohesive as possible.

Coupling, on the other hand, occurs when one element of a design depends on another in some way. Therefore, the greater the interdependence among elements, the higher the level of coupling. When possible, coupling should be avoided; a change in one element may necessitate a corresponding change in other elements that depend on that element. As its coupling is reduced, a design generally becomes more maintainable and extensible.

4.1.1 Increasing Cohesion

Each class in an object-oriented design should be as cohesive as possible. That is, each class should represent a single abstraction, or it should address a single general responsibility. A class that is not cohesive poses at least three problems, which follow:

- The class is more difficult to understand.

- You are assuming that the two (or more) abstractions represented by that class are always in a one-to-one relationship.

- You may have to specialize the class along different dimensions based on the different abstractions.

Consider an Account class that includes customer information as attributes, such as the customer's name, address, and tax identification number. The resulting class is not very cohesive because it embodies both the account and customer abstractions. In such a case, you are tacitly assuming that the two abstractions are in a one-to-one relationship. If you allow a customer to open multiple accounts, you will duplicate the customer's name, and so forth in each account. Furthermore, an account cannot have multiple owners because you can store information about only one customer in each Account instance.

The presence of two abstractions in the Account class also raises the possibility that you may have to specialize that class in two different ways, as shown in Figure 4.1. In particular, you may have specialization based on the different types of accounts, such as Cash Account and Margin Account (for stock trading), and based on the different types of customers, such as Individual Account and Institutional Account. You encounter a problem when you must *compose* the two dimensions (examples of this appear in Figure 4.2). The resulting hierarchy is a mess, and its multiple inheritance of implementation is not permitted in some languages (for example, Java and Smalltalk).

Even in languages that permit multiple inheritance, this type of specialization structure is problematic. The example contains an *inheritance diamond*, which is the diamond-shaped inheritance graph that results when a class (for example, Institutional Cash Account) inherits from two superclasses (Institutional Account and Cash Account) that in turn specialize a common superclass (Account). Such diamonds are confusing and lead to various implementation difficulties (Meyers 1995, 160–162).

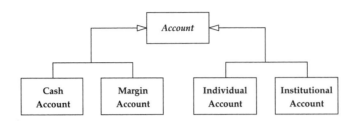

FIGURE 4.1 *Specializing an Account along two dimensions.*

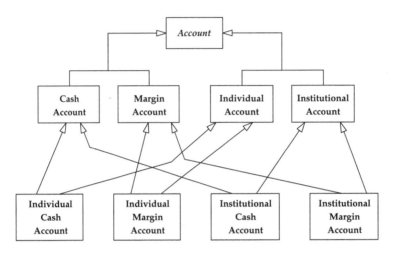

FIGURE 4.2 *Composing the dimensions.*

Separating the two abstractions, as shown in Figure 4.3, leads to a more cohesive design. You can relax the cardinality constraints (as shown in the figure) to allow a Customer instance to hold links to multiple Account objects and to allow an Account to have one or more Customers. In addition, you can specialize the two classes separately (allowing the composition to be via association rather than multiple inheritance), as illustrated by Figure 4.4.

FIGURE 4.3 *Separating the two abstractions.*

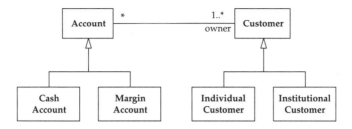

FIGURE 4.4 *Specializing the two abstractions.*

What rules can you apply to achieve class cohesion? One set of rules is analogous to those you use when *normalizing* a relational database. In fact, although you may think that the goal of normalization is to eliminate redundancy, a related effect of normalization is cohesive database tables (because each table defines the data for a single abstraction).

The normalization rules for first through third normal form can be summarized for class diagrams as follows (Shlaer and Mellor 1988, 42–46):

- An attribute should have a single value and should not have *structure* (that is, no repeating groups).

- An attribute should describe an instance of its containing class.

The preceding Account example violates the second rule because customer name, customer address, and so forth, do not truly describe an Account instance. Rather, each describes an instance of some other class, Customer, that should be introduced in the design shown in Figure 4.3.

As an example of the application of the first rule above, consider an account that can hold many different currencies. A *balance* attribute for the corresponding Account class would have as its value a list of <currency, balance> pairs that specify which currency and how much, respectively. To obtain a more normalized (and cohesive) solution, you introduce the Cash Asset class shown in Figure 4.5. In addition to describing the state of individual cash holdings, the Cash Asset class might offer class data and methods for converting between currencies.

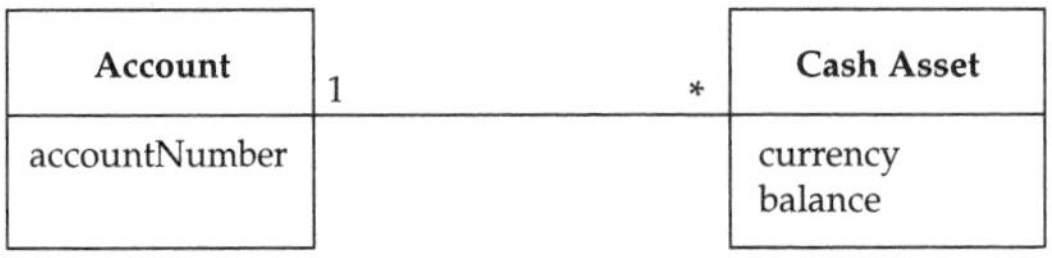

Account	1	*	Cash Asset
accountNumber			currency balance

FIGURE 4.5 *An Account with multiple currencies.*

As a final example of normalization, consider the model fragment in Figure 4.6. An instance of the Flight class represents a flight that has occurred and includes the flight number, the date of the flight, and the itinerary. Note, however, that as you fly a particular scheduled flight day after day you will be duplicating the itinerary in every instance. In the presence of such redundancy, you may wonder if the Flight class is truly just one abstraction. The answer, of course, is that it isn't; you are representing in one class both a flight schedule and an actual flight segment that has been flown. In other words, the Flight class in Figure 4.6 is not normalized.

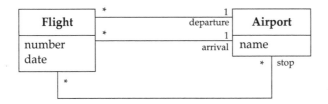

FIGURE 4.6 *An unnormalized model of airline flights.*

The normalized, more cohesive model appears in Figure 4.7. A Flight Schedule is an itinerary, whereas a Flight Segment represents one day's flying of a Schedule (and, therefore, contains any data unique to a particular flight, such as the crew).

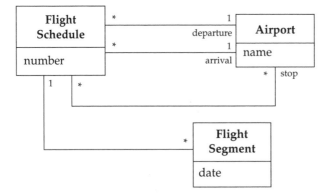

FIGURE 4.7 *The separation of flight schedules and actual flights.*

In summary, normalization is the process of eliminating redundancy. Redundancy wastes storage space and can lead to an update problem (because multiple areas must be updated, such as altering a customer's address that is stored in multiple Accounts). Normalization also makes models and designs more cohesive. Nonetheless, there is a tension between normalization, or cohesion, and efficiency. You sometimes "unnormalize" to improve execution performance, such as placing an owner's name and address in each of his or her Accounts so that you can access that information in the Account itself.

4.1.2   Reducing Coupling

Coupling in an object-oriented design is a measure of how much a class or an object knows about the world around it. You should strive to reduce coupling to limit the scope of change. If one object knows about another and the public interface of that second object changes, for example, the first object's implementation may be affected.

You have many forms of coupling in an object-oriented design. Following are four of the more basic forms:

- Identity coupling

- Representational coupling

- Subclass coupling

- Inheritance coupling

The four forms are discussed immediately below.

Identity Coupling

Identity coupling measures the level of connectivity of a design (de Champeaux, Lea, and Faure 1993, 245). If one object holds a reference (or pointer) to another, that object "knows" the identity of the other and, therefore, exhibits identity coupling. You reduce identity coupling by eliminating associations in your class diagram and by implementing associations in only one direction.

Representational Coupling

Representational coupling occurs whenever one object refers to another. The specificity (or implementation details) of the interface used in that reference determines the degree of coupling (de Champeaux, Lea, and Faure 1993, 242–244). The more precise the interface, the tighter the coupling. Accessing public data in another object is a very low-level, precise interface and, therefore, results in a very high degree of representational coupling.

In comparison, calling an *accessor method* that returns that data is a higher-level, more abstract interface and, thus, reduces the coupling (because the actual implementation of the data is hidden). Chapter 7, "Flexibility Guidelines for Dynamic Diagrams," outlines other ways of reducing representational coupling even further.

Subclass Coupling

When a client object refers to a subclass object through a subclass reference, rather than using a more general superclass reference, you have *subclass (or subtype) coupling* (de Champeaux, Lea, and Faure 1993, 244–245). A client should refer to the most general type possible, thereby de-coupling the client from the existence of specific subclasses. This general rule is captured in Figure 4.8. This is an aspect of what Robert C. Martin calls *dependency inversion* in his book *Designing Object-Oriented C++ Applications Using the Booch Method* (23). In this case, neither the client nor the subclass depends upon the existence of the other.

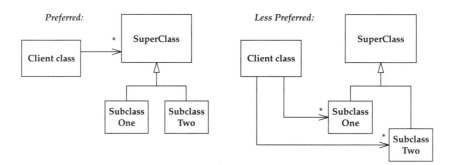

FIGURE 4.8 *Reducing subclass coupling.*

In the following Java code, which is repeated from Chapter 2, the Client class knows only about the File class:

```
class Client {
      public void handleFile (File f) {
            f.print();  // polymorphic print call
      }
  }
```

In reality, however, the File class is an abstract superclass. So, the `handleFile` method is passed a subclass instance reference (such as a reference to a Text File or an Image File), as shown in Figure 4.9. In this example, you are avoiding File subclass coupling because the Client is completely ignorant of those subclasses. As a result, you can introduce new File subclasses without altering the client code.

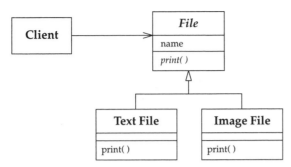

FIGURE 4.9 *Avoiding File subclass coupling.*

Obviously, you must create instances of specific File subclasses. Therefore, some of your code must be altered to reflect the introduction of new subclasses. To the maximum extent possible, however, you should strive to structure applications so that only a small portion of the application deals with specific subclass references (such as to create those instances), whereas the remainder of the application deals only with general superclass types.

An extension of this concept is the use of *interface classes* (or interfaces in Java) to define roles played by a class. An interface class is a class that has only public abstract methods; that is, it has no implementation of state or behavior. Chapter 9, "Reuse: Libraries, Frameworks, Components, and Patterns," discusses the use of interface classes in role-based design.

UML provides an «interface» class stereotype for such classes, as illustrated by the Printable class in Figure 4.10. Note that neither Printable nor its print method are italicized in the figure. The class and its methods are abstract by definition. So, there is no need to specify this property explicitly (although you may do so if you desire).

Another class may inherit and, hence, implement the interfaces defined in an interface class; in Java terminology, the class *implements* the interface. In Figure 4.10, for example, the Text File class implements the Printable interface. UML provides a special *realization arrow* to depict this relationship. The arrow is like the normal class specialization arrow, except that its shaft is dashed. It denotes the concept of a class realizing (that is, implementing) an abstract type.

Suppose you can modify your client code as shown in the following code and as depicted in Figure 4.11.

```
class Client {
      public void handleFile (Printable p) {
            p.print();
      }
  }
```

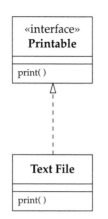

FIGURE 4.10 *An interface class.*

Now your client is coupled to a type that is even more general than File. (In fact, the File class may implement the Printable interface, although this is not included in the figure.) An instance of any class that implements the Printable interface can be passed to the client's handleFile method, such as the Tax Form class in Figure 4.11. (The instance passed to the client in Figure 4.9 is a File.)

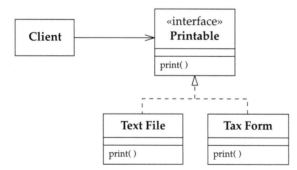

FIGURE 4.11 *Further reducing subclass coupling.*

Figure 4.12 offers an alternative UML depiction of references through interfaces:

- The *lollypop* denotes the implementation of an interface class.

- The circle represents the interface class and is labeled with its name (Printable).

The lollypop originates with the class (Text File) implementing that interface. The dependency from Client to the lollypop indicates that a Client instance references a Text File instance, but the type of that reference is Printable. In other words, a Client sees a Text File through the *portal* defined by the Printable interface class.

FIGURE 4.12 *A reference through an interface.*

Classes define abstractions, whereas interface classes define roles that classes play. A role is independent of any particular abstraction and, therefore, provides a more abstract type and, hence, a looser form of subclass coupling. Section 9.3.3, "Role Based Design," in Chapter 9 delves into this topic in more detail.

Inheritance Coupling

A subclass is coupled to its superclass through inheritance coupling. Furthermore, because class specialization is a relationship between classes (rather than instances), this coupling occurs at compilation time. Put another way, what a subclass inherits at compilation time cannot be discarded at execution time. Inheritance differs in this respect from aggregation, in which an object can add and dispose of its parts during program execution.

Suppose a Catalog Item (for example, a product listed in the DryGoods.com catalog) is allocated from company inventory. (For a description of DryGoods.com, see Section 1.1, "A First Functional Model," in Chapter 1, "System Functional Models.") In Figure 4.13, the Catalog Item inherits its inventory properties from an Inventory Item class. Note, however, that this solution assumes that once it is created as an item allocated from inventory, a Catalog Item will always be such an item.

What happens if DryGoods.com management determines that some Catalog Items should not be retained in company inventory but, rather, should be obtained from suppliers only when ordered? Those Catalog Item instances will still have the inventory properties inherited from the Inventory Item class.

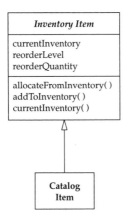

FIGURE 4.13 *Inheritance of a property.*

In the model in Figure 4.14, a Catalog Item object has an Inventory Item instance as an optional part. Some Catalog Items have such a part, whereas others do not. Furthermore, a Catalog Item can add or remove the part at execution time. In fact, a Catalog Item could have *multiple* inventories should the need arise. (A Catalog Item instance *delegates* any inventory requests to its Inventory Item part; if it has no such part, it ignores the request, throws an exception, or orders itself from its supplier.)

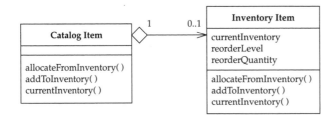

FIGURE 4.14 *Aggregation of a property.*

4.2   Class Generalization and Specialization

Chapter 2 described the concept of class generalization and specialization in Section 2.5, "Class Specialization." A superclass is a generalization because it defines properties that are common to its subclasses. A subclass, on the other hand, is a specialization of its superclass because it defines properties unique to that particular subclass—properties that do not also apply to the other subclasses.

What should cause you to introduce a generalization? When should you define a specialization? Under what conditions are generalizations or specializations unnecessary? The next section delves into these topics.

4.2.1   Introducing Class Generalization

A superclass defines a generalization (and supertype) of two or more subclasses. You generally introduce a superclass for either of two reasons:

- Two or more classes have common implementation.

- Two or more classes share a common interface.

The common implementation or interface is placed in a superclass and is shared by the classes through inheritance.

Figure 4.15 includes two classes, Book and Video, that have some common attributes and associations. In particular, each has an *itemNumber*, a *status*, a *title*, and a relationship with a Check Out Transaction. Obviously, you want to avoid implementing these properties in both classes. Figure 4.16 illustrates the introduction of a superclass, Lendable, that provides a single implementation of those common properties.

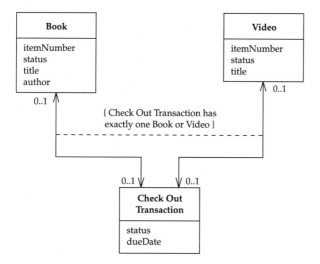

FIGURE 4.15 *Two classes with common implementation.*

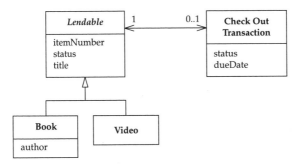

FIGURE 4.16 *Placing common implementation in a superclass.*

A serendipitous effect of adding the Lendable class in Figure 4.16 is that a Check Out Transaction holds a reference to a generic Lendable rather than to specific types of Lendables. This permits Transaction instances to deal with the future addition of new types of Lendables. Book and Video most likely share method interfaces that Lendable can use polymorphically, but this is not depicted in the figure.

You should also introduce a superclass to define a common interface, especially when a client can use that interface polymorphically. Figure 4.17 includes a set of File classes that all implement a common `print` interface. In Figure 4.18, this interface has been placed in a File superclass. A client can now print files without any awareness of the specific types of files. You are, thereby, reducing subclass coupling, as discussed previously.

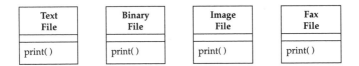

FIGURE 4.17 *Four classes with a common interface.*

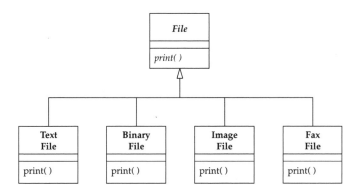

FIGURE 4.18 *Placing a common interface in a superclass.*

4.2.2 Introducing Class Specialization

In Chapter 2, Section 2.2.5, "Types of Class Specialization," outlines the ways in which a subclass specializes its superclass:

- It adds state information in the form of an attribute.

- It adds state information in the form of an association.

- It adds behavior in the form of a method (or by implementing an abstract superclass method).

- It replaces behavior by overriding a superclass method .

Therefore, you create subclasses when you have such specialization. As an example, suppose DryGoods.com offers three different ways of obtaining funds from customers: It can obtain funds directly from a credit or debit card, it can submit an invoice against an existing purchase order, or it can take funds from a cash account the customer maintains with the company.

You could lump these variations into a single Account class representing all the ways a customer can pay for an order. That class must, therefore, define all of the following properties:

- A credit (or debit) card number and expiration date (for the credit card case)

- A cash balance (for the cash account case)

- A reference to a Purchase Order (for the invoice case)

- An authorizeFunds method with conditional code for each of the three different ways of obtaining funds

- A `creditFunds` method with conditional code for each of the three ways of crediting funds back to an account

- A `depositFunds` and a `withdrawFunds` method used to add and remove cash (for the cash account case)

The result is a bloated, incohesive class.

As an alternative, you can introduce the three Account subclasses shown in Figure 4.19. The Account superclass defines the properties common to all accounts. Each subclass specializes the Account superclass because it specializes the implementations of the `authorizeFunds` and `creditFunds` methods. In addition:

- Credit Card Account adds attributes for the card number and expiration date of the card.

- Cash Account adds an attribute for the cash balance as well as methods to deposit to and withdraw from that balance.

- Invoice Account adds an association with a Purchase Order.

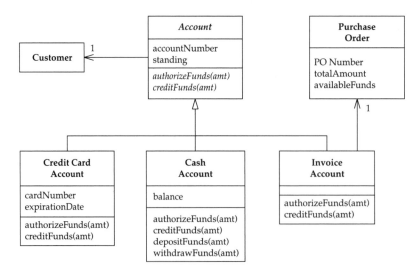

FIGURE 4.19 *Introducing specializations of the Account class.*

Observe that each subclass is specializing the Account class in at least one of the general ways outlined above.

A subclass typically should specialize its superclass in *some* way. You certainly want to avoid adding subclasses that differ only in the value of a *type* attribute. Consider the Order class in the stock-trading system developed in the previous chapter. You have both buy and sell Orders. Should you introduce Buy Order and Sell Order subclasses, as shown in Figure 4.20?

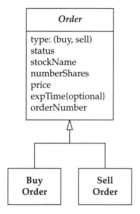

FIGURE 4.20 *Introducing specializations of stock-trading Orders.*

Before introducing these two types of specializations, you want to ensure that they differ in some way other than just the value of their inherited *type* attribute. (The values of that attribute for Buy and Sell Orders are *buy* and *sell*, respectively.) At first glance, Buy Order and Sell Order don't appear to specialize Order in any way. Neither of them add any new state (that is, attributes or associations), and (although the methods are omitted from the figure) neither add any new methods.

In this particular case, however, the two subclasses implement some methods differently. For example, each subclass implements an `execute` method (which is called when the Order is matched), but the two implementations differ. (A Buy Order adds stock to, and removes money from, its Account, whereas a Sell Order does the opposite.)

As a result, the two subclasses in this example specialize the superclass by adding behavior (in particular, by implementing an abstract superclass method) and, therefore, fulfill a purpose. The general point, however, is that you should consider whether proposed subclasses provide some specialization before you blindly add them to your design.

4.2.3 Avoiding Class Distinctions Based on State

One type of specialization you typically should avoid is distinguishing classes based on the different states of an instance. The class diagram in Figure 4.21, for example, defines Manager as a specialization of Employee because (in this system) a Manager is everything an Employee is and more. (The engineers and developers who take my courses rarely agree with this assessment.)

The problem with this approach, of course, is that an Employee may become a Manager (or vice versa), requiring that you delete the Employee instance and replace it with a Manager instance. Any client object holding a reference to that Employee object must update that reference, as the Employee object has *moved in memory*. In addition, if that client must invoke methods specific to the Manager class, it must store that new reference as a reference of type Manager (rather than of type Employee).

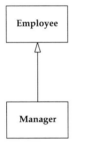

FIGURE 4.21 *An Employee specialization.*

Defining NonManagement Employee and Management Employee as subclasses of an abstract Employee class, as illustrated by Figure 4.22, obviously does not correct this problem. This is an example of *state subclasses* because each subclass represents an Employee in a particular state. Once again, as an Employee changes from one state to another (for example, from the nonmanagement to the management state), you must replace one instance with another.

One way of solving the problem in Figure 4.21 is to replace specialization with aggregation, as shown in Figure 4.23. When an Employee is promoted to management, it adds the optional Management Part. The Employee class has all interfaces for both regular employees and managers; the implementation of a management method is to test for the presence of the Management Part and (if present) to call the appropriate method in that Part. If managers and non-managers implement the same method interfaces in different ways, this solution can be extended to use the State design pattern (Gamma et al. 1995, 305–313), as depicted in Figure 4.24.

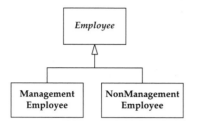

FIGURE 4.22 *State subclasses of Employee.*

FIGURE 4.23 *Replacing specialization with aggregation.*

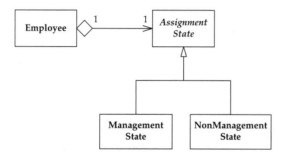

FIGURE 4.24 *Employing the State design pattern.*

4.2.4 Avoiding Concrete Superclasses

Consider Figures 4.21 and 4.22 again. Figure 4.21 has a concrete superclass, Employee, from which the Manager class is derived. Instances of the superclass represent regular employees, whereas subclass objects represent managers. In Figure 4.22, on the other hand, the abstract Employee class defines the properties of all employees, and instances of the Management Employee and NonManagement Employee subclasses are managers and regular employees, respectively.

The design in Figure 4.21 is simpler and, by that measure, preferable to the one in Figure 4.22. Unfortunately, what you gain in simplicity you sacrifice in flexibility. The solution in Figure 4.21 assumes that any property ascribed to a regular employee will also apply to a manager. Properties common to both managers and non-managers reside in the Employee class. Properties unique to managers appear in the Manager class. Properties unique to non-managers, on the other hand, have no place to reside.

The design in Figure 4.22 is more flexible in that you have a place for proper-ties unique to managers (Management Employee), properties unique to non-managers (NonManagement Employee), and properties common to both (Employee).

4.3 Specialization Versus Aggregation

As Figures 4.23 and 4.24 illustrate, an object can sometimes obtain its proper-ties through aggregation as well as through inheritance. The figures also demonstrate that in some cases, aggregation is preferable to inheritance because using specialization can produce negative consequences. In particular, the figures correct a situation in which the use of inheritance leads to the need to replace one instance with another as an object changes state.

This section describes three other situations in which aggregation may be preferable to class specialization. The first occurs when a class must be special-ized along different, orthogonal dimensions. That is, the class has different facets (or aspects), each of which must be specialized. A second is a design in which some, but not all, subclasses share a property. In the third case, multiple inheritance is used in a situation that, for both intuitive and technical reasons, calls for aggregation.

4.3.1 Avoiding Specialization Along Different Dimensions

As a general rule, you should specialize a class along only one dimension (that is, based on just one aspect of the class). Consider again Figure 4.1. The Account class has been specialized along two dimensions: by how trades are funded, and by who holds the account. That specialization looks reasonable until you must compose the dimensions.

Examples of the resulting composition are depicted in Figure 4.2. Observe that the composition mechanism is multiple inheritance (of implementation), a mechanism not available in some languages (such as Java and Smalltalk). Even when multiple inheritance is permitted, its use in this example produces messy diamond-shaped inheritance graphs. (See Section 4.1.1, "Increasing Cohesion," for additional discussion.)

To obtain a better solution, you can divide the aspects of the class into separate specialization hierarchies and compose the pieces using association (or aggre-gation), as shown in Figure 4.4. This example also illustrates that the resulting model is frequently more cohesive because the different aspects represent different abstractions (or responsibilities).

4.3.2   Placing Properties in the Correct Class

You should ensure that the properties (that is, the attributes, associations, and methods) of your classes are in the correct place in the class hierarchy. In particular:

- *A superclass property should be meaningful in all subclasses*: For the sake of simplicity, clarity, and cohesion, you generally do not want a subclass to inherit things it doesn't need. If a property applies to some (but not all) of the subclasses, you try to push that property down to the subclasses that need it.

- *A property that is common in two or more subclasses should be implemented just once*: This may entail pushing the property up to a common superclass.

The purpose of the Lendable class in Figure 4.16, for example, is to share the common attributes and associations of the Book and Video classes.

Sometimes a property's correct location is far from obvious. Figure 4.25 illustrates one of those nasty little situations where some (but not all) of the subclasses share a property. Subclasses B1 and B2 have a common method f (with the same implementation in both classes), whereas subclass B3 has no such method. You obviously want to avoid implementing f separately in both B1 and B2 (because modifying f will require changes to both classes), but where should you place the implementation of f?

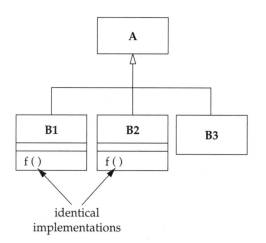

FIGURE 4.25 *A nasty little design problem: Where to place the common function.*

Perhaps the simplest solution is to place f in the superclass A, as shown in Figure 4.26. This solution requires that you override f with an *empty method* in B3, as shown in the figure. (I am ignoring C++-specific solutions, such as declaring f as private in A and declaring B1 and B2 as friends of A.) The result is that B3 has an interface (f) it should not have.

Although you should try to avoid such situations, you can normally tolerate them; after all, B3's f method doesn't do anything. This solution is unacceptable, however, if A is a concrete class (meaning that you can create instances of A). In that case, an instance of A incorrectly offers an interface for f, and invoking that method on such an instance has the same effect as invoking f on an instance of B1 or B2.

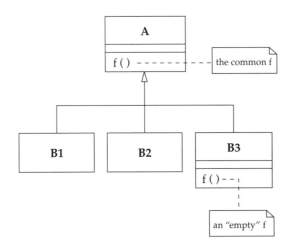

Figure 4.26 *Placing the common property in the superclass.*

Another obvious solution is the introduction of an *intermediate subclass* that inherits from A and from which B1 and B2 inherit, as illustrated by class B in Figure 4.27. As shown in the figure, that abstract class holds the implementation of f. This approach avoids the disadvantages of the previous solution in that f is defined only for B1 and B2 (and for B, but B is an abstract class).

Unfortunately, this solution doesn't scale very well. Suppose that B2 and B3 share an f' method absent in B1 and that B1 and B3 share an f" method not present in B2. As is apparent in Figure 4.28, the resulting design is a mess with inheritance diamonds "in spades." (An example of an inheritance diamond in this example is class B2's specialization of two superclasses, B and B', which in turn both specialize A.)

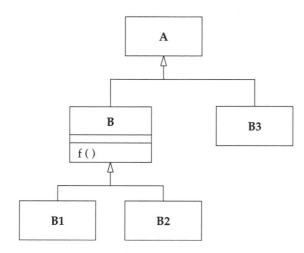

FIGURE 4.27 *Placing the common property in an intermediate subclass.*

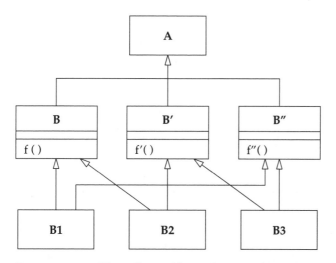

FIGURE 4.28 *The scaling problem with intermediate subclasses.*

Languages that support multiple inheritance of implementation allow a third solution, placing f in a *mix-in* class, such as M in Figure 4.29. B1 and B2 employ multiple inheritance to mix in the properties of M with those of A. This solution often scales better than the previous one because you can introduce multiple mix-in classes, as shown in Figure 4.30. The major disadvantage of this approach is its reliance on multiple inheritance of implementation, which is a feature not offered by all object-oriented programming languages. Furthermore, this solution grows ugly when the implementation of f relies on state information inherited from A.

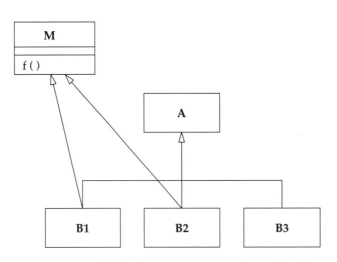

FIGURE 4.29 *Placing the common property in a mix-in class.*

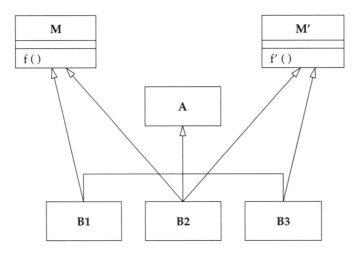

FIGURE 4.30 *The scaling of mix-in classes.*

A fourth solution utilizes aggregation rather than inheritance to share implementation. In Figure 4.31, the common implementation of f resides in *helper class* F. B1 and B2 implement f simply by calling f in F. The efficacy of this approach depends upon how f interacts with state information in B1 and B2.

Any state information accessed by f is passed as parameters. To alter the state of an instance of B1 or B2, however, f must call *set methods* in those objects, resulting in a somewhat unappealing design.

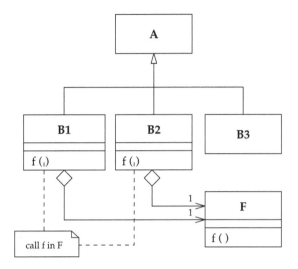

FIGURE 4.31 *Placing the common property in a helper class.*

Which solution is preferable? As the above discussion illustrates, the answer depends on several factors, which include: the nature of f, whether A is an abstract class, the degree of scaling required, and the implementation language to be used.

4.3.3 Misusing Multiple Inheritance for Aggregation

Multiple inheritance has gained an unsavory reputation. In fact, some organizations using C++ as their implementation language outlaw the use of multiple inheritance altogether. One cause of this state of affairs is the possibility of inheriting conflicting implementations. (Consider the example in Figure 2.39 in Chapter 2. If both Land Vehicle and Water Vehicle define a run method, but the two classes implement the method differently, then Amphibious Vehicle inherits two conflicting implementations of that method.) Another cause is the *misuse* of multiple inheritance.

Suppose you must develop an Automated Teller Machine class, and you already have Card Reader, Keyboard, Display Screen, and Cash Drawer classes. How do you incorporate those existing classes into your design? You could adopt an approach in which Automated Teller Machine inherits from those four classes, as shown in Figure 4.32.

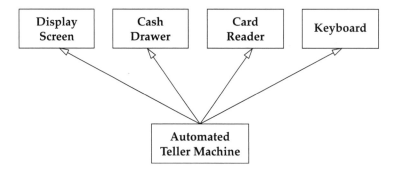

FIGURE 4.32 *Defining an Automated Teller Machine with multiple inheritance.*

This solution suffers from a conceptual flaw because an Automated Teller Machine is not a specialization of these classes in the normal sense of the term. Recall that class specialization is the "is-a-kind-of" relationship. Would you say that an Automated Teller Machine is a kind of Cash Drawer? Is it a kind of Card Reader? These are obviously not "is-a-kind-of" relationships. In this example, you are using class specialization merely for the convenience of implementation inheritance.

On a more pragmatic level, the design in Figure 4.32 is flawed because it exposes the interfaces of Cash Drawer, Card Reader, and so forth to clients of an Automated Teller Machine. All public methods in Cash Drawer are also public methods in Automated Teller Machine.

Note

As always, I am assuming C++ public inheritance. You could use private inheritance in this example. In almost every case where private inheritance is employed, however, one could obtain a more natural design by using aggregation in its place. This problem is such a case.

Suppose Cash Drawer has a public openDrawer method. That method is also public in the Automated Teller Machine, allowing an ATM client to invoke that method at any time. This is clearly undesirable. The drawer should be opened only if the ATM is in the appropriate state. You could override the openDrawer method in Automated Teller Machine to check the state of the ATM before opening the drawer, but you would have to override all such methods inherited from the four classes.

You can't claim that an Automated Teller Machine is a kind of Cash Drawer. When you can't say that a proposed subclass is a kind of its superclass, you should turn the question around and ask if the purported superclass is a part of the subclass. For example, can you say that a Cash Drawer is a part of an Automated Teller Machine?

The answer, of course, is affirmative, suggesting that what you have is aggregation rather than inheritance. Figure 4.33 contains the resulting design. In this solution, an Automated Teller Machine will expose its own set of interfaces, independent of those defined in Cash Drawer, Card Reader, and so forth.

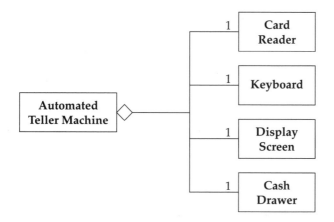

FIGURE 4.33 Defining an Automated Teller Machine with aggregation.

4.4 Aggregation

Some of the preceding examples employ aggregation. However, aggregation in UML has no semantics beyond those defined for association. Nonetheless, you can apply some simple guidelines that will make applications with aggregation more tolerant of change, and that will make the parts of an aggregate reusable in new contexts. The Automated Teller Machine examples used in this section are similar to those used by Arthur Riel in a discussion of designing flexible ATM components (203–209).

4.4.1 Hiding the Parts of an Aggregate

A basic goal of any software design, whether object-oriented or otherwise, is to limit the scope of change. You should strive to reduce coupling in an attempt to achieve this goal. In object-oriented design, you try to limit what a class knows about the world around it.

In an ideal world, the parts of an aggregate are *local* to that aggregate. Put another way, the parts should be hidden inside the whole; the outside world sees only the whole. This would permit you to alter or replace the parts without affecting anything beyond the aggregate whole. In Figure 4.33, for example, the outside world talks only to an Automated Teller Machine.

> **Note**
>
> *The "outside world" in this discussion is the banking software. The human at the ATM will obviously interact with the card reader, keyboard, and so forth.*

Where possible, you also should limit interactions between the parts. What happens when a human inserts a card into a card reader? The Card Reader instance could invoke a method in the Display Screen, informing the Screen to display its initial message, but the Card Reader is then coupled to the existence of a Display Screen. If you subsequently want to replace the Display Screen with a Speaker (in an ATM that "talks" to its customers), you must alter the Card Reader so that it interacts with a Speaker.

A more flexible design is one in which the parts interact only with the whole. When a card is inserted, the Card Reader interacts with the Automated Teller Machine; the ATM in turn calls the appropriate method in the Display Screen. Replacing a Display Screen with a Speaker requires changes to the Automated Teller Machine in any case, but will not affect the Card Reader.

4.4.2 Reusing the Parts of an Aggregate

Suppose you want to use your Card Reader class in different applications. In addition to ATMs, for example, you also develop software for toll booths. One form of toll booth requires that a person insert a card into a card reader; that card is then checked to determine whether it permits access through the gate. You would like to use the same Card Reader class for both ATMs and toll booths.

If a Card Reader invokes a method (for example, cardInserted) in its ATM when a card is inserted, then the Card Reader is coupled to the ATM. Attempting to use that Card Reader with a Toll Booth requires that you alter the Card Reader so that it holds a reference to a Toll Booth. You clearly want to avoid this situation.

You could alter the design so that the ATM (and the Toll Booth) constantly poll the Card Reader, checking to see whether a card has been inserted. This completely decouples the Card Reader from its whole, but it has the undesirable effect of requiring continual polling.

An alternative solution is the introduction of a Card Driven *interface class* from which both Automated Teller Machine and Toll Booth is derived, as illustrated in Figure 4.34. The Card Driven class defines the interface (`cardInserted`) on which Card Reader depends. The Automated Teller Machine and Toll Booth classes implement that interface. A Card Reader holds a reference to something of type Card Driven; it can refer to anything that implements the Card Driven interface.

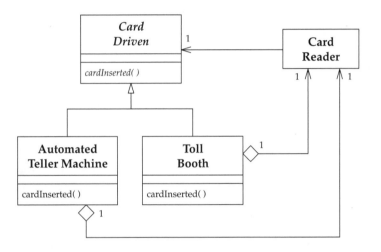

FIGURE 4.34 *Decoupling a Card Reader from its aggregate whole.*

You can think of the Card Driven class as defining a role that a class plays in a relationship with a Card Reader. Any class that implements the Card Driven interface plays that role. Alternatively, you can view Card Driven as a "receptacle" that is implemented by Automated Teller Machine and Toll Booth. A Card Reader can "plug in" to anything that implements that receptacle.

This example employs interface classes within the context of aggregation, but you can use them in any situation to reduce subclass coupling. In fact, you might even say that they eliminate *abstraction coupling* because the caller now depends only on a role played by the callee and not on the callee's specific abstraction. (Automated Teller Machine and Toll Booth are completely dissimilar with regard to the abstractions they represent.) Interface classes and their use in black-box frameworks is discussed further in Section 9.3.3.

4.5   A Summary of Guidelines

This chapter outlines several guidelines for flexibility, including the following:

- Keep classes cohesive. A class should represent a single abstraction. Applying data normalization rules can result in more cohesive classes.

- Reduce identity coupling by reducing the associations in your class diagram and by implementing associations in only one direction where possible.

- Reduce subclass coupling by pushing a client's knowledge of types as high up in the class hierarchy as possible. Wherever possible, a client should refer to a superclass rather than to specific subclasses.

- Move common interfaces and implementations to one place. You can move them to a superclass, or you can share implementation through the aggregation of a helper class.

- Avoid subclasses that do not specialize anything. In the typical case, a subclass should add a property or specialize a method. Avoid creating subclasses that differ only in the value of a type attribute.

- Make the properties of superclasses meaningful in all subclasses. You generally do not want subclasses to inherit things they don't need. Figures 4.27, 4.29, and 4.31 offer possible solutions for cases where some (but not all) subclasses share a property.

- Avoid specializing a class along multiple (orthogonal) dimensions. Composing the subclasses requires a diamond-shaped inheritance graph (and is not possible in languages that ban multiple inheritance of implementation).

- Use specialization only when you have an "is-a-kind-of" relationship.

- Avoid cases where an object must change its class dynamically (that is, where an object *migrates* from one class to another). This requires replacing one instance (and its references) with another. In particular, avoid specializing a class based on the states of its instances or the roles those instances play (as when the state or role changes, the class of the instance must also change).

- Avoid composition through multiple inheritance when what you have is aggregation. Using multiple inheritance means that the composite inherits all interfaces of its pieces. Use aggregation instead.

- Avoid concrete superclasses, as they are somewhat "brittle." Adding a property to the superclass introduces it in the subclasses, too.

- Don't forget that association (or aggregation) is sometimes an alternative to inheritance when sharing implementation. Use delegation through association where appropriate.

- Wherever possible, do not allow the outside world to see the parts of an aggregate. This allows the parts to change without affecting the outside world.

- Wherever possible, do not allow the parts of an aggregate to see one another. This allows one part to be replaced without affecting the others. (This may also aid with reuse because one part can be reused in other contexts without the other parts.)

- If the reuse of the parts is a goal, decouple the parts of an aggregate from their aggregate whole. If a part must interact with its whole, use an interface class to generalize the interface.

This chapter addresses guidelines for static modeling. Chapter 7 offers additional guidelines for the allocation of behavior to classes. Chapter 9 explains how to achieve additional flexibility in selected situations by using role-based design, applying design patterns, and so forth.

CHAPTER **5**

Dynamic Diagramming Notation

The development and documentation of an object-oriented application results in several artifacts. One is a model of the functional requirements of the application. As described in Chapter 1, "System Functional Models," use case diagrams and activity diagrams can be employed to describe the static (organizational) and dynamic (behavioral) aspects, respectively, of that model.

A second artifact is the design itself. Just as use case and activity diagrams are used to represent the static and dynamic aspects of the application's requirements, the design of the application can be described in terms of both static and dynamic views. Class and object diagrams, described in Chapter 2, "Class Diagramming Notation," are used to describe the static view of the design, whereas interaction and state transition diagrams, described in this chapter, can be used to represent the dynamic view.

The dynamic view of the design describes the temporal behavior (that is, the behavior over time) of that design. It focuses on the dynamics of object interactions and on the state-based behavior of the instances of various classes. Without this view, you have no description of what actually occurs as the system executes. While the dynamic view is sometimes omitted in projects as an attempt to "cut corners" and save time, it is as important as the functional and static views.

This chapter stresses the *notation* required of the dynamic model and the relevant *concepts* behind that notation. (Chapter 6, "Developing Dynamic Diagrams," focuses on the *process* of building this model.) It introduces two types of diagrams used in UML for dynamic modeling—interaction diagrams and state transition diagrams—and covers the following topics:

- *Describing use cases*: Scenarios are derived from use cases. To help you identify the different scenarios embodied by a use case, you may want to specify what the use case does and how it does it. Different ways of describing a use case, both operationally and declaratively, are illustrated. (Use case descriptions are normally a part of the functional model, covered by Chapter 1. Their notation appears in this chapter, however, because one form employs object notation described in Chapter 2.)

- *Scenarios*: A scenario is a use case instance. As such, it describes one path through a use case in terms of instances and their actions. The meaning and description of scenarios is discussed.

- *Depicting scenarios with interaction diagrams*: How objects interact in a scenario can be depicted graphically using an interaction diagram. The two forms of interaction diagrams, collaboration and sequence diagrams, are explained.

- *Collaborations provide the glue*: A collaboration describes a society of objects that interact to achieve some end. The concept is defined, and its use to relate use cases, scenarios, and interaction diagrams is outlined.

- *Additional features of interaction diagrams*: UML interaction diagrams include advanced features to specify iteration, branching, and so forth. The notation and use of these features is illustrated.

- *Class cards*: A class card (or CRC card) is a non-graphical alternative to a class diagram and interaction diagrams. The notation is explained, and its use and limitations are outlined.

- *State transition diagrams*: A state transition diagram can be used to specify the state-based behavior of a class of instances. The notation and its application to object-oriented design are discussed.

This chapter concludes with a summary and comparison of activity diagrams, interaction diagrams, and state transition diagrams.

5.1 Describing Use Cases

Recall from Chapter 1 that a use case is a system function. In particular, it models the way an actor interacts with the system. The notation for a use case in a use case diagram is a labeled oval. UML prescribes no additional syntax for specifying use cases. In most cases, however, you will want to provide a more detailed description of the use case's behavior. Analyzing and describing a use case helps you identify its various scenarios, which is an important step when building the dynamic view of the design.

Consider the Cancel Order Item use case in the DryGoods.com system as depicted in Figure 1.3 in Chapter 1, for example. What is involved in canceling an order item (that is, a line item in an order)? What steps must be carried out? The use case diagram provides only the use case's name and its (static) relationship with other use cases.

5.1.1 Describing Use Cases with Textual Specifications

A simple way to describe a use case is to supply a textual description. A textual description for the Cancel Order Item use case was provided in Section 1.1.2, "Use Cases in the Business View" in Chapter 1:

> The customer asks for an individual item in an order to be canceled. The item may be canceled only if it has not been shipped; in which case, the item is returned to inventory.

Observe that, because the Cancel Order use case *uses* the Cancel Order Item use case, this use case may also be triggered by a customer asking for an entire order to be canceled; in which case, the customer is implicitly asking for each individual item in the order to be canceled.

Note

You can solve this problem by further factoring the use cases. For example, you can define the Cancel Order Item use case so that it assumes the line item has been identified. You can then introduce a new use case, Identify Order Item, that handles that identification. When a customer cancels a single line item in an order, the Identify Order Item use case is followed by the Cancel Order Item. When an entire order is canceled, Cancel Order uses Cancel Order Item to cancel each of its line items. The triggering condition for Cancel Order Item, therefore, is the same in both cases.

This description is very general. It explains the context in which the use case occurs, but it provides few specific details about what must occur during the execution of the use case. To add those details, the textual description can be expanded to include an ordered list of steps, as shown in the following example, "Expanded Textual Specification for Cancel Order Item Use Case."

The following are the steps required of Cancel Order Item, assuming the customer has requested the canceling of a single item:

1. A customer asks a service representative to cancel an item in an order, providing an order number and an item number.

2. The service representative locates the order with that order number.

3. The service representative locates the line item in that order that corresponds to the specified item number.

4. The service representative cancels that line item.

5. The line item's quantity of its catalog item is returned to available inventory.

6. The customer's account is credited for the amount of that line item. (Assume that the customer's account was debited for the total amount of the order at the time the order was placed.)

Exceptions: One exceptional condition is when the order number is unknown. A second is when the order has no line item for the specified item number. A third is when the line item is no longer pending (because the item has been shipped or previously canceled).

The list of steps in "Expanded Textual Specification for Cancel Order Item Use Case" states, again in somewhat general terms, what has to be undertaken and in what sequence when canceling an order item. You can obviously hone this description to be as specific as you want regarding *how* the steps are accomplished.

5.1.2   Describing Use Cases with Activity Diagrams

What about a non-textual specification, such as a flow-chart? As described in Chapter 1, an activity diagram provides a graphical mechanism for describing the control flow of a use case. Figure 1.15 in Chapter 1, repeated here as Figure 5.1, contains an activity diagram for the Cancel Order Item use case. The activity diagram indicates that the order item (that is, line item) must be updated (to indicate that it is now canceled). If the item was not pending, the use case is completed. Otherwise, the customer's account must be credited and the requested inventory must be released. Furthermore, the latter two steps can occur in either order (or even in parallel).

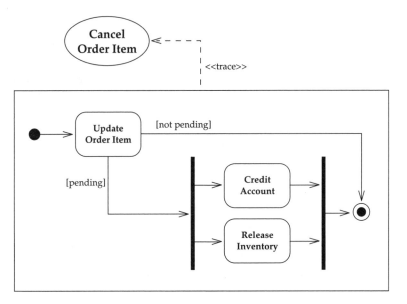

FIGURE 5.1 *The activity diagram for Cancel Order Item.*

Using a specification, described in Section 2.8.1, "Specifications," you can also introduce a non-UML diagram to describe a use case. (Recall that an off-the-diagram specification need not be textual.) For example, you can provide a data flow diagram that shows the data flows in the use case.

5.1.3 Describing Use Cases with Pre-Conditions and Post-Conditions

Both the textual list of steps and an activity diagram provide an *operational* description of the use case. That is, they specify *how* the use case is carried out by stating what must happen in what order. Suppose you wanted a more *declarative* specification that stated *what* must be done, but not necessarily how and in what order. One such specification is a statement of the use case's pre-conditions and post-conditions. In particular, you define three conditions:

- *The triggering condition*: What causes the use case to occur? In general, it can be triggered by the receipt of an event from an actor, by some internal system condition arising (such as a timer expiring), or by the execution of another use case (such as when another use case *uses* this one, or when this use case *extends* another). If the trigger is an event, the signature of the event should be stated. If it is an internal condition, the exact condition should be specified.

- *The pre-conditions*: They define what must be true before the use case is executed. Typically, these are conditions that are *tested* by the use case.

- *The post-conditions*: They specify what must be true after the use case is executed. These are conditions that are *effected* by the use case.

These three components can be described either textually or graphically. The following example, "Declarative Textual Specification for Cancel Order Item Use Case," contains a textual specification.

Declarative Textual Specification for the Cancel Order Item Use Case	
Name:	`CancelOrderItem`
Trigger:	Event from a Telephone Agent
	`cancelOrderItem(orderNumber: int, itemNumber: int)`
Preconditions:	There is an Order o with the given `orderNumber`.
	The Order has a Line Item li with the given `itemNumber`.
	li's status is pending.
Postconditions:	li's status is canceled.
	A `cancelInventoryRequest(inum, qty)` message is sent to the Product Warehouse, where `inum` is li's (catalog) item number and `qty` is li's quantity.
	A `creditAccount(anum, amnt)` event is sent to a Credit Authorization Agency caa, where `anum` is o's account number, `amnt` is li's total price, and caa is the Credit Authorization Agency responsible for that account number.
	An indication of success is returned to the Telephone Agent.

This particular specification covers only one triggering condition, when a Telephone Agent is requesting the cancellation. The Cancel Order Item use case may also be invoked as a part of the Cancel Order use case, because Cancel Order *uses* Cancel Order Item. You can expand the triggering condition in the figure to include that possibility; in which case, the first of the three pre-conditions is trivially true. Alternatively, you can factor the use cases further (as explained in a previous technical note).

The pre-conditions in the specification state what must be true to execute the use case. When designing for this use case, you must ensure that the order number is valid, the indicated order has a line item with the specified item number, and the line item is still pending. The post-conditions state what must be achieved by the use case. For this use case, they include sending events to two actor instances. Recall from Figure 1.22 in Chapter 1 that the Product Warehouse and Credit Authorization Agency objects referred to in the specification are instances of actor classes. Also recall from the discussion of that figure that a Product Warehouse is a legacy software system, whereas a Credit Authorization Agency is an external system.

If you prefer pictures to text, you can also cast this specification in terms of two object diagrams. One object diagram describes the trigger and pre-conditions, and the other defines the post-conditions. (Alternatively, you can separate the triggering condition and pre-conditions into separate object diagrams.)

Figure 5.2 contains the object diagram for the trigger and the initial configuration of the Cancel Order Item use case. The solid-headed arrow in the figure indicates an event emanating from the Telephone Agent instance; the arrow is labeled with the name of the event (cancelOrderItem) and its arguments. The remainder of the figure is standard object diagram notation (explained in Chapter 2). The diagram uses specific values for arguments and attributes (for example, an order number of 31546), but you could use generic placeholders (for example, orderNumber) in their place.

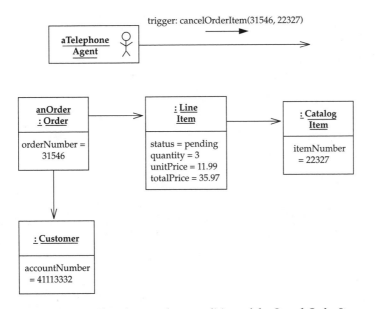

FIGURE 5.2   *The trigger and pre-conditions of the Cancel Order Item use case.*

Observe that the three pre-conditions specified in "Declarative Textual Specification for Cancel Order Item Use Case" are present in the object diagram. The diagram exhibits the existence of an Order instance whose order number is the one specified by the Telephone Agent (31546). Note also that the Order has a Line Item whose item number (shown in the Catalog Item to which the Line Item is linked) is the one specified by the Telephone Agent (22327). Furthermore, note that Line Item's status is pending.

The object diagram for the final configuration is shown in Figure 5.3. The post-conditions in the Cancel Order Item use case are all present in the diagram. The Line Item's status is now canceled, the Credit Authorization Agency for the Customer's account has been selected (using the prefix of the account number, 4111, as a key), the appropriate messages have been sent to the Product Warehouse and Credit Authorization Agency actor instances, and a response has been returned to the Telephone Agent. (The lollypop arrow indicates a return value.) Only one attribute value, the Line Item's status, has been altered in Figure 5.3. You could use a special font convention, such as bold or italics, to distinguish the attributes that change.

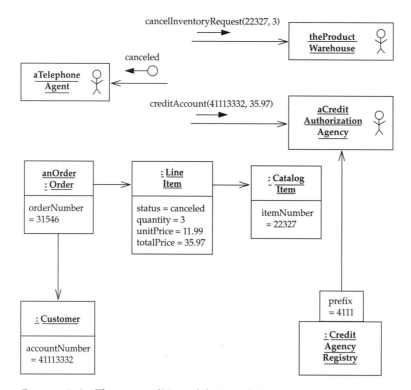

FIGURE 5.3 *The post-conditions of the Cancel Order Item use case.*

Compare the description in "Declarative Textual Specification for Cancel Order Item Use Case" to the graphical specification in Figures 5.2 and 5.3. One obvious distinction is that because it is an object diagram and, therefore, is cast in terms of particular instances, the graphical form is much more explicit and specific about details. It assumes the existence of certain classes and attributes. (Nonetheless, it is silent regarding how instances of those classes interact.) The textual form, on the other hand, says almost nothing about the existence of any classes or instances. (You can also extend the textual descriptions covered in Section 5.1.1, "Describing Use Cases with Textual Specifications," to include very specific details about classes and instances.)

Note

Whether you should include specific class and instance information in your use case descriptions is debatable. The advantage is the connection of use cases to the static design. That advantage is also the disadvantage because you are committing to particular classes.

This decision may depend in part upon whether you produce your use case model before, during, or after the development of your class diagram. (Although the use case model precedes the class diagram in a typical development effort, a project implementing a library of reusable classes or rebuilding an existing system might elect to defer use case analysis.)

5.2   Scenarios

Speakers use the term *scenario* to mean many different things. In UML, however, the term denotes a single concept: A scenario is a *use case instance*. Whereas a use case describes a system function, a *scenario* represents a single execution path through a use case. Furthermore, although a use case may describe its behavior in very general terms, a scenario defines its execution path in terms of the actions of and interactions between *objects* (not classes).

Consider the Cancel Order Item use case discussed in the preceding section. This use case has several possible execution paths; for example, the order number or item number may not be found, the Line Item may not be in a pending state, and so forth. The primary execution path—the one that occurs when things work as desired—is described by the following example, "Primary Execution Path of Cancel Order Item Use Case."

Primary Execution Path of Cancel Order Item Use Case

1. The Telephone Agent uses an Order Registry to look up the Order object with order number 31546. The Order Registry returns a reference to the Order with that order number.

continues

2. The Telephone Agent tells the Order to cancel the Line Item for item number 22327.

3. The Order finds the Line Item for that item number and tells it to cancel itself.

4. The Line Item's status is pending. It changes its status to canceled.

5. The Line Item tells its Catalog Item to add its quantity (3) back to inventory.

6. The Catalog Item tells its Product Warehouse to cancel the inventory request for this order, providing its item number and the quantity.

7. The Line Item returns a Status object to the Order that indicates that it has canceled itself, and that includes its total price: $35.97.

8. The Order asks its associated Account to prepare a refund of $35.97 for that Account.

9. The Account creates a Credit Refund instance initialized with the account number (41113332), the amount of the refund ($35.97), and a link to the proxy for the remote Credit Authorization Agency for this Account. (This scenario ignores the details of how a reference to that proxy is obtained.) The Account returns to the Order a reference to that Credit Refund instance.

10. The Order tells the Credit Refund to execute.

11. The Credit Refund tells the Credit Authorization Proxy to credit an account, providing the account number and the amount of the credit.

12. The Credit Authorization Proxy connects to the remote Credit Authorization Agency and tells it to credit an account, providing the account number and the amount. The remote Agency returns an acknowledgment of success, which the proxy returns to the Credit Refund instance.

13. The Credit Refund returns to the Order.

14. The Order returns an indication of success to the Telephone Agent.

These steps provide a textual outline of the scenario, describing how objects act and interact and in what sequence. This form is not defined by UML, but it is frequently a very useful way of communicating the specific details of each scenario. Forcing yourself to put these details on paper guarantees that you have carefully considered exactly how your design will work.

How do you describe a scenario in UML? UML provides a specific type of diagram, the *interaction diagram*, as a graphical means of depicting object interactions in a scenario.

5.3   Depicting Scenarios with Interaction Diagrams

An interaction diagram is a graphical representation of how objects interact with one another in a scenario. Unlike the textual scenario on which it is based, however, an interaction diagram depicts only the communication between objects. What an object does internally is not shown.

Objects communicate in an interaction diagram by sending messages. Sending a message is an abstract concept that may be implemented in any of several ways. In the typical case, it corresponds to invoking a method (or calling a member function), where the message name is the name of the method. In other cases, it may indicate sending a message, event, or signal, such as an inter-process message or a signal sent over radio waves.

A message may carry data with it. Whereas sending a message entails invoking a method, the data items are the parameters being passed. For example, a Telephone Agent object might send an Order object a cancelLineItem message with the data value 22327 (an item number).

UML provides two forms of interaction diagrams: the collaboration diagram and the sequence diagram. The two forms contain almost the same information, but they present it in two different ways:

- A collaboration diagram is *spatially* oriented with an emphasis on the links between objects.

- A sequence diagram is organized *temporally* with the focus on the order in which messages are sent between objects.

Figure 5.4 contains the collaboration diagram for the scenario for canceling an order item, described textually in the preceding section. The objects, links, and qualifier values are depicted as they are in an object diagram. Superimposed over that basic object diagram are the messages sent from one object to another. The solid-headed, simple-shafted arrows indicate the sending of messages (or invoking of methods) and are labeled with the message (or method) name. The lollypop arrows designate returns and are labeled with the return value. A message name may be followed by a parenthesized list of values passed with the message. For example, the lookupOrder message includes as data 31546 (the order number).

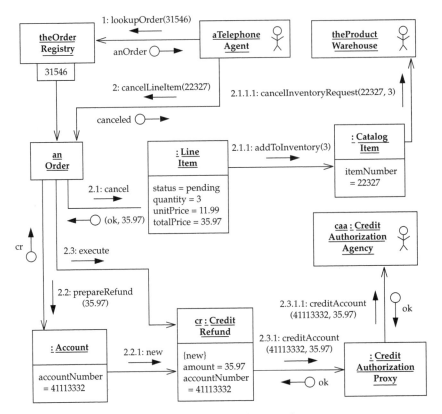

Fɪɢᴜʀᴇ 5.4 *The collaboration diagram for the scenario.*

A number specifying the relative sequencing of the message precedes each message name. In the figure, the message numbered 1 (lookupOrder) is sent before any of the other messages. Nested numbering is used to indicate nested calls. Messages 2.1, 2.2, and 2.3, for example, are sent by an Order (in that sequence) during its handling of message 2.

Where an object is passing or returning a reference to another object, the name of that other object is used. In the figure, for example, theOrderRegistry instance is returning (from lookupOrder) a reference to the Order object. The label on the return arrow, anOrder, designates that a reference to the object of that name is being returned. (This is a convention employed in this book. It is not defined in UML. As an alternative, you can also use an unfilled circle on the lollypop arrow to indicate that a reference is being returned and a filled circle when a value is returned.)

> **Note**
>
> *Using nested numbers permits the addition of lower-level details without renumbering all messages in the diagram. Suppose, for example, that you decide later to add some detail about how a Credit Refund instance is created. For example, you want to show that, during the construction (and initialization) of the Refund instance, a Credit Agency Registry is consulted to obtain a reference to the appropriate Credit Agency Proxy. This becomes message 2.2.1.1 in the figure, and no other messages need to be renumbered.*
>
> *In other notational schemes where messages were numbered sequentially with simple integer values, adding a message in the middle of the control sequence required renumbering all messages that followed it.*
>
> *Some CASE tools automatically number messages in collaboration diagrams, and some will also generate textual documentation from collaboration (and sequence) diagrams.*

The sequence diagram for the same scenario is given in Figure 5.5. (Due to space limitations, the Catalog Order's cancelInventoryRequest message to the Product Warehouse and the Credit Authorization Proxy's creditAccount message to the Credit Authorization Agency are omitted from the picture.) The dashed vertical lines are object *lifelines*; each is headed by its object and represents the lifetime of that object's participation in this scenario. Although none in the figure do so, the objects at the head of a lifeline may include a second compartment that lists values for its attributes (just as some of the objects in the collaboration diagram in Figure 5.4 include attribute values).

The solid-headed, solid-shafted arrows indicate messages sent and are labeled with the message and its data (if any). The dashed-shafted stick-headed arrows show return of control. When a value is returned, the return arrows may be labeled with return followed by the value(s) in parentheses. When no value is returned, you may omit them, or you may include them either unlabeled or labeled just with return.

Time passes as you proceed "down the page" in a sequence diagram. So, the relative ordering of messages is specified by the relative vertical positions of the messages in the diagram. With the exception of object creation (covered below), the horizontal position of an object lifeline has no special significance; likewise, the fact that some lifelines appear below others (such as the Line Item and Customer instances residing in the same column) has no semantic importance. In addition, a message may be sent from left to right or vice versa, which is illustrated in Figure 5.5.

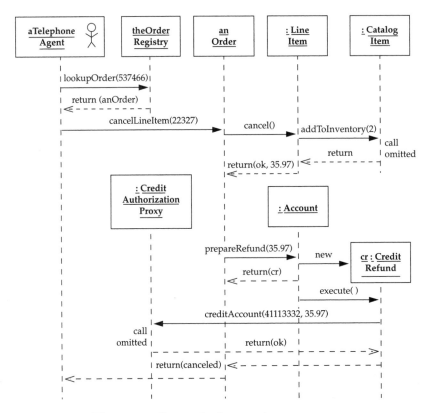

Figure 5.5 *The sequence diagram for the scenario.*

The collaboration and sequence diagrams in Figures 5.4 and 5.5, respectively, provide essentially the same information, but in different forms. The collaboration diagram is oriented spatially, meaning that you can see the object and link topology at a glance. To determine the sequencing of the messages, however, you must inspect the message numbers. The sequence diagram, on the other hand, is laid out in the temporal plane. This enables you to pick out the ordering of messages quickly, but you must study the message arrows to discover how objects are linked to one another.

Note

Some CASE tools will produce one diagram from the other. That is, they will take a sequence diagram as input and produce the corresponding collaboration diagram, or vice versa. This fact underscores the point that the two diagrams are different presentations of the same basic information.

Interaction diagrams are important because they show patterns of object interactions. That is, they specify how objects interact over time to achieve some
end. They also indicate what an individual object does in terms of the messages
to which it responds (or, alternatively, of the methods it offers). Therefore,
when an object receives a message in an interaction diagram, its class must
define that method (in the third compartment of the class in the class diagram).

In the diagrams in Figures 5.4 and 5.5, for example, aTelephoneAgent sends a
lookupOrder message to theOrderRegistry. As a result, in the class diagram for
this system, the Order Registry class must list lookupOrder as one of the methods in its third compartment. This method is included in the Order Registry
class shown in Figure 5.6. In general, the methods listed in a class are the
accumulation of all the messages received by instances of that class across all
scenarios.

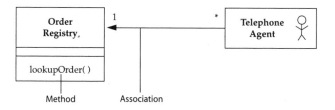
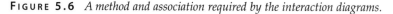

F IGURE 5.6 *A method and association required by the interaction diagrams.*

Interaction diagrams also tell you what associations must exist in your class
diagram and in which direction those associations must be implemented.
When one instance sends a message to another, the two objects must have a
link, meaning that their classes must have an association. Furthermore, the link
must exist from the first to the second object, meaning that the association must
(at a minimum) be directed from the first object's class to the second object's
class.

Because aTelephoneAgent instance sends a message to theOrderRegistry
instance, there must be a link from the former to the latter. In fact, this link is
represented explicitly in the collaboration diagram in Figure 5.4. An association
must, therefore, exist from the Telephone Agent class to the Order Registry
class, as also shown in Figure 5.6.

In summary, your class diagram must be consistent with your interaction diagrams in the following ways:

- Any object in an interaction diagram must be an instance of a class in the class diagram.

- When an object receives a message, that object's class must include the name of that message as one of its methods in its third compartment in the class diagram.

- When one object sends a message to another, the first object has a link to the second. The class diagram must include an association between the two objects' classes. Furthermore, the association must be directed from the first object's class to the second object's class.

Some CASE tools include an application that will diagnose any inconsistencies between the diagrams. Some also provide an option to automatically add a method to a class when an instance of the class receives that message in an interaction diagram.

5.4 Collaborations Provide the Glue

Consider Figures 5.2 through 5.5 again. The before and after views in Figures 5.2 and 5.3 are remarkably similar to the interaction diagrams in Figures 5.4 and 5.5. For the most part, the same set of objects and links are depicted in all four figures. The first two figures are a static view of the before and after configurations of the Cancel Order Item use case that assumes the normal case, namely that the item is successfully canceled. Figures 5.4 and 5.5 show how objects interact in the scenario for that normal case. As a result, the interaction diagrams in those two figures begin and end in the configurations depicted in Figures 5.2 and 5.3, respectively.

This raises an interesting point. Suppose that, for each interaction diagram you draw, you wish to illustrate the starting and ending object diagrams. How do you tie the interaction and object diagrams together? UML provides a construct called the *collaboration* that you can use for this purpose.

A collaboration groups a "society" of classes or objects that achieve some purpose together. A collaboration is indicated by a dashed oval labeled with the name of the collaboration, as shown in Figure 5.7. It is not a part of any particular diagram, but its static and dynamic manifestations are a class or object diagram and an interaction diagram, respectively. The former indicates what entities participate in the collaboration.

These objects or classes in a collaboration may span different layers or subsystems. The interaction diagram shows how those objects interact during the collaboration. The static view of the collaboration in Figure 5.7 is the combination of object diagrams in Figures 5.2 and 5.3, whereas the dynamic view is either of the interaction diagrams in Figures 5.4 and 5.5.

Canceling a
Pending Item

FIGURE 5.7 *The collaboration for a Cancel Order Item scenario.*

In general, you can represent each scenario as a collaboration. A use case, then, has a set of collaborations—one for each of the use case's interesting scenarios. Each collaboration has the following:

- A textual specification of the scenario, which outlines the steps in the scenario. (Specifications were discussed in Section 2.8.1.)

- One or more object diagrams that specify the objects that participate in the scenario and their links with one another.

- A collaboration and/or sequence diagram specifying the interactions between objects in the scenario.

Figure 5.8 depicts these relationships.

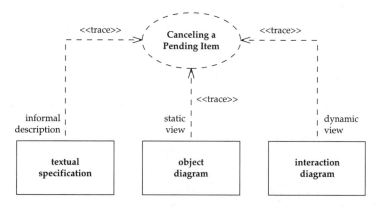

FIGURE 5.8 *The views of a collaboration for a scenario.*

5.5   Additional Features of Interaction Diagrams

Figures 5.4 and 5.5 illustrate the rudimentary features of collaboration and sequence diagrams. This basic notation is sufficient for typical situations. In some cases, however, you may want to depict additional interaction patterns such as iteration, branching, and object creation and destruction. For example, how do you show that an object is created during the scenario described by the interaction diagram? (Figures 5.4 and 5.5 include the creation of an object, a Credit Refund instance although that notation has yet to be explained.) How do you indicate that one object *conditionally* sends a message to another, and the conditions under which the message is sent?

One of the contributions of UML is that while these additional constructs are uncommon in older object-oriented design notations, UML offers specific syntax for them. Interaction diagrams may include iteration of message sending, conditional message sending, and object creation and destruction. Collaboration diagrams may also indicate how links are implemented, whereas sequence diagrams may include timing constraints.

5.5.1   Iteration

Consider an Order that has several Line Items. When the Order is canceled, it must cancel each of its Line Items. An interaction diagram for such a scenario could include multiple Line Item objects with the Order sending a cancel message to each of them. It would be simpler, however, to depict this as iteration; that is, a cancel message, shown once, may be sent multiple times.

UML provides notation for interaction in both collaboration and sequence diagrams. Figure 5.9 illustrates the use of iteration in a collaboration diagram. In the figure, aTelephoneAgent looks up an Order using an order number and then cancels the Order. The Order sends a cancel message to each of its Line Items. In this scenario, each Line Item is still pending. Therefore, it releases its allocated inventory by sending an addToInventory message to its Catalog Item.

The asterisk after message number 2.1 indicates that the message will be sent multiple times. The bound of the iteration is specified in the parentheses that follow the asterisk. The bound in the figure indicates that the Order sends the message to each of its Line Items. (UML does not prescribe any particular syntax for iteration bounds.) The stacking of those objects denotes the fact that multiple Line Items and Catalog Items are involved in this scenario.

The analogous iteration in a sequence diagram is shown in Figure 5.10 (except that the sequence diagram omits the looking up of the Order). The rectangle encloses the area to which the iteration is applied. The bound of the iteration is included in the upper left corner of the rectangle. (You can imagine the rectangle being "unfolded" that many times.) Once again, the stacking of Line Items and Catalog Items indicates that several instances of each are involved.

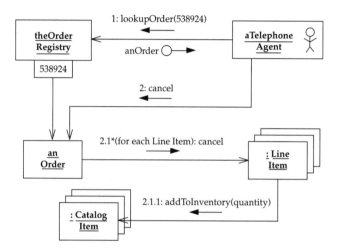

FIGURE 5.9   *Iteration in a collaboration diagram.*

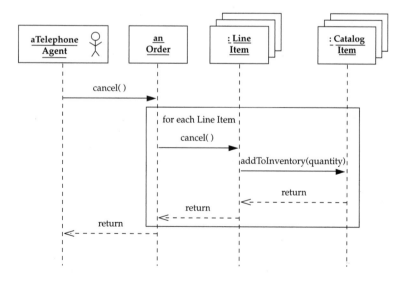

FIGURE 5.10   *Iteration in a sequence diagram.*

5.5.2 Conditional Messages and Branching

In some cases, you may want to specify that one object sends a message to another only if some particular condition holds in the sending object. The sender evaluates the condition and determines whether to send the message based on the result. A collaboration or sequence diagram can show such conditional sending of a message.

Consider the scenario depicted in Figures 5.9 and 5.10. It assumes that all Line Items are still pending because each tells its Catalog Item to add its quantity back to inventory. If the Line Item were already shipped or previously canceled, however, it would simply return instead. Suppose you want to depict the fact that a Line Item sends the addToInventory message only if its status is pending. The collaboration diagram in Figure 5.11 includes that depiction.

Note that, unlike its corresponding message in Figure 5.9, the addToInventory message in Figure 5.11 is prefaced by [status == pending]. The square brackets denote an enclosed guard, which may be any boolean-valued expression. (UML does not define syntax for the expression; this example uses a C-style comparison.) The message will be sent only if the guard is true. In other words, each Line Item sends the addToInventory message only if its status attribute is equal to pending.

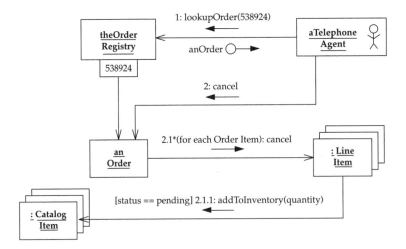

FIGURE 5.11 *Conditional messaging in a collaboration diagram.*

The syntax for a conditional message in a sequence diagram is exactly the same as that in a collaboration diagram. That is, the guard within square brackets precedes the message. Figure 5.12 contains the sequence diagram for the scenario depicted in Figure 5.11. The guard in the figure appears above the message rather than before it due to space limitations. In general, the guard appears *before* its message.

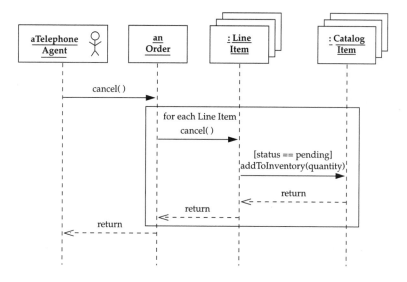

FIGURE 5.12   *Conditional messaging in a sequence diagram.*

The examples in Figures 5.11 and 5.12 show the conditional sending of a message. By including multiple messages with mutually exclusive guards, it is also possible to show more general branching.

Consider the handling of a mail order. A mail order agent enters the order into the DryGoods.com system (introduced in Chapter 1) and then commits it. The first step in the committing of the order is to authorize the amount of the purchase against the credit or debit card number listed in the order. If this authorization is approved, the line item(s) in the order should be committed. If it is denied, an external customer relations system must be informed of the problem.

Figures 5.13 and 5.14 contain the collaboration and sequence diagrams, respectively, for this scenario. In the collaboration diagram, the Mail Order asks a Credit Authorization object to authorize the purchase and receives a boolean-valued result. The assignment notation before the message name indicates that the Order stores the result of the authorization request in an authorized variable. Observe that the diagram includes two succeeding messages numbered 1.2, each with a different guard. If the authorized variable is true (meaning that the purchase was authorized), the Order sends a commit message to its Line Item. If that variable is false, the Order sends an unfundedMailOrder message to the Customer Relations system.

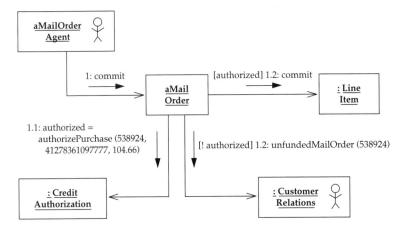

FIGURE 5.13 *Branching messaging in a collaboration diagram.*

The sequence diagram depicts the same branching logic. The Mail Order asks the Credit Authorization object to authorize the purchase and receives a boolean-valued result: authorized. The Order then has two guarded messages sent from the same point of origin. The fact that the messages originate from the same point indicates that no time passes between the testing of the two guards. In other words, the Mail Order tests the authorized variable and, based on the result, sends one of the two messages.

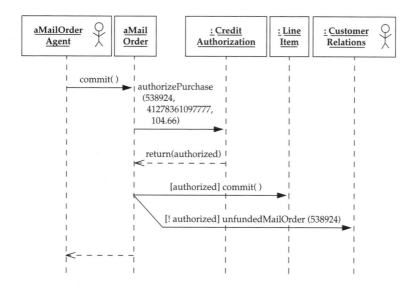

FIGURE 5.14   *Branching messaging in a sequence diagram.*

Note that, after the branching calls in Figure 5.14, the Mail Order object will have two different returns of control (one each from the Line Item instance and the Customer Relations actor object). How do you show both returns? Showing one below the other is misleading because the two are not related temporally; instead, they exist in two completely different flows of control. To depict them both, you separate the Mail Order's lifeline into two parts, as shown in Figure 5.15. The two lifelines are rejoined to show that the two paths share subsequent interactions. You also separate an object's lifeline when you have two different *calls* to the object in different branch paths.

When you have branches like those shown in Figures 5.13 and 5.14, or conditional messages like those in Figures 5.11 and 5.12, you are incorporating two scenarios into one diagram. Figures 5.13 and 5.14, for example, describe the case where a Mail Order is authorized, as well as the case where the authorization is denied. You should use such branching judiciously because the interaction diagram can become very complex.

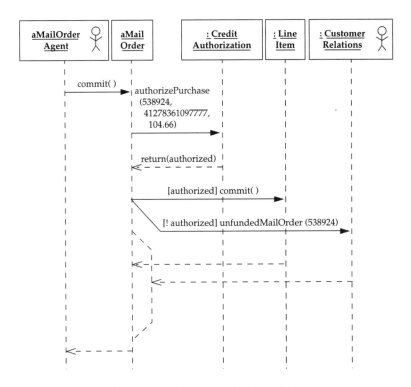

FIGURE 5.15 *Showing multiple lifelines in a branching sequence diagram.*

Suppose, for example, that each branch in Figures 5.13 and 5.14 (that is, committing a Line Item and handling an unfunded Mail Order) requires several steps. The resulting diagram might be extremely confusing. In such a case, you can always separate the diagram into two parts, one for each branch. For this example, one interaction diagram would depict the case where you receive true from the Credit Authorization, while another would depict the steps required when you receive false.

Also note that the two guards in the figures are mutually exclusive; only one of the guards can be true. What if you have overlapping guards? If more than one guard evaluates to be true, both branches are taken. In other words, you have concurrency. Chapter 8, "Architectural Models," discusses this situation.

5.5.3 Object Creation and Destruction

It is often useful to indicate when an object may be created or deleted (or both) during a scenario. For example, in a scenario where an Order adds a Line Item to itself, you might want to show that the Line Item object is being created during that scenario. Likewise, you might want to indicate that an Order deletes a Line Item during a scenario.

An object that is created or deleted during a scenario can include a new or destroyed property, respectively, in the corresponding collaboration diagram. Figure 5.16 depicts a scenario in which an Order creates a new Line Item. The new property in the Line Item instance indicates the creation of that object during the scenario. The figure uses a new message for the creation (corresponding to the new operator in C++ or Java), but this is not prescribed by UML. (An instance creation method in Smalltalk, for example, can have any name.)

Figure 5.17 contains a collaboration diagram for a scenario in which an Order is deleting one of its Line Items. (This might occur during the order entry phase when a customer decides he or she doesn't really want that fancy umbrella after all.) The Order, upon being told to remove the Line Item for a particular catalog item number, finds that Line Item and deletes it. The destroyed property indicates that the Line Item is being deleted during the scenario. The diagram uses delete, the C++ operator, as the message name for deletion, but again, this name is not required by UML. The diagram also ignores how the Order finds the Line Item with the correct catalog item number.

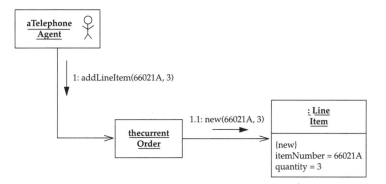

FIGURE 5.16   *Object creation in a collaboration diagram.*

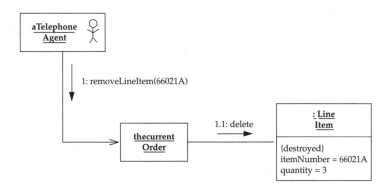

FIGURE 5.17   *Object destruction in a collaboration diagram.*

If an object is both created *and* deleted during a scenario, it is labeled either with both new and destroyed or simply with transient (which is shorthand for new and destroyed). Links in a collaboration diagram can also be annotated with the new and destroyed properties to show that they are created and destroyed during a scenario. In Figure 5.18, for example, the link from the Telephone Agent to the Order has been annotated to show that the Telephone Agent obtains that link in this scenario. (The figure is otherwise identical to Figure 5.9.)

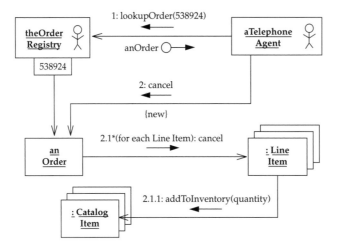

FIGURE 5.18 *Link creation a collaboration diagram.*

To show that an object is created in a sequence diagram, the creating message terminates at the edge of the object's rectangle (rather than on the object's lifeline). Figure 5.19 contains the sequence diagram equivalent of the collaboration diagram in Figure 5.16. The diagram indicates that the Order is creating the Line Item with the *new* message, in that the message terminates at the edge of the Line Item object's rectangle.

When an object is deleted in a sequence diagram, the deleting message ends the object's lifeline. This termination is further emphasized with an X at the end of the lifeline. (This distinguishes object deletion from the case where the object's participation in the scenario has ended, but the object still exists.) The sequence diagram in Figure 5.20 models the same scenario as does the collaboration diagram in Figure 5.17. The Order is deleting the Line Item in the diagram.

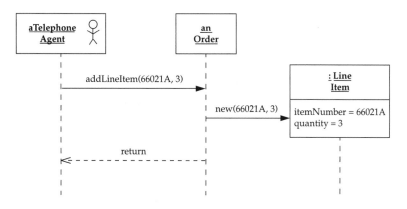

FIGURE 5.19 *Object creation a sequence diagram.*

> ### Note
>
> *Depicting object destruction is most useful when you are using an implementation language, such as C++, that requires the programmer to delete objects explicitly. Developers using languages like Java and Smalltalk, in which objects are automatically deleted through a process called garbage collection, seldom worry about such matters. (They worry instead about disposing of object references once they are no longer needed.) They might use the object destruction notation in a case where they know that, by virtue of one object "forgetting" another, the second object is now eligible for garbage collection.*

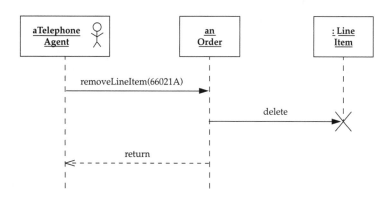

FIGURE 5.20 *Object destruction a sequence diagram.*

5.5.4 Timing Constraints

In some situations, such as in the development of real-time applications, you may want to specify the maximum or minimum time bounds between two points in a scenario. A sequence diagram is temporally oriented and, therefore, can include timing constraints. (A collaboration diagram, on the other hand, is organized spatially and, therefore, does not include such constraints.)

Because time passes from the top to the bottom of a sequence diagram, the vertical axis can be calibrated with specific time intervals. Alternatively, points in the diagram can be annotated with *timing marks*; then, these marks can be included in constraints that specify temporal requirements. Figure 5.21 illustrates the use of timing marks. Two marks, a and b, annotate the sending of an authorization request and the return result from that request. The constraint in the diagram states that the time from a to b must be less than 10 seconds.

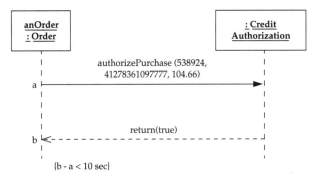

FIGURE 5.21 *Timing constraints in a sequence diagram.*

You can annotate a sequence diagram with any constraint involving any combination of timing marks. For example, you can specify that the sum of the times across two different intervals is less than (or greater than) some bound, or that one temporal interval is greater than another. In typical cases, however, you want to specify a minimum or maximum bound across a single interval. For that type of constraint, UML provides the abbreviated form illustrated in Figure 5.22. You simply bracket the interval and label the bracket with the minimum or maximum bound.

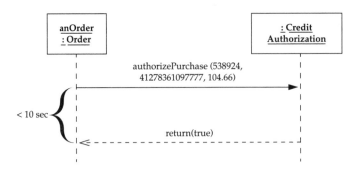

FIGURE 5.22 *An abbreviated form of timing constraints.*

5.5.5   The Origin of Links

Because a collaboration diagram is a spatial representation, it can include an indication of how one object obtains a link to another in that scenario. The role at the target end of the link is annotated with one of the following stereotypes:

«association»: The client object has a field holding a reference to the target object (or the client has a reference to a container object holding the reference to the target object).

«global»: The client object obtains a reference to the target object from a global variable (or from a public static field in a class).

«local»: The client object has a reference to the target object in a local variable of a method, most likely because the client called a method in some other object and received the reference as a return value.

«parameter»: The client object receives a reference to the target object as a parameter in a call to a client method.

«self»: The client object references itself through an implicit or explicit this or self reference (depending upon the implementation language).

If no stereotype is listed, «association» is assumed.

In Figure 5.23, the collaboration diagram from Figure 5.18 has been extended to include the implementation of the links. The Telephone Agent stores a reference to the Order Registry in a field. Likewise, each Line Item contains a field that refers to the Line Item's Catalog Item. The Order instance includes a field that points to a container object that in turn holds references to the Order's Line Items. On the other hand, a Telephone Agent obtains a reference to the Order as a return value from the lookupOrder call.

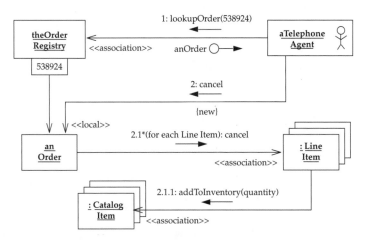

FIGURE 5.23 *The implementation of links in a collaboration diagram.*

5.5.6 Activations

You may encounter situations in which you would like to depict exactly when an object is in control. A sequence diagram can include *activations* that indicate the intervals of control for each object in the diagram. Figure 5.24 illustrates a scenario in which an Order consisting of a single Line Item is canceled.

The sequence diagram in the figure has been augmented to include each object's activations. The shaded regions along an object's lifeline indicate intervals during which that object is executing (or is in a thread or process that is swapped out but otherwise would be executing). The unshaded rectangles indicate the intervals during which an object has made a blocking call and is awaiting the return. (A blocking call is one in which the caller is suspended while the called method executes. This topic is discussed in Chapter 8.)

Note

Using a shaded activation to indicate that the caller is executing is not standard in the current version of UML. UML uses only unshaded activations to indicate that an object is either executing or blocked. Nevertheless, I find this distinction to be an extremely useful extension to the standard notation.

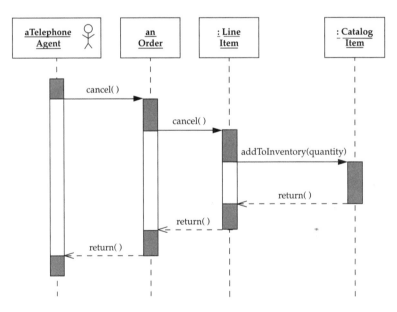

FIGURE 5.24 *Activations in a sequence diagram.*

When an object calls a method in itself, the calling method is blocked awaiting the return from the called method. Stacking one activation on top of another depicts this simply, as shown in Figure 5.25. The calling activation remains shaded because the object retains control.

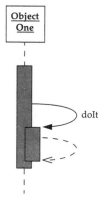

FIGURE 5.25 *Stacking activations for reflexive calls.*

5.6 Class Cards

The class-diagramming notation described in Chapter 2 provides a means of defining the static properties of classes. The interaction diagrams described in the preceding section allow you to describe the dynamic interactions of those classes. The graphical nature of these diagrams provides a "big picture" view of classes and scenarios. Nonetheless, some projects prefer a "lighter weight" notation for brainstorming, working with business analysts, and so forth. Class cards are one such notation.

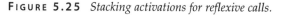

Note

Class cards are not an integral part of UML. Nonetheless, several books describing their use during object-oriented analysis and design have been published. Refer to the following list:

> *Bellin, D. and S. Simone. 1997.* The CRC Card Book. *Reading, Mass.: Addison-Wesley.*

> *Taylor, D. 1995.* Business Engineering with Object Technology. *New York: John Wiley & Sons, Inc.*

> *Wilkinson, N. 1995.* Using CRC Cards: An Informal Approach to Object-Oriented Development. *New York: SIGS Books.*

> *Wirfs-Brock, R., Brian Wilkerson, and Lauren Wiener. 1990.* Designing Object-Oriented Software. *New Jersey: Prentice-Hall.*

continues

Class cards remain a popular alternative to graphical notation. For this reason, you may encounter class cards in your work. Therefore, a basic description of the notation is included in this section. Class cards are described here, rather than in Chapter 2, because their more robust form, class-responsibility-collaboration (CRC) cards, include a modicum of dynamic information in the form of collaborations.

When you employ class cards, you develop one card for each class in your application. The physical medium can be as simple as sheets of paper or white index cards. Each class card lists the *responsibilities* of a class, which are what an instance of the class must know and what it must be able to do. What an instance must know is the state information it must retain—in other words, its attribute values and links to other objects. What it must do is its list of methods.

Figure 5.26 includes a sample class card for the Line Item class in the DryGoods.com system. The figure also shows the normal class diagram notation for the same class. As you can see, the two representations of the class contain the same information (although the class card version may seem a little less formal in its presentation).

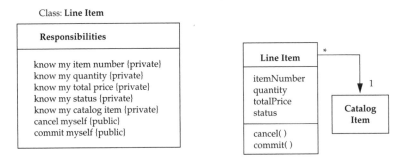

FIGURE 5.26 *A class card and its class diagram equivalent.*

To provide at least the rudiments of a dynamic view, class cards are often extended to include object *collaborations*. A collaboration occurs when one object must invoke a method in (or send a message to) another. When an object responsibility is a method (rather than state information), a separate column on the class card can be used to indicate with what other objects this object must collaborate to fulfill that responsibility. To be more precise, the class names of those other objects are listed.

Figure 5.27 indicates that when a Line Item commits and cancels itself, it must collaborate with its associated Catalog Item. This type of card is frequently referred to as a *class-responsibility-collaboration card*, or *CRC card* for short.

Class: **Line Item**

Responsibilities	Collaborations
know my item number {private} know my quantity {private} know my total price {private} know my status {private} know my catalog item {private} cancel myself {public} commit myself {public}	Catalog Item Catalog Item

FIGURE 5.27 *Adding collaborations to a class card.*

The class card in Figure 5.27 indicates that a Line Item calls a method in a Catalog Item when committing or canceling itself. What the class card fails to specify, however, is what Catalog Item method is called. Furthermore, if an object collaborates with multiple other objects when carrying out a responsibility, you do not see the order in which those collaborations occur. UML interaction diagrams provide a more complete picture of system dynamics because they depict exactly what methods are called (or what messages are sent) in a particular scenario and in what order. In addition, you can deduce a skeletal implementation of a method by considering what that method does in all the interaction diagrams in which it is called.

5.7   State Transition Diagrams

UML provides three forms of dynamic diagrams: activity diagrams, interaction diagrams, and state transition diagrams. Activity diagrams, described in Chapter 2, are used to model the dynamics of use cases. An activity diagram is a type of flow chart of the use case. An activity diagram can also be used at a higher level (for example, to specify use case sequencing) as well as at a lower level (for example, to show the steps in an individual activity). It is an abstract view of behavior, however, because it leaves open the question of who carries out each activity.

An interaction diagram, described earlier in this chapter, specifies how objects interact in a particular scenario. As such, it indicates what object methods are called in which order in that particular scenario. On the other hand, it says nothing about what an object does internally, or how an object may change internally over time.

A state transition diagram, discussed in this section, describes the state-based behavior of a class of instances across all scenarios. Although you could draw a state transition diagram for any class, the diagrams for many classes would be relatively uninteresting. An object has meaningful state-based behavior if you can say one of the following:

- The object passes through a set of states.

- Some of the object's behaviors are meaningful in some states but meaningless in others. In other words, whether the object responds to a particular request depends upon the state it is in.

- The object's methods must be executed in a particular order.

Consider an Automated Teller Machine class in a remote banking application. An ATM instance is always in a state in which it expects only one or two of its methods to be invoked. First it's in a state where it expects a card to be inserted, then (after the card is inserted, and it reads the information from the card), it's in a state where it expects a PIN to be entered, and so forth. You could draw a state transition diagram for the ATM class that depicts those states and transitions.

A Bank Account class, on the other hand, has no analogous conditional behavior. It is always in a state in which any of its methods (to deposit money, to withdraw money, or the check the balance) can be invoked. Put another way, you can call a Bank Account's methods in any order. For example, you can request two deposits, followed by three withdrawals, followed by a query, followed by another withdrawal, and so on. Therefore, a state transition diagram for the Bank Account would be uninteresting because it would consist of a single state.

A state transition diagram consists of one or more state machines.

5.7.1 Events

State machines communicate by sending events to one another. The precise interpretation of an event is left open by UML. In some cases, an event may correspond to a signal, such as a hardware interrupt. In other situations, it may correspond to a message, such as a method invocation or an inter-process message.

An event may be accompanied by data. Recall that a Catalog Item in the DryGoods.com system represents an item listed in (and, therefore, sold through) the catalog. Suppose a Catalog Item has a state machine. That state machine may receive an `allocateFromInventory` event, which represents a method invocation that is requesting inventory. That event always includes the quantity to be allocated as data.

5.7.2 States

A state is an abstraction of an object's state. It can represent particular values for a subset of the object's attributes and links. A transition between states, therefore, represents some change in those values.

A state is depicted in UML as a *capsule* with a name and/or a set of actions. The general form is shown in Figure 5.28. Either the name or actions may be omitted. An initial starting point and final ending point are indicated using a solid circle and a bull's eye, respectively.

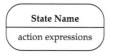

F I G U R E 5.28 *The state notation.*

Under the standard interpretation of state transition diagrams, time passes in states. (Transitions are assumed to be almost instantaneous.) *Activities* are behaviors that take non-negligible time and, therefore, must be executed within states. An *action*, on the other hand, is a behavior that takes very little time and, hence, can be executed during a transition. Examples of actions are setting an attribute value and generating an event (or message) to another state machine.

There are four ways actions can be taken within states:

- *An action can be taken upon entry to the state, regardless of how the state is entered.* The action expression for an entry action is the entry keyword, followed by a slash (/), followed by a description of the action. Upon entry to the Count Pings state in Figure 5.29, for example, the variable i will be set to 0.

- *An action can be taken on exit from the state, no matter how the state is left.* The syntax is the exit keyword, followed by a slash, followed by the action. Upon exit from the Count Pings state in Figure 5.29, the value of i will be displayed.

- *Another state machine can be invoked while in the state.* For this, the do keyword is used with the name of that other state machine listed after a slash. During the Count Pings state, the ComputeJ state machine will be executed. (This machine must have an initial state and a final state.)

- *An event can be received in place in the state (that is, without leaving the state), thus triggering an action.* The event name and action are separated by a slash. In Figure 5.29, for example, ping is the name of an event. When that event is received in the Count Pings state, the variable i is incremented. (No state transition occurs.)

UML doesn't specify a syntax for action expressions. Figure 5.29 uses C-style syntax.

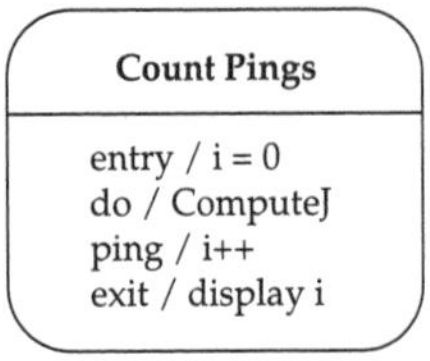

Figure 5.29 *An example of a state.*

All of the expressions outlined above are *action* expressions. Activities have been de-emphasized in the current UML state machine formalism. An activity can be specified only as an amalgam of actions.

5.7.3   Transitions

A transition is the movement of an object from one state to another. It is assumed to take almost no time. In a state machine, a transition is depicted as a directed edge between the source and destination states. The transition occurs as a result of some triggering condition, and that condition normally labels the transition. Possible triggers for a transition include the following:

- The receipt of an event

- The receipt of an event and a guarding condition

- A condition becomes true

- A certain amount of time passes

One trigger is the receipt of an event. Figure 5.30 contains a state machine for a type of answering machine often found at movie theaters. The answering machine is initially in the Idle state. When it receives a `phoneRings` event, it moves to the Playing state (where it answers the phone and plays its message). It remains in that state (playing its message) until it receives a `callerHangsUp` event; at that point, it moves back to the Idle state.

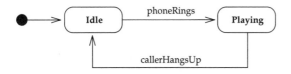

FIGURE 5.30   *Transitions triggered by events.*

The receipt of an event together with a guarding condition can also trigger a transition. That is, the event must be received *and* the condition must be true for the transition to be taken. The condition is included within square brackets after the event. Figure 5.31 depicts the two possible states of a Catalog Item instance. An `allocateFromInventory` event sent to the instance includes the requested quantity of inventory as data. When a Catalog Item in the Available state receives such an event, *and* the desired quantity is more than the quantity in stock, a transition to the Back-Ordered state occurs.

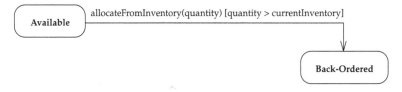

FIGURE 5.31 *A transition triggered by an event and a guard.*

Guarding conditions can also be included when events are received in place in a state. Figure 5.32 describes the Available state in the state machine for a Catalog Item. When a Catalog Item instance in that state receives an `allocateFromInventory` event for which the requested quantity is no more than the quantity in stock, that requested amount is subtracted from the quantity in stock.

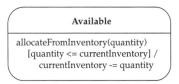

FIGURE 5.32 *An internal action triggered by an event and a guard.*

An internal condition rather than the receipt of an event can trigger a transition. The condition is included as a `when` clause that labels the transition. In Figure 5.33, for example, the transition from the Available to the Back-Ordered state occurs when the current inventory reaches zero. Note that a `when` condition differs from a guarding condition in that the former is evaluated constantly, whereas the latter is evaluated only once. The guarding condition in Figure 5.31, for example, is evaluated only once, when the `allocateFromInventory` event is received. The condition in Figure 5.33, on the other hand, is evaluated continually in the Available state.

FIGURE 5.33 *A transition triggered by a condition.*

An additional possible triggering condition for a transition is the passing of a specified period of time. (These are sometimes called *time-out transitions*.) The period is specified as part of an `after` clause. Figure 5.34 indicates that the object in the Await Reply state will, after 10 seconds, take a transition to the Resend Request state.

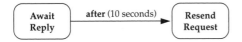

FIGURE 5.34 *A transition triggered by the passage of time.*

A state machine can execute actions while taking a transition. Recall, however, that an action must take almost zero time. During a transition, therefore, an object can carry out only behaviors that require negligible time, such as setting attribute values, sending events, and so forth. The actions taken during a transition are separated from the triggering condition by a slash. In addition, for any action that sends an event, regardless of whether the action is taken during a transaction or within a state, the event name is preceded by a carat (^).

Figure 5.35 indicates that a transition from the Back-Ordered state to the Available state occurs when an `itemAvailable` event is received. Furthermore, during that transition, the current inventory is increased. It also specifies that during both transitions from the Available state to the Back-Ordered state, a `backorderItem` event will be sent to the Warehouse. When an event is generated, the receiver may be shown using the *dot notation* (the receiver and the event name separated by a dot), as shown in the diagram. If no such receiver is specified, the assumption is that the event is being broadcast.

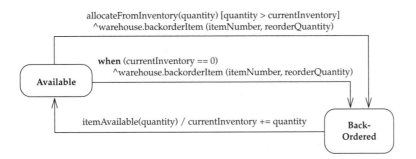

FIGURE 5.35 *An action taken during a transition.*

Observe that the two transitions into the Back-Ordered state in Figure 5.35 execute the same action, that of sending the `backorderItem` event to the Warehouse. Assuming that those transitions are the Back-Ordered state's only two incoming transitions, the action can be specified as an entry condition for the state instead. This alternative model in shown in Figure 5.36, the complete state machine for a Catalog Item.

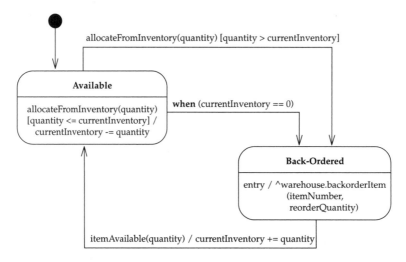

FIGURE 5.36 *A state machine for a Catalog Item.*

5.7.4 Composite States

The UML state machine syntax includes the full Statechart notation (Harel 1987). An important grouping feature of Statecharts is the *composite state*. A composite state is composed of a collection of lower-level sub-states that share semantics. For example, all of the sub-states may have the same outgoing transition. The states outside the composite state in some cases may ignore the internal details of the composite state and interact with it as a single state.

Figure 5.37 includes a composite Pending state in a state machine for an Order. That state in turn consists of two lower-level states, Entered and Funded. The transition to the Canceled state, enabled by the receipt of a `cancel` event, originates from the Pending composite state. This transition can occur from either of the two internal states. (If a `cancel` event occurs while the Order is in the Open, Fulfilled, or Canceled state, on the other hand, it is ignored. The Telephone Agent is entering an Order in the Open state. It can be aborted, in which case the Order instance is deleted, but it cannot yet be canceled.) The state machine in the figure otherwise has the normal semantics already discussed.

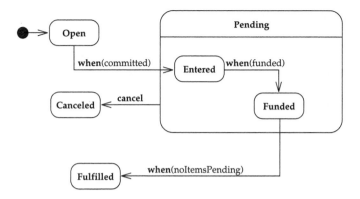

FIGURE 5.37   *A composite state.*

The external states sometimes may view the composite state as a single state. One such case is when an external state has a transition into the composite state (rather than into one of its internal sub-states). In Figure 5.38, for example, the Open state has a transition into the Pending state. In these situations, the composite state must have an initial internal state, and execution starts at that initial state. In this example, the Pending state has an initial internal state, Entered. The state machines in Figures 5.37 and 5.38 have identical semantics.

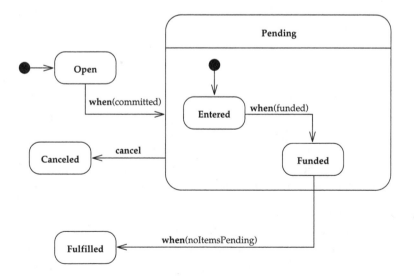

FIGURE 5.38   *A transition into a composite state.*

When a transition leaves a composite state, the state may also retain a history of its internal location, allowing a subsequent transition to return to that location. In Figure 5.39, for example, the circled *H* in the Pending state is an internal *history state*. When a transition leaves the Pending state, that history state remembers the internal state from which the transition left. On any subsequent transition into that history state, control resumes in the remembered internal state.

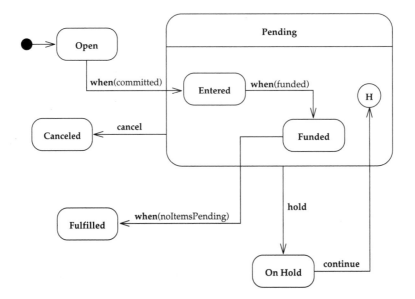

FIGURE 5.39 *A history state.*

In the example in Figure 5.39, an Order in the Pending state can be placed on hold. At that point, all activity on the Order is suspended. If the Order is taken off hold (through the receipt of a `continue` event), however, the Order resumes its previous state. If the Order was in the Entered state when put on hold, for example, it will be in the Entered state when continued.

5.7.5   Parallel States and State Machines

Like the Statecharts on which they are based, UML state transition diagrams can include parallel state machines and parallel states. The state transition diagram for a Catalog Item shown in Figure 5.40 includes two internal state machines that execute in parallel. The dashed line is included to emphasize the concurrency.

From a logical point of view, when you create a Catalog Item instance, an instance of each of the two state machines starts executing in parallel. One state machine represents the Catalog Item's inventory aspect, which flips between the Available and Back-Ordered states. (This is essentially the state machine in Figure 5.36, although some of its details have been omitted in this figure.) The other machine indicates that a Catalog Item may ping-pong back and forth between being listed in the catalog and being unlisted.

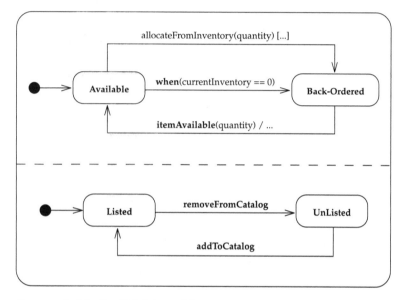

FIGURE 5.40 *Parallel state machines.*

Note that parallel state machines for a class typically indicates a lack of cohesion for that class. In other words, the presence of parallel state machines indicates that an instance of the class engages in different, unrelated activities. To increase the cohesion of the Catalog Item class, you could move the inventory management responsibility into a separate Inventory Item class. Consult Section 4.2.4, "Inheritance Coupling," in Chapter 4, "Flexibility Guidelines for Class Diagrams," for further discussion of this separation. Of course, this is merely a guideline because some classes, such as facades, participate in various types of activities (Gamma et al. 1995, 185–194).

The transitions in a state machine can also *split* and *join*, resulting in parallel states. Figure 5.41 is a partial state machine for a Line Item. When canceled, a Line Item undertakes two concurrent activities: it tells the appropriate Credit Agency to credit the customer's account, and it tells its Catalog Item to return its quantity back to inventory. The solid bars in the figure are synchronization bars; they have the same semantics as synchronization bars in activity diagrams. The two internal Canceling sub-states can, therefore, execute in parallel (as emphasized by the dashed line between them). Both states must complete before the Line Item enters the Canceled state.

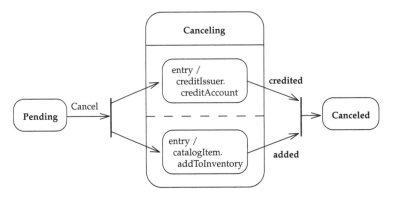

FIGURE 5.41 *Parallel states in a state machine.*

5.8 A Summary of UML Dynamic Diagrams

UML provides three different types of dynamic diagrams: activity diagrams, interaction diagrams (of which collaboration and sequence diagrams are two particular sub-types), and state transition diagrams. While together they form a dynamic model of the system, these three types differ from one another in what they depict and to what they are applied:

- *Activity diagram*: An activity diagram is a workflow view. It depicts a set of activities that must be carried out, together with the temporal sequencing of those activities and the conditions under which they occur. It says nothing about what objects are involved. It, therefore, can be used for everything from showing the sequencing of use cases to flowcharting an individual method.

- *Interaction diagram*: An interaction diagram indicates the sequencing of object interactions in one scenario. It shows exactly which objects respond to which requests, as well as the results of those requests, in that scenario. On the other hand, the internal state of an object, as well as how that state may change during the scenario, is not shown.

- *State transition diagram*: A state transition diagram is used to show the state-based behavior of a class of instances across all scenarios. Whereas the scope of an interaction diagram is a single scenario, a state machine is tied to one class. It specifies the states through which an instance of that class may pass, the messages to which that instance will respond in each of those states, and the conditions that cause the instance to pass from one state to another.

An interaction or state transition diagram can be very precise or relatively abstract. A challenge for the designer is to find the appropriate level of detail given the phase of development. Too much detail too early can stall a project, whereas insufficient detail later often prolongs the implementation effort.

CHAPTER 6

Developing Dynamic Diagrams

Chapter 5, "Dynamic Diagramming Notation," described the concepts and notation for two types of dynamic diagrams: interaction diagrams and state transition diagrams. The former describes how objects interact during a scenario, while the latter models the state-based behavior of a class of instances. These diagrams, together with specifications, such as descriptions of use cases and scenarios, provide you with a rich dynamic model of your application.

How is such a model developed? What steps do you employ? One way that you can develop a dynamic model is to adopt a top-down approach that originates from use cases. It is top-down because you start with general items, use cases (that is, system functions), and you walk through scenarios to identify very specific items, object methods and required links between objects. As an alternative, you can take a more bottom-up approach by starting with specific object responsibilities (that is, methods, attributes, and links) and then use scenarios to validate and expand those responsibilities.

Note that the top-down and bottom-up approaches seek to achieve the same end. The goal of each is to identify the required links between objects, the methods each object must have, and, to some extent, what each method must do. Furthermore, the design artifacts are often the same for each approach although use cases are de-emphasized in the bottom-up approach. The artifacts include:

- *A list of use cases (system functions) and their descriptions*: The use cases describe functional requirements. Designers who use bottom-up, responsibility-driven design sometimes ignore an application's use cases. Furthermore, if you are developing a library of reusable classes, the ultimate use cases may not be apparent.

- *A set of scenarios (use case instances) for each use case*: When described in text, these contain information the interaction diagrams may not include, such as how individual objects change internally.

- *An interaction diagram for each scenario*: These describe the object interactions required to carry out that scenario.

- *State transition diagrams for state-based classes*: These are recommended for classes with interesting state-based behavior.

- *Additions and modifications to class diagrams*: These include methods, associations, and the directions in which associations must be implemented.

The two approaches differ primarily in their starting points and directions. The top-down approach employs use cases to drive the overall process. So, it moves from the general (use cases) to the specific (methods). The bottom-up approach, on the other hand, uses object responsibilities (attributes, links, and methods) as its starting point. So, it moves from the specific to the general.

This chapter describes both approaches, and each is illustrated with a short example. For the top-down approach, the stock-trading system introduced in Section 3.2, "Developing a Class Diagram Using Abstraction," in Chapter 3, "Developing Class Diagrams," is used. The bottom-up approach is used to develop a part of a dynamic model for the library system from that same chapter.

- *Top-down design of system dynamics*: One approach for developing system dynamics entails starting with use cases and, by analyzing the required steps in each use case, identifying individual object behaviors. This approach is explained and illustrated with a stock-trading example.

- *Bottom-up design of system dynamics*: An alternative approach is to concentrate first on the behaviors of individual objects and, then, to use scenarios to validate the list of such behaviors. This approach is described and illustrated with a library example.

- *Developing state-based object dynamics*: Regardless of which approach for analyzing system dynamics you use, you may want to develop state transition diagrams to model the state-based behavior of some classes of objects. How to choose which classes require such diagrams, as well as how to develop those diagrams, are explained.

Although the class diagramming and dynamic modeling approaches are discussed in separate chapters, the two activities do not occur sequentially. Static and dynamic models are typically developed in parallel. More specifically, you develop a partial class diagram, work through the dynamics, revise and expand the class diagram, work through the dynamics again, and so on.

6.1 Top-Down Design of System Dynamics

The top-down approach starts with use cases and "drills down" in each to determine the associations and methods required in the class diagram. The steps in this approach are as follows:

1. Identify the use cases of system behavior.

2. Specify and refine each use case. The use case specification can take any of several different forms, as described in Section 5.1, "Describing Use Cases," in Chapter 5.

3. Define a scenario for each "interesting path" through the use case. If you draw an activity diagram to "flowchart" each use case, for example, each of its paths defines a scenario.

4. Draw an interaction diagram for each scenario.

5. Identify object methods from object interactions in the interaction diagrams. If an object of class C receives event e in an interaction diagram, then class C should list method e in its third compartment in the class diagram.

6. Define each state-based object's behavior with a state transition diagram using interaction diagrams for guidance. Typically, any events consumed and produced by the state transition diagram are messages to and from that object in the interaction diagrams. (Coverage of this subject is deferred to Section 6.3, "Developing State-Based Object Dynamics," later in this chapter.)

6.1.1   Identifying Use Cases

The top-down approach employs use cases as its starting point. Therefore, it is imperative that you produce a complete list of use cases. Chapter 2, "System Functional Models," outlined Jacobson's approach for use case identification, which is to determine how each actor interacts with the system (Jacobson et al. 1992, 155). In particular, you first identify the actors, and then you enumerate the interactions with the system initiated by the actor and the interactions with the actor initiated by the system. Each of those interactions is a use case (or a part of a use case).

Jacobson's approach is not the only way of identifying use cases, however. There are other approaches you can use, either in preference to Jacobson's method (perhaps because you aren't certain what actors you have), or in combination with his approach (as completeness checks to ensure that you have identified all use cases). Two such alternatives are as follows:

- Assuming you have a partial class diagram, consider the life cycles of each class of object. For each class in the system, what use cases cause an instance of the class to be created? What use cases cause an instance to be deleted? What use cases cause its attribute values and links to change over time?

- Examine the verb phrases in the problem statement as possible indications of use cases. In particular, you consider any verb phrase that entails an action. If the action is performed by this system, you ensure that it is fulfilled as one or more use cases.

Consider again the class diagram for a stock-trading system developed in Chapter 3, Section 3.2, "Developing a Class Diagram Using Abstraction." The final class diagram, originally depicted in Figure 3.7, is repeated in Figure 6.1. Figure 6.1 also includes the Buy Order and Sell Order subclasses introduced in Figure 4.20. Recall that this class diagram was developed by abstracting from domain expertise. As a result, the use cases for this system remain undiscovered.

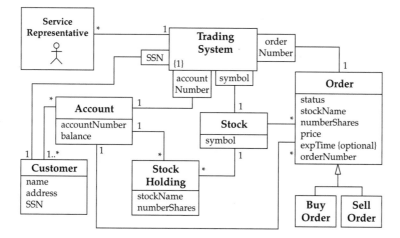

FIGURE 6.1   *The class diagram for the stock-trading system.*

To apply Jacobson's approach to obtain use cases for this problem, identify the actors first. In this problem, at this level of abstraction, the only actor is the Service Representative. Furthermore, because the Service Representative initiates all interactions between the system and a Service Representative, you must only ask yourself, "What does a service representative ask or tell the system to do?"

A Service Representative can do any of the following:

- Enter a buy order

- Enter a sell order

- Cancel an existing order

- Create a new account

- Execute a transfer of stock into the system

- Execute a transfer of stock out of the system

- Execute a transfer of cash into the system

- Execute a transfer of cash out of the system

- Issue a query to obtain information about an existing account, order, or customer

Each of these distinct activities corresponds to a use case. However, this list of use cases may not be complete. How can you be certain you've thought of every interaction involving an actor? What if some system actions don't involve any actors?

As a completeness check, you can consider which use cases act on an instance of each class in the class diagram in Figure 6.1. In particular, which use cases cause an instance to be created or destroyed? Which ones cause an instance's attribute values and links to change?

Note

The discussion of the stock-trading system both in Chapter 3 and here ignores the issue of persistence. All objects are assumed to be in memory. Therefore, destroying an object entails removing all traces of it from the system. If persistence were included here, destroying an object would imply removing it from the database. (It might still exist in some remote, almost inaccessible data warehouse.) For persistent objects, identify the use cases that cause those objects to be removed from memory or from the database.

Consider the Trading System class. Any instances of this class are created during system initialization, and they are not destroyed until system termination. It is generally a good idea to include initialization and termination as use cases so that you can model the required sequence of activities. How does the state of a Trading System instance change over time? Such an instance has no attributes, and its links change only as Customers, Accounts, Stocks, and Orders are added and removed. The creation and destruction of instances of those classes will be considered when those classes are analyzed.

Two new use cases have been identified:

> Start up the system
>
> Shut down the system

What about instances of the Customer class? They are created at the request of Service Representative. So, you need to add a use case to handle the addition of a customer to the system. Customer instances are also destroyed at the request of a Service Representative, so you need a use case for that. How can a Customer instance's state change? Its name attribute can change when a customer asks to have his or her name changed in the system. Hence, you need to add a use case for that. Likewise, the address attribute can change due to a customer request. Therefore, you must introduce a use case for that change. Because social security numbers are used as keys to identify Customer instances, changing a social security number probably requires creating a new Customer instance.

A Customer instance's state includes its links to Accounts. Those links to Accounts can change because a customer can be added to or removed from an account. Therefore, you need use cases for these two functions. Analyzing the Customer class has resulted in the addition of the following six use cases:

Add a new customer

Remove an existing customer

Change a customer's name

Change a customer's address

Add a customer to an account

Remove a customer from an account

Consider the Account class. An instance of the Account class is created when a new account is created. This use case was identified when the Service Representative's interactions with the system were considered. An Account instance is destroyed when an account is removed from the system. So, you must add a use case for that.

An existing Account instance has an account number, which is a key for the account and never changes. It also has a balance, which can rise or fall because money is transferred into or out of the account. Transferring money into and out of an account are already listed as use cases. Can an Account's balance change for any other reason? Yes, it can go up or down when a sell or buy order is executed against the account. Therefore, you need a use case for matching orders. Note that this use case extends the use cases for entering a buy and sell order because entering an order sometimes includes the matching behavior (in particular, when the Order just entered can be matched with an existing Order).

If this system dealt with dividends or charged accounts with a periodic service fee, you would also recognize the need for those use cases while analyzing what changes occur to the balance of an Account. An Account instance also has a set of links to Customers, Orders, and Stock Holdings. Changes to the former were addressed when considering the Customer class. An Account adds and removes links to Orders and Stock Holdings when those objects are created and destroyed. These actions will be addressed when considering the Order and Stock Holding classes.

The analysis of the Account class uncovered the following use cases:

Close an existing account

Execute orders (match buy orders to sell orders)

Next, consider the Stock Holding class. An instance of this class is created or deleted because a customer buys stock for the first time or sells his or her last shares of the stock, respectively. This is part of matching orders, which is already listed as a use case. An instance is also created or deleted because a customer transfers shares of a stock into or out of the system. These two use cases have already been identified. A Stock Holding instance can also be created or deleted if one company is purchased by another, or if one company spins off another. These changes will be discussed when analyzing the Stock class.

How can a Stock Holding's state change? Assume that its stock name is fixed. Its number of shares can increase or decrease when the customer buys or sells shares, which is handled by the use case for matching orders. The number of shares can also change because of a split (either a regular split or the dreaded reverse split). You, therefore, need a use case for applying a stock split. A Stock Holding also has links to an Account and to a Stock, which never change.

Just the following use case was added during the analysis of the Stock Holding class:

Apply a stock split

The next class to analyze is the Stock class. What would cause the system to create a Stock instance? This occurs when a company goes public or is spun off from the parent company. You probably want two separate use cases for these two functions. A Stock instance will be removed when a company goes bankrupt, in which case its holdings disappear, or when a company's stock is converted into shares of another company during a takeover. You also need use cases for these situations.

A Stock instance has links to Stock Holdings and to Orders. Any links it has to Stock Holdings exist as long as the Holdings exist (and the creation and destruction of Holdings has been discussed). Any links it has to Orders most likely exist as long as the Orders are open. Changes to the state of an Order are addressed in the following discussion of the Order class.

The following four use cases were identified during the analysis of the Stock class:

Add a security

Remove an existing security

Spin off a security

Convert one security into another

The last classes to consider are the Order class and its two subclasses: Buy Order and Sell Order. Note that the two subclasses do not introduce any new attributes or associations. Therefore, you need to consider only how an instance of those two subclasses is created or deleted. A Buy Order or Sell Order instance is created when a buy or sell order is entered in the system, respectively; these two use cases have already been listed. Is such an instance ever removed? Obviously, removing an Order when it is executed, canceled, or expired is not desirable, because any subsequent queries about the Order would be impossible. You might want to remove Buy and Sell Orders from the database some number of months or years after those Orders are resolved; in which case, you would add such a use case to the list.

How can an Order instance's state change over time? Its links to a Stock and to an Account never change. (It is always placed for the same security and placed on the same Account.) It status attribute can change in three ways. It changes from open to executed when the Order is matched, and matching orders is on the list of use cases. It changes from open to canceled when the Order is canceled, and this use case is also on the list. It can also change from open to expired when the order expires (that is, when the expiration time of an Order is reached). Therefore, a use case to expire an order must be added to the list.

The number of shares of an Order can change due to a stock split; that use case has already been noted. Likewise, its offered price never changes except due to a stock split. Its expiration time can probably change; a customer can call and ask that the expiration time of an Order be extended, for example. That use case, which is to change an order's expiration time, must be added to the list.

The two following use cases have been added as a result of the analysis of Order, Buy Order, and Sell Order:

Expire an order

Change an order's expiration time

Considering the actors' interactions with the system resulted in a partial list of use cases. This inspection of classes has added several use cases to that list. The complete list follows:

Enter a buy order

Enter a sell order

Cancel an order

Open a new account

Close an existing account

Transfer cash into an account

Transfer cash out of an account

Transfer stock into an account

Transfer stock out of an account

Query the properties of an account

Query the properties of an order

Query the properties of a customer

Start up the system

Shut down the system

Add a new customer

Remove an existing customer

Change a customer's name

Change a customer's address

Add a customer to an account

Remove a customer from an account

Execute orders (match buy orders to sell orders)

Add a security

Remove an existing security

Spin off a security

Convert one security into another

Expire an order

Change an order's expiration time

Apply a stock split

To this point, two approaches have been used to identify use cases: analyzing how actors interact with the system, and considering the lifecycles of instances of of each class. If you have a problem specification, a third possible approach is to isolate the verb phrases in that particular specification and then determine what use case (if any) is suggested by each verb phrase. A written specification for this system was given in Chapter 3, Section 3.2.1, "Determining Classes Using Abstraction. The first paragraph of that specification follows:

> You are to develop a small stock-trading system. Customers place buy and sell orders and securities transfers with service representatives; then, the service representatives enter those orders into the system. The system is closed, meaning that all buys are matched with sells within the system. (This system does not use orders placed with any other system.)

The first sentence is obviously a global statement of work and is not a use case. The second sentence states:

> Customers place buy and sell orders and securities transfers with service representatives; then, the service representatives enter those orders into the system.

This sentence outlines the entering of orders and transfer requests in the system. A service representative can enter two kinds of orders, buy and sell orders, and these two use cases are already listed above. Likewise, a service representative can place four kinds of transfers (cash in, cash out, stock in, and stock out); all four of those use cases have already been identified.

The third sentence follows:

> The system is closed, meaning that all buys are matched with sells within the system.

The closed nature of the system is a constraint on the system, not an indication of a use case. The phrase, "all buys are matched with sells," however, suggests the matching of orders, which is already on the list of use cases.

The final sentence follows:

(This system does not use orders placed with any other system.)

This, again, is a constraint on the system, not a description of required functionality. Although it is not included here, the analysis of the other five paragraphs in the problem specification, likewise, uncovers no additional use cases.

At this point, you have a list of use cases. You may have enumerated that list by any combination of the following:

- Identifying the actors' interactions with the system

- Analyzing the life-cycles of classes in the system

- Isolating the verb phrases in the problem specification

You can now transform the list into a use case diagram, the notation for which was explained in Chapter 1, "System Functional Models." A use case diagram for the stock-trading system is given in Figure 6.2.

NOTE

At first glance, the use case diagram in Figure 6.2 seems complex due to the large number of use cases it includes. You can group these use cases into packages, where each package represents a functional area. The use cases that create and alter Customer instances, for example, could be placed in a Customer Management package. These packages appear in a use case diagram. This would simplify the figure because at the first level you would see only the packages. (When you open a package, you would see its constituent use cases.) The package notation is described in Section 8.1, "Logical Architecture," of Chapter 8, "Architectural Models."

Observe the Expire Order use case in the figure. It is neither associated with another use case, nor with any actor. This use case is triggered not by an actor but by an internal system condition (probably by the expiration of a timer). Such a use case is called a *hidden use case* (Larman 1998, 43). Its presence is not necessarily a sign of a problem because you occasionally have use cases that are triggered by some internal system condition and are carried out by the system without the participation of any actor.

Note

The Expire Order use case is associated with an actor if you elect to model the order database or the timer as an actor. The decision to employ a timer is a design detail. Therefore, timers are at a much lower level of abstraction than the other elements of Figure 6.2. Likewise, databases are often omitted from initial use case diagrams because they are simply a mechanism to achieve persistence.

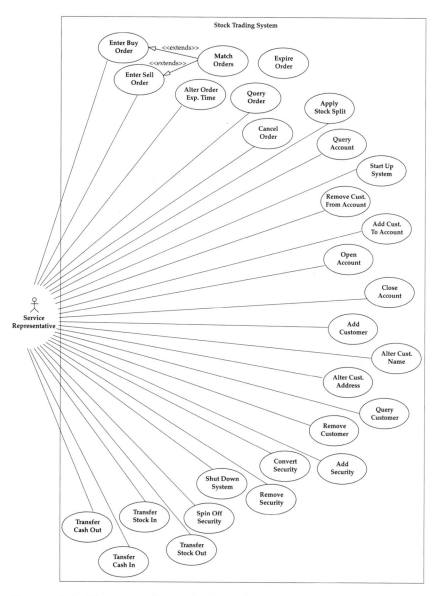

FIGURE 6.2   *The use case diagram for the stock-trading system.*

6.1.2   Describing Each of the Use Cases

You have identified a set of use cases, each of which represents a system function. The next step in the top-down process of dynamic design is to identify a set of "interesting scenarios" for each use case. Preparing a careful description of each use case can help facilitate that process. As discussed in Chapter 5, Section 5.1, "Describing Use Cases," the details of a use case can be modeled using the following:

- A textual paragraph outlining the use case

- A textual list of behavioral steps in the use case

- An activity diagram that flowcharts the use case

- A list or diagrams of the pre- and post-conditions of the use case

The process of describing a use case and modeling its scenarios will be illustrated for the first use case identified for stock trading: Enter Buy Order. A paragraph describing that use case follows:

> Entering a buy order entails taking information from a service representative and entering a new buy order in the system. The account number and stock name provided by the service representative must be verified as being known to the system. The system must also verify that the account with that account number has sufficient funds for the buy. Finally, a buy order is created.

The paragraph above offers only a sketchy outline of the use case. Designing interaction diagrams for this use case requires a more detailed discussion of the use case than the paragraph provides. The description above can be refined to add specificity, such as breaking the use case into a list of steps:

1. A Service Representative tells the system to enter a buy order, providing an account number, a stock name, a number of shares, a price, and (optionally) an expiration time.

2. The system checks to see that the account number is legal. (If it is not, an error is diagnosed.)

3. The system checks to see that the stock name is legal. (If it is not, an error is diagnosed.)

4. The system checks to see that the account with the given account number has sufficient cash to fund the order. (If it is not, an error is diagnosed.)

5. The system creates a new buy order with the provided stock name, number of shares, price, and expiration time. The status of that order is open.

6. The system generates a unique order number for the order and returns that order number to the Service Representative.

As an alternative to (or an augmentation of) a list of steps, you may choose to draw an activity diagram for the use case. In addition to offering a graphical rather than a textual view, an activity diagram allows non-sequential control flows to be specified. Figure 6.3 contains one possible activity diagram for the Enter Buy Order use case. Observe from the figure that the account number and stock name can be checked in either order (or in parallel) but that the order is created only if the account number and stock name are legal and the account has sufficient funds to cover the order.

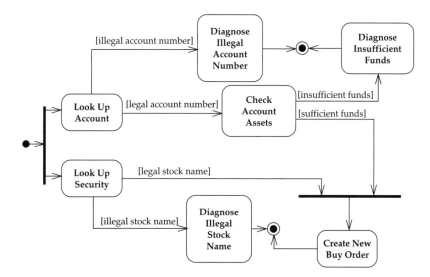

FIGURE 6.3 An activity diagram for the Enter Buy Order use case.

The textual list of steps previously described and the activity diagram in Figure 6.3 are *operational* specifications because they describe the temporal ordering of the steps that must be undertaken to fulfill the use case. Suppose you desire a more *declarative* specification that indicates only *what* must be accomplished (but not necessarily how or in what order). As discussed in Chapter 5, Section 5.1.3, "Describing Use Cases with Pre-Conditions and Post-Conditions," such a specification typically answers the following questions:

- *What triggers the use case?* When a use case is triggered by a message from an actor, you should indicate the message (or event) and any accompanying data. When a use case is triggered by an internal system condition, you should specify the condition.

- *What is the starting configuration?* In other words, what are the pre-conditions of the use case? These are typically conditions that must be checked.

- *What is the ending configuration?* That is, what are the post-conditions of the use case? These are typically effects that must be achieved.

This declarative specification can be documented either by text or with an object diagram. The following example, "A Declarative Description of the Enter Buy Order Use Case in Text," contains a textual description of the trigger, pre-conditions, and post-conditions of the Enter Buy Order use case.

A Declarative Description of the Enter Buy Order Use Case in Text	
Name:	EnterBuyOrder
Trigger:	*An event from a Service Representative* enterBuyOrder (acctNumber, stockName, numberShares, offeredPrice, <optional> expirationTime)
Preconditions:	stockName *must be a key for a known Stock,* s acctNumber *must be a key for a known Account, a* a's *balance is at least* numberShares ___offeredPrice
Postconditions:	*A new Buy Order,* bo, *must be created* bo's numberShares, offeredPrice, *and* expirationTime *must be set to the values provided in the triggering event* bo *must be linked to Stock* s *and Account* a bo's *status must be open A unique order number must be assigned to* bo *and returned to the Service Representative*

If you have an initial class diagram, you can also describe the pre- and post-conditions in object diagrams. Figure 6.4 defines both the trigger and the pre-conditions of the Enter Buy Order use case, whereas Figure 6.5 specifies the post-conditions. Figure 6.4 indicates that the trigger is an enterBuyOrder event from a Service Representative. It shows that the acctNum and sName (account number and stock name) values, which are included as parameters with that event, must be qualifiers for a known Account and Stock instance, respectively, and that the balance of that Account must be at least as much as the provided numShares (number of shares) multiplied by the buyPrice.

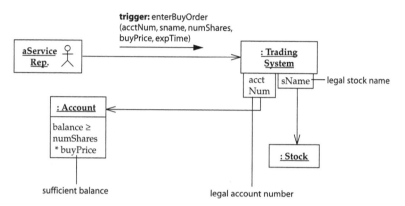

FIGURE 6.4 *An object diagram for the starting configuration of the use case.*

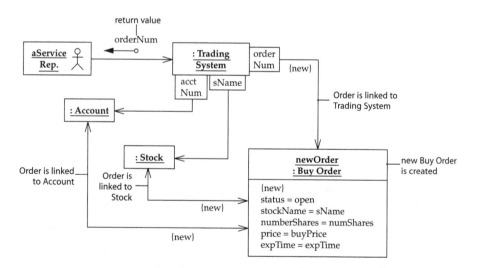

FIGURE 6.5 *An object diagram for the ending configuration of the use case.*

Figure 6.5 indicates that a Buy Order object must be created, the object's attributes must be initialized in a particular way, and the object must be linked to the Account and Stock instances from Figure 6.4. It also shows that a key for the Order, an orderNum (order number), must be created and returned to the Service Representative. Note that the sName, numShares, buyPrice, and expTime values to which the Buy Order's attributes are initialized are the parameters of the enterBuyOrder event in Figure 6.4.

6.1.3 Identifying and Modeling Scenarios

At this point, you have a set of use cases and their descriptions. The next step in the top-down dynamic design approach is to identify and model the set of scenarios required by each use case. Recall that a scenario is a use case instance and describes one interesting execution path through, or one possible outcome of, a use case in terms of objects and their interactions. In general, a use case may have multiple possible paths and may give rise to many scenarios. For example, when a use case is modeled with an activity diagram, each distinct path through that activity diagram represents a scenario.

Given its above specifications, the Enter Buy Order use case clearly has four interesting execution paths through it, which follow:

- The provided account number is determined to be illegal.

- The provided stock name is determined to be illegal.

- The provided account number is legal, but the indicated account cannot fund the purchase.

- The account number and stock name are legal, the account can fund the purchase, and the order is entered.

For this particular use case, one scenario describes the normal (or correct) path through the use case, whereas the other scenarios describe error cases. Although having only a single normal scenario for a use case is very common, it is not universal.

Modeling each scenario entails drawing an interaction diagram for it and, optionally, writing a textual specification of it. In turn, the interaction diagrams can help you identify required object methods and links.

The scenario for the case where the account number is illegal follows:

1. A service representative asks the system to enter a buy order and provides the account number, stock name, number of shares, offering price, and expiration time.

2. The system determines the account number is illegal and informs the service representative of the error.

A sequence diagram for this scenario is given in Figure 6.6. The diagram does not depict the mechanism used by the Trading System to search for the Account with the specified account number. The class diagram in Figure 6.1 includes a qualified association from the Trading System to the Account class, which is keyed by account number, indicating that such a mechanism must exist. At this point in the development process, however, the choice of an implementation of that mechanism has been deferred.

FIGURE 6.6 *A sequence diagram for the first scenario for entering a Buy Order.*

Observe that, as a result of this scenario and sequence diagram, the association between the Service Representative and Trading System classes must be directed toward the Trading System class (to permit Service Representative instances to send messages to the Trading System instance). Furthermore, the Trading System class must include the method being invoked (or message being sent), enterBuyOrder. Those additions are highlighted in Figure 6.7.

FIGURE 6.7 *Class diagram additions for the first scenario.*

The second scenario for the Enter Buy Order use case follows:

1. A service representative asks the system to enter a buy order and provides the account number, stock name, number of shares, offering price, and expiration time.

2. The system determines the stock name is illegal and informs the service representative of the error.

A sequence diagram for this scenario is shown in Figure 6.8. The actual mechanism used to search for a Stock with the indicated stock name is not shown. This scenario requires no additional extensions to the class diagram.

FIGURE 6.8 *A sequence diagram for the second scenario for entering a Buy Order.*

The third scenario for the Enter Buy Order use case follows:

1. A service representative asks the system to enter a buy order and provides the account number, stock name, number of shares, offering price, and expiration time.

2. The system determines that the account number and stock name are keys for a known Account and Stock, respectively.

3. The system checks and finds that the Account can't fund the purchase.

4. The system informs the service representative of the problem.

Figure 6.9 contains a sequence diagram for this scenario. The Trading System finds the Account instance with the specified account number and then checks that Account's balance against the amount required for the stock purchase (the number of shares times the buy price). In this scenario, the balance is insufficient to cover the purchase; so, an error is returned to the Service Representative.

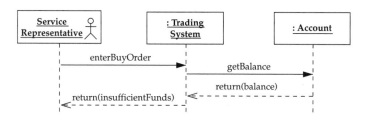

FIGURE 6.9 *A sequence diagram for the third scenario for entering a Buy Order.*

Figure 6.9 requires two additions to the class diagram. The association between the Trading System and Account classes must be directed toward the Account class, and the Account class must include a getBalance method. These changes are shown in Figure 6.10.

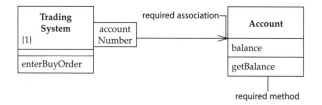

FIGURE 6.10 *Class diagram additions for the third scenario.*

Note

In the sequence diagram in Figure 6.10, the Trading System is using an Account's balance to determine whether the Account can fund the buy order. This allocation of behavior violates a basic tenet of object-oriented design, namely that state variables and the methods that operate on those variables are assigned to the same class. The design in the figure is, therefore, less extensible than it could be. This example is revisited in Chapter 7, "Flexibility Guidelines for Dynamic Diagrams."

The final scenario for the use case follows:

1. A service representative asks the system to enter a buy order and provides the account number, stock name, number of shares, offering price, and expiration time.

2. The system determines that the account number and stock name are keys for a known Account and Stock, respectively.

3. The system checks and finds that the Account can fund the purchase.

4. The system creates an order number with which to index the new Order to be created.

5. The system creates the new Buy Order with the proper attribute values and links.

6. The system returns the order number to the service representative.

Figure 6.11 includes a sequence diagram for the scenario. Observe that the Buy Order instance is being created by the Trading System. Because each Stock and Account instance must maintain a list of the Orders placed against it (so that, for example, a Stock instance can match its Orders), the Trading System concludes by informing the Buy Order's Stock and Account instances about the new Order and passing each a reference to the Order.

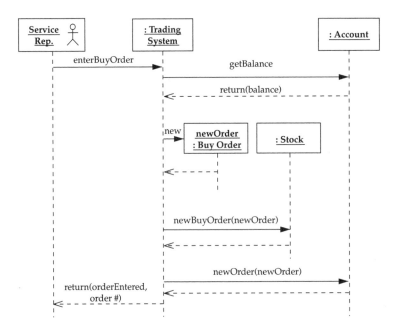

FIGURE 6.11 *A sequence diagram for the fourth scenario for entering a Buy Order.*

If an appropriate Sell Order already exists in the system, the new Buy Order can be matched immediately. Match Order is a conditional extension of the Enter Buy Order use case (see Figure 6.2) and is not included in this scenario.

The descriptions, scenarios, and sequence diagrams for one use case, Enter Buy Order, are presented here. To complete the design of the dynamics for the stock-trading system, you continue this process for each use case by determining what scenarios are required and then draw an interaction diagram for each scenario. From the scenarios and their interaction diagrams, you ascertain what methods and associations are required.

NOTE

Only one of the four sequence diagrams for the Enter Buy Order use case describes a normal situation (that is, a situation in which an order is successfully entered into the system). Some projects cut corners by describing and diagramming only the normal scenarios for each use case. That is, they ignore the scenarios that describe error cases. While you may not want to draw interaction diagrams for the error cases, you should still analyze those scenarios and document (perhaps with a textual note) what error handling is required. Doing so now, while the scenarios are fresh in your mind, is usually preferable to revisiting each use case during system implementation. It also allows the error-handling behavior to be reviewed with the rest of the design, rather than being thrown together at the last minute.

6.2 Bottom-Up Design of System Dynamics

The preceding section describes a top-down approach to the design of system dynamics in which you start with use cases and work down toward individual methods. An alternative approach is responsibility-driven design, in which you begin by identifying the responsibilities (state and behavior) of each type of object and then work upward (Wirfs-Brock, Wilkerson, and Wiener 1990, 61–105). This process is the opposite of the top-down approach because it starts with specific object methods and then uses scenarios primarily as a validation (rather than a discovery) mechanism.

The following are the steps in the bottom-up approach:

1. Identify the classes in the system. You can use noun phrases or abstraction to do this, as described in Chapter 3.

2. Make a list of the responsibilities of the objects of each class. An object's responsibilities are what it must know and do (that is, its state and behavior), as discussed in Chapter 5, Section 5.6, "Class Cards." You can depict your classes and responsibilities with a UML class diagram.

3. Identify interesting scenarios that you will use to validate your enumeration of responsibilities. To do this, you can first identify and model the use cases, as described in Section 6.1.1, "Identifying Use Cases," earlier in this chapter, or you can simply dream up individual scenarios.

4. Draw an interaction diagram for each scenario, validating that you have all necessary responsibilities. Add (or rearrange) responsibilities as necessary.

You apply this approach repeatedly, identifying responsibilities, drawing interaction diagrams, adding responsibilities, and redrawing the interaction diagrams, until you have what you believe is a complete set of responsibilities.

6.2.1 Identifying Classes and Responsibilities

Recall the library system described in Chapter 3, Section 3.1, "Developing a Class Diagram from Noun Phrases," which allowed library members to borrow books and videos from a lending library. Suppose you want to apply this bottom-up approach to develop a design of the dynamics of that system.

The first step is to develop a static model in terms of classes and responsibilities. To identify the classes for this system, you can use any of the three approaches outlined in Chapter 3. That chapter used this example to illustrate identifying classes from noun phrases. As an alternative to that discussion, however, suppose you have no written specification of the system and want to use abstraction instead. Furthermore, assume you want to use the Fusion method's set of identification keys: physical objects, people and organizations, and abstractions (Coleman et al. 1994, 38–39).

The physical objects for this application follow:

Book, each instance of which is a physical copy of a book.

Video, each instance of which is a physical copy of a video.

Library Card, each instance of which represents a card issued to a library member.

The people and organizations follow:

Library Member, each instance of which is a member of the library (holding a library card).

Library, the lending library that owns the books and videos.

Clerk, the class of actors who use the system. Each instance will be a presentation interface (such as a GUI).

Two general abstractions exist in this domain, which follow:

> *Work,* which is a book or video title. *Charlotte's Web* is a Work, for example, while a physical copy of *Charlotte's Web* is a Book.

> *Loan Transaction,* an instance of which describes a Library Member's borrowing of a Book or Video.

Next, you identify the responsibilities for each class (that is, the state and behavior that an instance of that class must have). The responsibilities of Book follow:

- It must know its unique item number.

- It must know its status: whether it is checked out or available. This can be achieved by having a Book refer to its currently active Loan Transaction when a Book is checked out.

- It must be able to check itself out.

- It must be able to check itself in.

A Video has essentially the same responsibilities, suggesting the need for a generalization, a Lendable class, in which to place the common properties. The Book and Video classes are specializations of Lendable. Are those subclasses required? At the moment, they introduce no additional responsibilities to those defined in Lendable, and it is unclear that any such distinctions will be required in the future. Therefore, those two classes are omitted from the design.

A Library Card has a membership number and perhaps an expiration date. It must be able to renew itself, and it must be linked to its owning Library Member.

A Library Member's responsibilities follow:

- It must know its name, address, and the other personal information required for each member.

- It must be able to update that personal information (such as when a person changes address).

- It must know how many books or videos it currently has checked out (to ensure that it never has more than ten total items borrowed from the library).

- It must know whether any of the items it has checked out are overdue (to ensure that it can borrow no additional items while it has an overdue item).

The latter two responsibilities could be generalized and restated as follows:

It must retain links to the Lendables (Books and Videos) it currently has checked out.

It must indicate whether the member is in good standing (meaning that the member has fewer than ten items checked out and has no overdue items).

A Library instance will serve as a facade (Gamma et al. 1995, 185–193), providing the Clerks access to the system. It, therefore, must have the methods that allow a Clerk to check out and check in a Lendable. It must also access Book and Video instances based on an item number, it must access Library Cards using a membership number, and it must locate Works based on a title and, perhaps, other criteria.

An instance of Work must know its title and any other information you wish to retain about the book or video. It must also keep links to its physical copies (that is, to its Lendable instances) to support certain queries. You may eventually want to specialize this class, creating Book and Video subclasses that hold information specific to those types of items. (For example, a Book has an author, whereas a Video has a producer, director, and cast.) These subclasses are not included in the current design, however.

A Loan Transaction must be linked to the Lendable that is borrowed, and to the borrowing Library Member. It must also have the due date of the Lendable, and it must be able to indicate whether it is overdue.

Figure 6.12 contains an initial class diagram for this application.

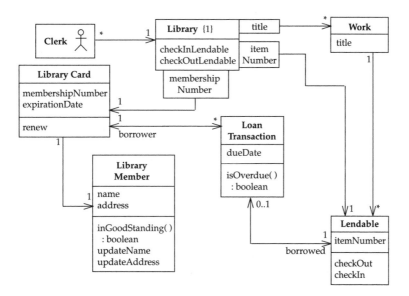

FIGURE 6.12 *An initial class diagram for the library system.*

6.2.2   Validating the Model

Now, use scenarios to validate and flesh out your class diagram. Consider a case where a member checks out a book. The scenario follows:

1. The Clerk asks the system to check out a book to a member. The Clerk provides the member's membership number and the book's item number.

2. The system determines that the member with that membership number is in good standing (that is, the member has no overdue books or videos and has fewer than ten items currently checked out).

3. The system checks out the book to the member.

Despite the lack of detail in this description, you can use your class diagram to help you produce a sequence diagram for this scenario. Obviously, the Library uses the membership number to identify a particular Library Card instance. Observe from Figure 6.12, however, that the Library must somehow access the related Library Member instance to obtain the member's standing. This can be accomplished in either of the following two ways:

- The Library can ask the Library Card if the member is in good standing. In turn, the Library Card delegates that request to the Library Member (and returns the result to the Library). In that case, the Library Card class must include a method to return its Library Member's standing.

- The Library can ask the Library Card for a reference to its Library Member. Then, the Library asks the Library Member for its status. This requires a method in the Library Card to obtain its Library Member, as well as an association from the Library class to the Library Member class.

An alternative approach is to remove the Library Card class altogether by merging its properties into Library Member, as shown in Figure 6.13. The argument against this solution is class cohesion: The two classes represent two different abstractions and, therefore, should be separate. In this application, however, the two classes may be a single abstraction.

A Library Card and Library Member will always be in a one-to-one relationship. (If a Library Member could hold multiple Library Cards, for example, you most likely have two different abstractions.) Furthermore, the behavioral distinction between the two concepts isn't very clear. A Library Card is responsible for the library membership itself, whereas a Library Member handles information about the person holding the card. Is a member's standing a property of the Library Member or of the Library Card?

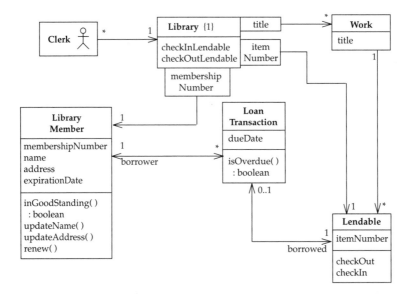

FIGURE 6.13 *A modified class diagram with no Library Card class.*

In turn, this suggests a fourth solution in which Library Card is replaced with Library Membership. The Library Membership class maintains the standing of the membership, whereas the Library Member class retains information about the person owning the membership. This solution, shown in Figure 6.14, is the one adopted for this application. (The Library instance must still access a Library Member's name and address to answer queries, to mail notices, and so on, but how that is accomplished is deferred for now.)

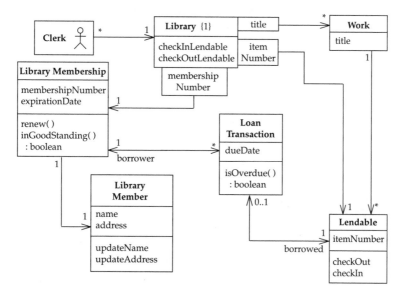

FIGURE 6.14 *A modified class diagram with a Library Membership class.*

When asked by a Clerk to check out a Lendable, the Library uses a membership number to find the appropriate Library Membership instance and then checks that instance's standing. Consider the scenario outlined above in which the Membership is in good standing. Once that standing is ascertained, the Library looks up the Lendable (a book instance in this case) with the specified item number and tells that Lendable to check itself out. The Lendable must then create a Loan Transaction instance.

Observe from the class diagram in Figure 6.14 that the Library Membership instance must be updated to include a reference to the Loan Transaction, as such an instance holds links to all currently active Loan Transactions that apply to it. Assuming that the Lendable creates the Loan Transaction instance, who should inform the Membership object about the new Loan Transaction? At least three options exist, which follow:

- The Library calls the Lendable's checkOut method, passing a reference to the Library Membership instance. The Lendable creates the Loan Transaction object, initializing it with references to the Lendable and the Library Membership instances. Then, the Lendable informs the Library Membership instance about the new Loan Transaction. Note that this solution requires an association from Lendable to Library Membership, thereby increasing identity coupling.

- The Library calls the Lendable's checkOut method, passing a reference to the Library Membership instance. The Lendable creates the Loan Transaction object, initializing it with references to the Lendable and the Library Membership instances. During that initialization, the Loan Transaction constructor informs the Library Membership instance about the new Loan Transaction. This also requires an association from Lendable to Library Membership, even though the coupling is weaker because the Lendable object never calls any methods in the Membership instance. (It merely hands the Library Membership reference to the Loan Transaction.) This type of reference is sometimes called an *opaque reference* (or *opaque pointer*) (Lakos 1996, 247–257).

- The Library creates the Loan Transaction instance, initializing it with references to the Lendable and the Library Membership instances. Then, it informs both the Lendable and the Library Membership objects about the new Loan Transaction. This solution eliminates any relationship between Lendable and Library Membership, but it requires an association from Library to Loan Transaction, which might otherwise be unnecessary. It also requires that the Library interrogate the Lendable before creating the Transaction to ensure that the Lendable can be checked out and to determine the due date.

Having the Library Membership create the Loan Transaction is also an option. Although, that solution requires an association from Library Membership to Lendable, *and* it requires that a Lendable be queried to see that it is available and to obtain its due date. In short, it has all of the disadvantages of the above three choices but without any obvious advantages.

The second approach is adopted here. It requires an `addLoanTransaction` method in the Library Membership class that is called by a newly created Loan Transaction. It also requires the opaque reference from Lendable to Library Membership. Furthermore, when the Loan Transaction is created, its `dueDate` attribute must be initialized using a value provided by the Lendable.

> **NOTE**
>
> *The approach adopted for this design makes use of an opaque reference. Such references are extremely valuable in C++ designs because they reduce compile-time coupling and, therefore, can decrease the number of classes that must be recompiled when the interface of another class is modified. John Lakos explains the use of opaque pointers for this purpose in his book (1996, 247–257).*

How does a Lendable determine its due date? Assume that books and videos have different loan periods. The description in Chapter 3 stated that books are loaned for two weeks, whereas videos are loaned for three days. Suppose, however, that different videos are loaned for different periods. A new video might be available for only two days, whereas an old Jerry Lewis movie is loaned for a week. In that case, the loan period is dependent on the particular title and, therefore, is part of the state of a Title; furthermore, a Lendable must access that period when calculating its own due date.

The class diagram must, therefore, be extended to include a `loanPeriod` attribute and query method in the Title class, and to include an association from Lendable to Work. Those changes, as well as the `addLoanTransaction` method in the Library Membership class and the opaque reference from Lendable to Library Membership, have been introduced in the class diagram in Figure 6.15.

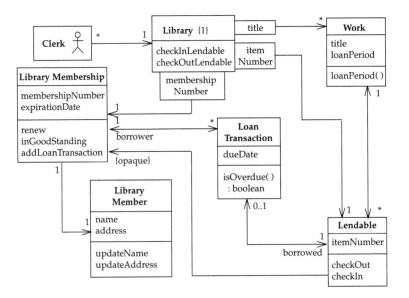

FIGURE 6.15 *A modified class diagram with check out additions.*

A sequence diagram for this scenario is shown in Figure 6.16. A detailed textual description of the scenario depicted by this diagram follows:

1. The Clerk tells the Library to check out a Lendable, providing the membership number of the person checking out the book, 40779, and the Lendable's item number, 3122465.

2. The Library looks up the Lendable instance with item number 3122465. In this scenario, that Lendable is a book, theBook. The mechanism used to achieve this search is not depicted in the sequence diagram. (This is a low-level detail that can be added later.)

3. The Library looks up the Library Membership instance with membership number 40779. In this scenario, such an instance exists. Again, the exact mechanism used for this step is not shown in the diagram.

4. The Library calls the Library Membership object's `inGoodStanding` method to determine if the membership is in good standing. That method must validate that the Membership has no more than ten Lendables checked out and that no checked out Lendables are overdue. In this scenario, the Membership has no Lendables currently checked out, so the method returns `true`.

5. The Library tells the Lendable instance (`theBook`) to check itself out while passing it a reference to the Library Membership instance.

6. The Lendable instance invokes its Title instance's `loanPeriod` method to obtain its loan period, which is 14 days.

7. The Lendable creates a Loan Transaction instance, passing its constructor (or "initializer" for languages without constructors) the due date and references to the Lendable and Library Membership objects.

8. The Loan Transaction instance sets its `dueDate` attribute to the provided value, and it stores the links to the Lendable and Library Membership. (This assignment of values is internal to an object and doesn't normally appear in a sequence diagram. If you want to indicate the internal behavior of an object in an interaction diagram, you can add a note or annotate the diagram.)

9. The Loan Transaction constructor (or "initializer") invokes the Library Membership's `addLoanTransaction` method while passing a reference to itself. Then, the Library Membership stores that link in its list of transactions. (Again, this internal action doesn't appear in the sequence diagram.)

10. The constructor returns to the Lendable. The Lendable returns an indication of success to the Library Membership instance.

11. The Library returns an indication of success to the Clerk.

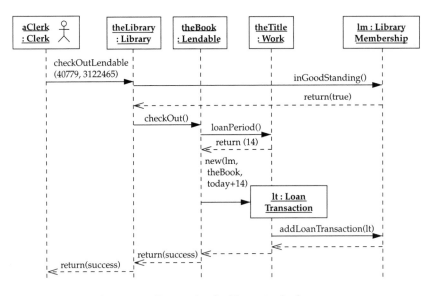

FIGURE 6.16 *A sequence diagram for checking out a book.*

Other scenarios and sequence diagrams, not included here, cover other scenarios involving checking items out, scenarios for checking items in, and so forth. Consider a scenario for sending out a notice about an overdue Lendable. Suppose, for example, a person keeps a book beyond the book's due date. You might want the system to create a list of all overdue books. Each item in the list should include the membership number of the person who has overdue items, as well as the item number and due date of each overdue book. A textual description of that use case follows:

1. A Clerk asks the Library instance to list overdue Lendables.

2. The Library iterates through its list of membership numbers, looking up each Library Membership, and then asking that Library Membership instance to create an overdue notice.

3. Each Library Membership iterates through its currently active Loan Transactions, asking each to create an overdue item notice.

4. Each Loan Transaction checks its status. If it is overdue, it returns an Overdue Item Notice that contains its item number (obtained from its Lendable) and its due date.

5. If a Library Membership has any overdue items, it returns an Overdue Notice that includes its membership number and the Overdue Item Notice for each of its overdue items. (Otherwise, it returns nothing.)

6. The Library returns a list of information returned from the Library Memberships to the Clerk.

This use case requires several additions to the class diagram. The Library class must have a listOverdueLendables method, the Library Membership class must have a createOverdueNotice method, and the Loan Transaction class must include a createOverdueItemNotice method. You also need an Overdue Notice and an Overdue Item Notice class that defines such notices. (A Library Membership with overdue items will create and return an instance of the former, whereas an overdue Loan Transaction will create the latter.)

Figure 6.17 contains a class diagram with those additions. You might want to omit the Overdue Notice and OverdueItemNotice classes at this level because they define the details of how notice information is handed around in the system. (You would add them later when you specify the finer details of the design.) Nevertheless, they are included in the figure (although their properties are omitted). The figure also elides the properties of the Library Member class and omits the association from Library Membership to Overdue Item Notice.

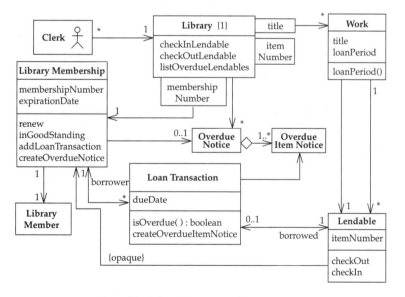

FIGURE 6.17 *A modified class diagram with overdue notice additions.*

A collaboration diagram for this scenario is shown in Figure 6.18. When you modify a class diagram to incorporate features required by one interaction diagram, you must also check your existing interaction diagrams to see if they, too, must be modified. The additions to the class diagram required for this scenario do not require any additions or modifications to the sequence diagram in Figure 6.16.

NOTE

Many CASE tools for object-oriented design include tools that, at your option, will check the consistency of your class diagram and interaction diagrams. For example, they will diagnose situations in which a sequence diagram includes a message that does not appear as a method in the receiving instance's class in the class diagram.

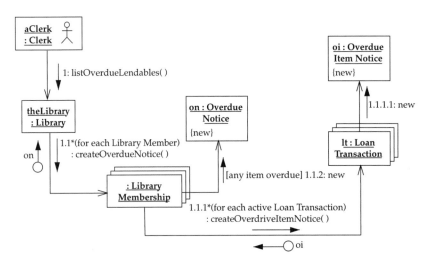

FIGURE 6.18 *A collaboration diagram for creating overdue notices.*

When employing this bottom-up approach to design system dynamics, continue developing scenarios and sequence diagrams for the various system behaviors. As you do this, make any required modifications to the class diagram and to the existing sequence diagrams. Continue this process until you believe you have analyzed all of the system's behaviors.

NOTE

The class diagram developed for the library system in this section is an elaboration of the class diagram for the same problem developed in Chapter 3, Section 3.1, "Developing a Class Diagram from Noun Phrases." The class diagram in Chapter 3 (specifically Figure 3.1) is derived from the noun phrases in a description of the desired library system. It, therefore, contains only classes that correspond to noun phrases in that description.

This example illustrates that, as you design a system, you may discover abstractions or functional requirements in the problem domain that do not appear in the original problem specification. If your goals include producing a specification of the system as built, you may want to repeatedly update that specification throughout the design phase.

6.3   Developing State-Based Object Dynamics

Regardless of which approach you use to analyze and model system dynamics, you may want to model the state-based dynamics of individual instances. You do this by producing a state transition diagram for each class whose instances have interesting state-based behavior. To determine which instances have such behavior, consider each class in the system and ask yourself the following questions:

> Does an instance of that class pass through a set of states?
>
> Are some of an instance's behaviors meaningless in some states?
>
> Must an instance's methods be executed in a particular order?

If you answer "yes" to any one of these questions, the instances of that class have some state-based behavior that you may want to model with a state transition diagram.

Consider the factory control system described in Chapter 3, Section 3.3, "Developing a Class Diagram from Use Cases." The final class diagram for that application, originally included in Figure 3.13, is repeated here in Figure 6.19. Which classes could benefit from state transition diagrams?

The actor classes, Operator and Failure Monitor, are outside the system. Therefore, their internal behavior is of no interest. A Log Entry is the data logged when a Machine changes state. Once created, it doesn't change, and it obviously has no state-based behavior. Likewise, the Log instance also has no state-based behavior. It has only one method, `logStateChange`, and that method can be called at any time. (Assume that the Log is always available. That is, assume it cannot be turned on and off.)

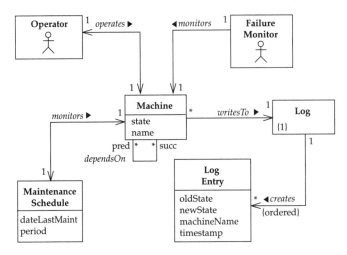

FIGURE 6.19 *The class diagram for the factory control system.*

Machine instances obviously have state-based behavior. A major emphasis of this application is the tracking of state changes in factory machines. You can draw a state transition diagram with a state for each of the six states in which a Machine can reside, which are: running, waiting, idle, down for scheduled maintenance, down for unscheduled maintenance, and off. That diagram will show what state changes are permitted and what triggers each of them.

The remaining class in Figure 6.19 is Maintenance Schedule. Does a Maintenance Schedule instance have state-based behavior? It can be in either of two possible states: timing and idle. In the timing state, it is running a timer indicating when scheduled maintenance is due. When that timer expires, it enters the idle state in which it does nothing.

What is the state transition diagram for a Maintenance Schedule? If you have developed interaction diagrams, you can use those diagrams to help you derive the state transition diagram. A Maintenance Schedule participates in two sequence diagrams. In the first, shown in Figure 6.20, the Maintenance Schedule's timer expires (or, as the annotation in the sequence diagram indicates, the date calculated by adding its `dateLastMaintenance` and its `period` has been reached). It informs its related Machine that scheduled maintenance is due, after which it is idle.

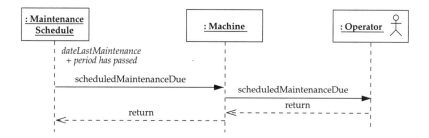

FIGURE 6.20 *A sequence diagram involving a Maintenance Schedule.*

The second sequence diagram involving a Maintenance Schedule is shown in Figure 6.21. In this scenario, an Operator places a Machine in scheduled maintenance. In turn, the Machine tells its Maintenance Schedule to start the maintenance cycle, which causes the Maintenance Schedule to set its dateLastMaintenance attribute to that moment in time. In effect that restarts the timer. (The Machine undertakes other actions, such as logging a state change, but those are omitted from the diagram.)

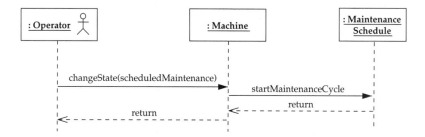

FIGURE 6.21 *Another sequence diagram involving a Maintenance Schedule.*

Armed with those two sequence diagrams, you can derive the state transition diagram shown in Figure 6.22. A Maintenance Schedule should probably start in the Timing state because, most likely, you want a Machine's maintenance timer to start running when its Maintenance Schedule is created. Upon entry to that state, the Maintenance Schedule should set its dateLastMaintenance attribute to now, which has the effect of starting a timer.

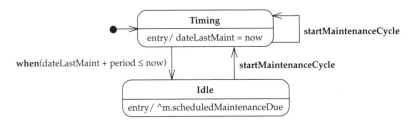

Figure 6.22 *A state transition diagram for a Maintenance Schedule.*

When does a Maintenance Schedule leave that state? Look at Figure 6.20, and you will see that the reason for this state change is the expiration of the Maintenance Schedule's timer. In particular, its `dateLastMaintenance` plus its `period` is now (or in the past). As the figure indicates, when that state change occurs, the Maintenance Schedule must send a `scheduledMaintenanceDue` message to its Machine. The transition and its trigger are, therefore, included in the state transition diagram. Furthermore, upon entry to the `Idle` state, the Maintenance Schedule sends its Machine (`m`) the required message.

What causes a Maintenance Schedule to leave the `Idle` state? The sequence diagram in Figure 6.21 indicates that such a state change occurs because the Maintenance Schedule receives a `startMaintenanceCycle` message. Therefore, this transition and its trigger must be included in the state transition diagram. Furthermore, when receiving that message, the Maintenance Schedule must start its timer. This is already handled by the entry condition in the `Timing` state.

The transitions between the `Timing` and `Idle` states have been identified, but is the state transition diagram complete? For each possible combination of incoming message and internal state, it is generally a good idea to consider what should occur if that message is received while in that state. In this state transition diagram, you have only two states (`Idle` and `Timing`) and one incoming message (`startMaintenanceCycle`). The receipt of that message while in the `Idle` state triggers the transition described in the preceding paragraph. What happens if that message is received while in the `Timing` state?

As indicated by Figure 6.21, a Machine sends a `startMaintenanceCycle` message to a Maintenance Schedule because the Operator placed the Machine in scheduled maintenance. If the Maintenance Schedule receives such a message while it is in the `Timing` state, the Operator decided to place the Machine in scheduled maintenance before the timer expired. Should this be allowed? It seems most likely that such an action should be permitted and, when it does occur, that the Maintenance Schedule should simply restart its timer. (In other words, it should set its `dateLastMaintenance` attribute to now.) Therefore, a self-loop from the `Timing` state to itself, enabled by the receipt of that message, must be included in the state transition diagram.

The point of this discussion is not to explain Maintenance Schedules but to illustrate how the information present in sequence diagrams can help you develop state transition diagrams.

CHAPTER 7

Flexibility Guidelines for Dynamic Diagrams

One of the most difficult facets of object-oriented design is to formulate a good allocation of behavior to classes. It is also one of the most important because a proper allocation of behavior contributes to the flexibility of a design more than any other principle, guideline, or tactic. A poor assignment of behavior often leads to cascading changes as the design is extended—introducing a modification or extension in one area of the design has effects on other areas.

This activity can be especially challenging for designers with prior experience in other, non–object-oriented design approaches. The intuition you may use to decompose behaviors in structured design, for example, leads to a somewhat inflexible object-oriented design. Although control is often centralized during structured design, the object-oriented designer strives to distribute control, thereby increasing the extensibility of the resulting design.

Those experienced in structured design often attempt to define a class for each function rather than introducing a class for each entity. Likewise, data modelers are accustomed to thinking about data and the code that operates on it as separate parts of a design. In object-oriented design, however, you attempt to allocate data and its code to the same class.

This challenge is complicated by the tension between extensibility and reuse of the software because increasing extensibility often reduces reusability and vice versa. To promote extensibility, a class encapsulates the application-specific behaviors required of that class. A class designed for reuse, on the other hand, should be as independent of any particular application as possible. This chapter offers a set of guidelines that, when applied, increases the flexibility of the resulting design. It also discusses the trade-off between extensibility and reusability.

Chapter 9, "Reuse: Libraries, Frameworks, Components, and Patterns," describes various types of reuse in detail. This chapter addresses the following topics:

- *Class and method cohesion*: A class should represent a single abstraction. From a behavioral point of view, the methods of a class should engage in a single, general type of responsibility. Likewise, each method should have a single purpose. These principles, aimed both at extensibility and reusability, are explained and illustrated.

- *Distributing behavior*: If an object has the state required to perform an activity, that object should also have the behavior for that activity. This principle, a cornerstone of object-oriented design, is explained in terms of a group of complementary guidelines, and its efficacy in producing extensible designs is illustrated by several examples.

- *Extension versus reuse*: Taken to an extreme, keeping state and behavior together can lead to very extensible designs but at the price of reducing the reusability of individual classes. This trade-off is examined, and alternative guidelines for promoting reusability are described.

Note that these are just guidelines. You will find exceptions to their application, some of which are noted in this chapter. For example, a façade class (Gamma et al. 1995, 185–193) is, by some measures, not a very functionally cohesive class, but nonetheless it is an important tool for reducing coupling.

The guidelines described in this chapter are equally significant for both *control-oriented* and *information-oriented* applications. The examples in the chapter are drawn from both types of software.

Note

A control-oriented application's major task is to control the operation of another application or system. The factory control system in Section 3.3, "Developing a Class Diagram from Use Cases," of Chapter 3, "Developing Class Diagrams," is one example.

The major goal of an information-oriented system is the retention and processing of data. Three examples of this are the DryGoods.com system for processing orders introduced in Chapter 1, "System Functional Models;" the library application in Chapter 3 in Section 3.1, "Developing a Class Diagram from Noun Phrases;" and the stock-trading system from Section 3.2, "Developing a Class Diagram Using Abstraction."

7.1 Class and Method Cohesion

Cohesion is a measure of how diverse an entity's features are. The more diverse the features are, the less cohesive the entity is. In an object-oriented design, each class should be highly cohesive; it should represent a single abstraction (or family of similar abstractions in the case of a superclass). Section 4.1.1, "Increasing Cohesion," in Chapter 4, "Flexibility Guidelines for Class Diagrams," discussed how applying database normalization rules to a class promotes cohesion of the state (data) defined in the class. Class cohesion also has a behavioral side; a class (or, more precisely, its instances) should engage in just one general type of responsibility. Each method defined in a class should also be cohesive in that it should carry out a single specific function.

7.1.1 Class Cohesion

Recall the factory control system analyzed in Section 3.3 in Chapter 3. The class diagram for that system, presented originally in Figure 3.13 and repeated here as Figure 7.1, includes a Machine class describing factory machines and a separate Maintenance Schedule class that defines the maintenance schedule for a Machine. In the initial factory control system, the relationship between Machine and Maintenance Schedule is always one-to-one and symmetric (that is, a single Machine and a single Maintenance Schedule are linked to one another). Why include a Maintenance Schedule class? Why not place the maintenance-timing behavior in the Machine class?

Section 3.3.3, "Completing the Use Case Class Diagram," in Chapter 3 addressed that question by analyzing the basic responsibilities of instances of the two classes. A Machine is responsible for responding to stimuli and determining if a state change is warranted. A Maintenance Schedule is responsible for producing a stimulus. These two responsibilities are different. Therefore, blending the two responsibilities into the Machine class results in a class that, from a behavioral point of view, is not as cohesive as it should be.

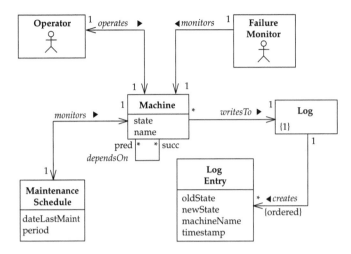

FIGURE 7.1 *The class diagram for the factory control system.*

What are the implications of ignoring cohesion and placing the maintenance-scheduling behavior in the Machine class? One important result is that the design is difficult to extend with new ways of determining when maintenance is due. For example, suppose that in the future you have alternative ways of determining whether maintenance is due; consider the following:

- In some cases, maintenance is scheduled based on the wear of a machine part. A sensor takes readings of that wear. Determining when maintenance should occur entails interacting with that sensor and interpreting its readings.

- Some machine parts degrade as a function of the temperature and humidity in the factory. Maintenance is scheduled based on cumulative (not cumulus!) atmospheric conditions since the last time maintenance was performed.

If you assign the maintenance scheduling activity to the Machine class, that class becomes a mess when these additions are introduced. It must include behavior for all the different variations of ascertaining when maintenance is due. You might be inclined to specialize the Machine class based on these variations: one subclass does timer-based scheduling, one does wear-based scheduling, and so on. That option evaporates, however, if some factory machines have multiple maintenance schedules of different types. (Consider a machine with a timer-based schedule for oiling the machine, a wear-based schedule for replacing its clutch, and so forth.)

This example emphasizes another implication of ignoring cohesion; when you place the machine and maintenance schedule abstractions in a single class (Machine), you are assuming those two abstractions will *always* be in a one-to-one relationship. Allowing multiple maintenance schedules per machine results in a messy Machine class. Allowing multiple machines per maintenance schedule is not possible.

To analyze the behavioral cohesion of your classes, try to write a one-sentence characterization of the responsibilities of each class in your design. Those characterizations for the (non-actor) classes in the factory control system are:

> *Machine*: responds to external stimuli and determines what state changes those stimuli require
>
> *Maintenance Schedule*: produces a stimulus when maintenance on a machine is due
>
> *Log*: adds log entries to the log of machine state changes
>
> *Log Entry*: provides access to an entry in the log

If you have a characterization that describes multiple types of activities, consider separating those activities into distinct classes. For example, if you merge maintenance scheduling into the Machine class, your description of that class is:

> *Machine*: responds to external stimuli, determines what state changes those stimuli require, and keeps track of when scheduled maintenance is due

This compound sentence contains two different responsibilities and, therefore, suggests that this single class should be separated into two parts (responding to stimuli and determining when maintenance is due).

These one-sentence characterizations form a starting point. As you subsequently assign behaviors to classes, make sure you abide by those characterizations. For example, suppose you had not yet identified the need for a Maintenance Schedule class, but you had correctly characterized the responsibilities of the Machine, Log, and Log Entry classes as given above. When you analyze the requirement to determine when maintenance on a Machine is due, where do you place that behavior? That responsibility doesn't seem to match the description of any of the existing three classes. At that point, therefore, you introduce a new class, Maintenance Schedule, to house the new responsibility.

For many applications, design is a continuing activity. To allow for future maintenance and extension, you should introduce these single-sentence class descriptions into comments in your source code. This exposes future designers and maintenance programmers to your intentions for each class and may help them determine whether a proposed addition to a class is appropriate.

Class cohesion is a guideline that you may decide to ignore from time to time. One such case, which was mentioned at the beginning this chapter, is the introduction of a façade class (Gamma et al. 1995, 185–193). Such a class provides external clients a single point of access to a subsystem or component. It, therefore, provides method interfaces for all the use cases exported by the subsystem or component, and if those use cases engage in different types of activities, the façade is not functionally cohesive.

Improving system performance is another situation analogous to the reason that database administrators sometimes define unnormalized databases. You may find that placing two functions together, rather than separating them in different classes (and, therefore, in different instances during system execution), will increase the system's execution speed. An object can carry out two functions in one place as a result of a single function invocation, rather than delegating part of that responsibility to a second object through a second function call. If rapid system execution is a major objective, you may find that, in some portions of your design, cohesive classes are a luxury you cannot afford.

7.1.2   Method Cohesion

Each class or instance method should also be cohesive in that should carry out one function. This is analogous to functional cohesion in structured design (Yourdon and Constantine 1978, 115–118). You generally should avoid defining a method that is engaged in several types of activities. For example, a Machine's changeState method (invoked by an Operator) should be limited to actions involved with changing the Machine's state (and the immediate effects of that state change). It should not be instigating actions that have nothing to do with changing the Machine's state.

One reason for method cohesion is to reduce cognitive complexity: A cohesive method is simpler and, therefore, easier to understand. This is a benefit to the individual who develops and maintains the class and to the person who designs and implements client code.

To increase method cohesion, you can apply the approach that was outlined previously for classes to methods. In other words, you can write a one-sentence characterization of each method's basic function and then guard against placing any other type of activity in that method.

7.2 Distributing Behavior

A basic tenet of object-oriented design and programming is that an object with the state required to carry out some activity should also have the behavior for that activity. That is, you want to locate the state and the behavior on that state in the same class. You can assert this tenet in several ways:

- You should distribute behavior as evenly as possible. Attempt to avoid *dumb objects*, which merely hold data and provide accessor methods (that is, reading and writing methods) for that data. Also, eschew objects that form islands of control.

- You should avoid the use of a controller, or what Arthur Riel calls a "god class" (1996, 32). A *controller object* is one that asks for state information from another object and then uses that state information to make a decision or perform a calculation. Because the queried service object has the state to carry out that activity, it should also have the behavior. The client object should tell that service object to make the decision or perform the calculation, which separates the client from any knowledge about how the service object effects that computation.

- You should reduce representational coupling. This form of coupling, first introduced in the "Representational Coupling" section in Chapter 4, measures how general (or abstract) the interface used by the client object is (deChampeaux, Lea, Faure 1993, 242–244). The more an interface exposes the service object's internal details, the more specific it is; hence, the degree of representational coupling is higher.

  Obtaining the values of specific state variables (either by loading them directly, or by using accessor methods) implies that the client is strongly coupled to the service object because the values and intent of those state variables are exposed to the client. Raising the level of the interface to something more abstract than accessor methods reduces representational coupling.

- Use an assertive style rather than an inquisitive style of programming. A client object tells a service object what it wants that object to do, rather than asking for information from that object.

These guidelines sound very similar, as indeed they should. They are different manifestations of the same tenet: an object with the state required by some activity should carry out that activity. The following examples illustrate the benefit derived from following these guidelines.

7.2.1 An Elevator Control Example

Consider two alternative designs for an elevator control system. In each design, the class diagram with no methods is the same. Each design has an Elevator class, in which each instance retains the current state of the corresponding elevator, such as its current location, direction, and so forth. It also has an Elevator Control System class, a single instance of which maintains a list of elevators and receives incoming requests when buttons are selected. This fragment of the class diagram is shown in Figure 7.2.

FIGURE 7.2 *A partial class diagram for an elevator control system.*

How does the Elevator Control System assign an Elevator to an incoming request? In one possible design, it iterates through the Elevators, asking each Elevator for its current location, direction, and so on. (Recall from Section 5.5.1, "Iteration," of Chapter 5, "Dynamic Diagramming Notation," that the rectangle in the figure encloses the body of an iteration with the iteration bound indicated in the upper left corner of the rectangle.) It then uses that information to determine which Elevator is closest (by some metric) and assigns the request to that Elevator.

The methods required for this design are included in the class diagram in Figure 7.3. Figure 7.4 contains a sequence diagram for a fragment of a scheduling scenario. (The italicized text in Figure 7.4 indicates areas where details have been omitted. The Elevator Control System's interactions with the Request instance are also elided.)

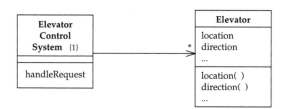

FIGURE 7.3 *One allocation of behavior to Elevators.*

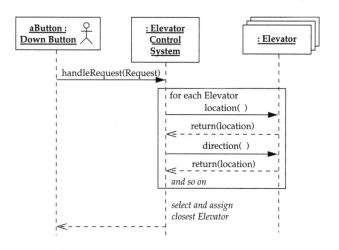

FIGURE 7.4 *A first sequence diagram for scheduling Elevators.*

An alternative design is one where the Elevator Control System asks each Elevator to compute its proximity to a request. Using its location, direction, and so forth, each Elevator returns (perhaps as an integer value) that measure. The behavior required for this solution is shown in Figure 7.5, and a scenario fragment is depicted in Figure 7.6. (The Elevator instances' interactions with the Request object are omitted from the figure.)

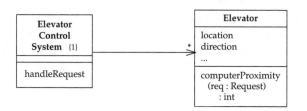

FIGURE 7.5 *An alternative allocation of behavior to Elevators.*

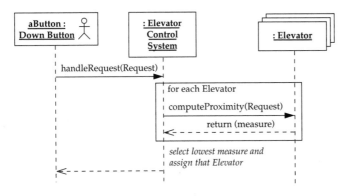

FIGURE 7.6 *A second sequence diagram for scheduling Elevators.*

Note

This discussion ignores some additional complexities of any elevator-scheduling scheme, whether centralized or distributed, that handles multiple Elevators. For example, when an Elevator is assigned a new request, some of the Elevator's existing assignments may have to be reconsidered. Suppose an Elevator on the 11th floor moving downward is assigned a new request from someone on the 9th floor that wants to go down. Existing assignments to this Elevator for stops below the 9th floor may now be closer to some other Elevator. For the sake of simplicity and brevity, the discussion here focuses only on selecting an Elevator for a new request.

Which design is more flexible? In the first design, the Elevator Control System is acting as a controller. It asks each Elevator for information about the Elevator's current state and, then, uses that information to determine how close the Elevator is to the person requesting to be picked up. Any variations to Elevators that affect the way Elevators are assigned requests will require new state variables in the Elevator class, as well as additional behavior in the Elevator Control System to use the values of those variables.

In contrast, an Elevator in the second design, using the values of its state variables, makes its own determination of the proximity of a request. This is a more extensible allocation of behavior because introducing new variations of Elevators will frequently be local to the Elevator class. Because the Elevator Control System knows nothing about how Elevators determine their proximity to a pick-up request, it will not change when different types of Elevators make that determination in different ways.

Suppose, for example, that you want to extend this system to work in a building in which some elevators cannot stop on all floors. In the first design, you must extend the Elevator class to include both an instance variable, enumerating the floors on which an Elevator can stop, as well as an accessor method, indicating whether an Elevator can stop on a specified floor. You must also modify the `handleRequest` method in the Elevator Control System class so that it ensures (for each Elevator) that the Elevator can stop on the floor from which this request originated. In the second design, on the other hand, you must introduce the instance variable enumerating the floors and alter the `computeProximity` method so that it returns a huge number (or perhaps -1) when the Elevator cannot stop on that floor. These changes are both local to the Elevator class; the Elevator Control System class remains unaltered.

As a second example, consider extending the system to handle elevators that are out of service. The first design requires adding a boolean-valued state variable and corresponding accessor method to the Elevator class, indicating whether the Elevator is in service. It also requires introducing code in the Elevator Control System's `handleRequest` method to obtain and test that variable's value. Contrast that with the second design, where that instance variable is added to the Elevator class, and the Elevator's `computeProximity` method is extended to check that variable (and to return a huge number if the Elevator is out of service). Once again, the first design requires modifications to two classes, whereas the second design requires changes only to the Elevator class.

Consider one final extension, the introduction of service elevators. A service elevator can handle a pick-up request, but it moves more slowly than a normal elevator. Both the Elevator Control System and Elevator classes must be modified in the first design. Each Elevator must maintain an indication of whether it is a regular or service elevator, and the Elevator Control System must use that new information in its `handleRequest` method. Only the Elevator class in the second design must be changed because the `computeProximity` method will return a higher value if the Elevator is a service elevator.

For each of these suggested extensions, the first design requires a change to both the controller and controlled classes, whereas the second design, with a more intelligent Elevator class, requires modifications only to that class. As these examples illustrate, the second design is more extensible than the first because changes that are local to one class in the second design cause cascading effects in the first. The two designs differ in the degree that they adhere to the guidelines previously cited:

- The second design keeps state and behavior together; an Elevator has both the required state variables and corresponding behavior to compute its proximity to a request. In the first design, the Elevator has the state variables, whereas the Elevator Control System has the behavior.

- You are distributing behavior more evenly in the second design. In the first design, Elevators are dumb. They are simply repositories for state variables, providing only the accessor methods for those variables. The Elevator Control System is doing everything. In the second design, however, the two classes share the scheduling behavior. Each Elevator computes its proximity to a request, and the Elevator Control System uses the results of those computations to select the closest Elevator.

- The Elevator Control System in the first design is a controller. It is requesting state information from an Elevator and using that to compute the cost of assigning a request to that Elevator. Why not simply tell the Elevator to compute that cost? That approach, taken in the second design, reduces the degree to which the Elevator Control System is a "god object." (It still remains a controller because it must take the proximity results from all Elevators and choose the closest one. Selecting an Elevator, however, requires state information from all Elevator objects. A design completely void of a controller must chain the Elevator objects together; a pick-up request is handed down the chain, and each Elevator determines if it is closer than the currently closest Elevator.)

- The degree of representational coupling is lower in the second design than in the first. Through its use of accessor methods, the Elevator Control System in the first design is dependent on the existence and meaning of particular Elevator state variables. This is a relatively high level of representational coupling because anytime new state variables and their accessor methods are added to the Elevator class, the Elevator Control System class must be extended to employ those methods. In the second design, the Elevator Control System depends only on the fact that an Elevator can compute its proximity to a specified request.

- The first design is inquisitive in its tone because the client object (Elevator Control System) is asking the service object (Elevator) about its current state. In contrast, the second design is more imperative in style; the client object tells the service object to carry out a service.

The second design also allows for a greater degree of parallelism. Because an Elevator is doing most of the work required to calculate its proximity to a request, placing each Elevator instance on its own processor implies that all of those calculations could occur in parallel. This level of parallelism is not possible in the first design. An even distribution of behavior frequently produces this effect.

When analyzed for extensibility, the second design is preferable to the first. Is the first design superior to the second in some other respect? In some cases, you might select a more centralized allocation of behavior to achieve some sort of performance optimization. Suppose, for example, that the Elevator instances run on cards that have few available CPU cycles. In that situation, you might want those instances to perform as little computation as possible, so the first design is the preferred assignment of behaviors to classes.

7.2.2   A Heating and Cooling Example

Consider another example, this one borrowed from Riel (1996, 37–39). Suppose you must develop a heating and cooling system for buildings. Two of the classes in your system are Flow Regulator, which is responsible for opening and closing vents to permit or restrict the flow of warm or cool air into rooms, and Room, an instance of which represents a physical room. Focusing exclusively on the heating side of this application, the rule for heating a room in the initial system is that if a room's current temperature falls below its desired temperature and the room is occupied, heat must be routed to the room.

Obviously, each Room instance must maintain, as part of its state, its current and desired temperatures and an indication of if it is occupied. (Assume that each physical room includes a motion detector.) Suppose that the Flow Regulator calls Room instance methods to obtain those three values and applies the rule specified above. Figures 7.7 and 7.8 contain a partial class diagram and a sequence diagram, respectively, for this design.

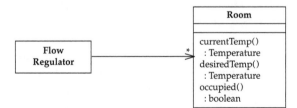

FIGURE 7.7   *One allocation of behavior to Rooms.*

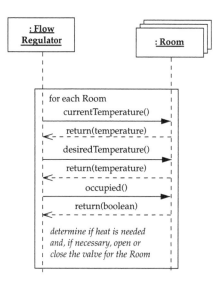

FIGURE 7.8 *A first sequence diagram for determining if Rooms require heat.*

The Flow Regulator in this design is a controller. To be specific, it is querying the state of each Room and, then, using the results to decide whether the Room requires heat. This design is somewhat difficult to extend because altering the rules under which Rooms must be heated requires modifications to both the Room and Flow Regulator classes. Suppose, for example, that some Rooms must be heated whenever the current temperature falls below the desired temperature, regardless of whether the Room is occupied. This change requires that you add a type attribute to each Room (indicating whether it is a "heat only if occupied" Room or a "heat regardless of whether occupied" Room) and that you introduce behavior in the Flow Regulator class to obtain and test the attribute's value.

A more complicated extension is one where Rooms are heated during certain time intervals, regardless of their current temperatures. To allow this, the Room class must be modified (perhaps through the introduction of subclasses) to indicate whether the Room is of this new type and, if so, to include the time ranges during which it must be heated. In addition, the Flow Regulator must be altered to include behavior that will check those time ranges for that variety of Room. In each of these extensions, new state variables and their accessor methods must be added to the controlled class, Room, and new behavior to use those state variables must be added to the controller, the Flow Regulator.

Rather than have the Flow Regulator use a Room's state to decide whether the Room needs heat, why not have the Room make that decision? Consider an alternative allocation of behavior in which the Room class includes a heatRequired method. The Flow Regulator periodically invokes this method in each Room instance and, depending upon the result, opens or closes the valves for that Room. Figures 7.9 and 7.10 depict the class diagram and a sequence diagram, respectively, for that design. This solution requires that the Flow Regulator poll the Rooms. An even better design (although not pictured here) is one in which the Room informs the Flow Regulator when it requires heat and when that heat should be discontinued.

FIGURE 7.9 *An alternative allocation of behavior to Rooms.*

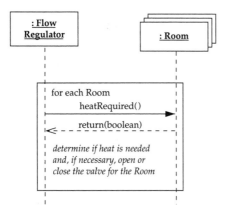

FIGURE 7.10 *A second sequence diagram for determining if Rooms require heat.*

This solution is more extensible than the first design because the two additions proposed above require modifications only to the Room class. The heatRequired method can take into account, based on the type of the Room, whether the occupied state variable should be considered, or whether various time ranges must be checked. No changes to the Flow Regulator are required when adding either feature.

You can also compare the two designs using the guidelines outlined at the beginning of this section. The second design has a more even distribution of behavior. Rooms and the Flow Regulator share the work in that design, whereas a Room instance in the first design is nothing but a stupid repository of state variables. The second design does a better job of co-locating state and behavior (in the Room class). It reduces the representational coupling of a Flow Regulator to a Room (by providing a more abstract interface, heatRequired), and it is more imperative in its style (because a Flow Regulator tells a Room to determine when heat is required).

If you have parallel hardware available in this system, distributing the required behavior evenly across the Flow Regulator and Room classes allows for a greater degree of parallelism. The many Room instances can execute their heatRequired methods in parallel, and the Flow Regulator can respond to one Room's request for heat as other Rooms continue to execute that method.

7.2.3 Two Stock-Trading Examples

The elevator control and heating and cooling applications above are both examples of control-oriented systems. Nonetheless, the same principles also apply to other kinds of systems. Recall the stock-trading application introduced in Section 3.2, "Developing a Class Diagram Using Abstraction," in Chapter 3. Figure 7.11 contains the class diagram for that application, originally shown in Figure 3.7 and subsequently extended with Buy Order and Sell Order subclasses.

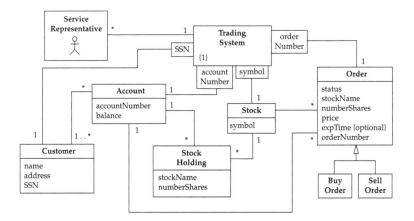

FIGURE 7.11 *The class diagram for the stock-trading system.*

Consider the Cancel Order use case, which is triggered when a customer calls and asks a Service Representative to cancel the Order with a specified order number. This use case has at least three interesting scenarios:

- An Order with the specified order number cannot be found.

- An Order with the specified order number is found, but its status is not *open*. (The Order has been executed, it has expired, or it has been previously canceled.)

- An Order with the specified order number is found; its status is *open*, and the Order is canceled.

Figure 7.12 contains a partial sequence diagram for the third scenario. The Service Representative invokes the Trading System object's cancelOrder method, passing an order number. The Trading System looks up the Order with that order number. It then calls the Order's getStatus method and (in this scenario) determines that the Order is still open. It then invokes the Order's cancel method. (Any interactions initiated by that cancel method are omitted from the figure.)

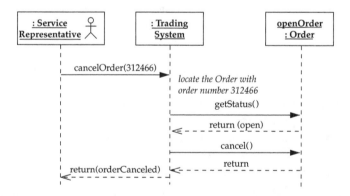

FIGURE 7.12 *A first sequence diagram for canceling an open Order.*

With this allocation of behavior, the Trading System instance is behaving as a controller object. It asks an Order for the Order's status and, then, uses the resulting value to determine whether the Order should be canceled. Why not simply tell the Order to cancel itself and let the Order check its status as part of the implementation of its cancel method, as illustrated in the sequence diagram in Figure 7.13? Note that because the Order checks it status internally, that behavior is not apparent in the diagram.

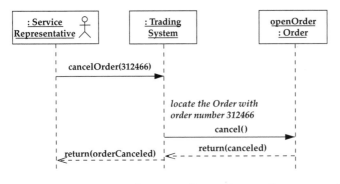

FIGURE 7.13 *A second sequence diagram for canceling an open Order.*

As was true in the prior examples, the designs outlined by these two sequence diagrams differ in their extensibility. Suppose that you must introduce in this system a new status value, onHold. An Order is on hold when the customer wants to reconsider it. While in that state, it can be canceled or expired but not executed (that is, matched). How would this affect the two designs? In the design indicated by Figure 7.12, the Order class must be altered to include the new status value. In addition, the Trading System's cancelOrder method must be modified to check for the new status value, onHold. In the design in Figure 7.13, on the other hand, the modifications (for this scenario) are local to the Order class.

At this point, you may be thinking, what's the big deal? After all, for the scenario depicted in Figure 7.12, you only have to make a small change in one place in the Trading System to deal with Orders that are on hold. If you adopt this style of design and programming, however, you will have *many* places in your code where a client object queries an Order for its status and, then, uses the resulting value to make a decision. Each time you introduce a new status value (or remove an old one), you will have to inspect all of those places.

Because this is a concurrent application (due at least to the presence of multiple Service Representatives beating on the system at the same time), the second sequence diagram is also preferable to the first based on the type of locking each requires. In the design in Figure 7.12, the Trading System must grab a lock on the Order before checking its status and, then, hold that lock until the Order is canceled to prevent another client from altering the Order during that interval. For the design in Figure 7.13, however, only the Order's cancel method must be atomic. As a result, the Order can lock itself internally during the execution of that method. The latter is the preferred locking scheme for reasons that are covered in the next chapter.

This is a general phenomenon, not an isolated example. Because they read and then alter other objects, controllers operating in concurrent environments often must grab and hold locks on those objects. Replacing a controller with a client that simply tells each service object to perform a service often means that only the individual services must be atomic. Therefore, the service objects can lock themselves internally during the execution of those methods. Because locking at the method level is superior to alternative locking schemes, concurrent systems designs with an even distribution of behavior offer this additional advantage over their controller-oriented counterparts.

As a second example from the stock-trading application, consider entering a new Buy Order into the system. Section 6.1.3, "Identifying and Modeling Scenarios," of Chapter 6, "Developing Dynamic Diagrams," developed the scenarios and sequence diagrams for the Enter Buy Order use case. The sequence diagram for the scenario in which a new Buy Order is successfully created appeared in Figure 6.12 and is repeated here as Figure 7.14. When asked to enter a buy order, the Trading System first looks up the Account with the specified account number. Then, it obtains the balance of the Account to ensure the Account can fund the desired stock purchase. (Recall that this system requires that you fund all Buy Orders from cash in an existing Account.)

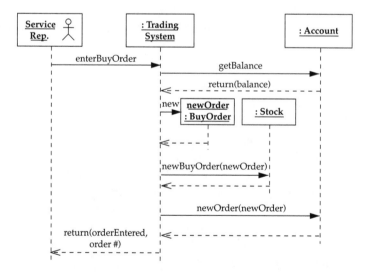

FIGURE 7.14 *A sequence diagram for successfully entering a Buy Order.*

The Trading System is again acting as a controller. It is querying the balance of an Account and using that information to decide whether the Account can fund the stock purchase. The Trading System is now dependent upon what parts of an Account are used to fund Buy Orders. When an Account funds Buy Orders in new ways, you must modify both the Account and Trading System classes.

The use of an Account's balance to fund Orders is flawed. Suppose you have $10,000.00 in your Account, and you attempt to place a Buy Order totaling $7500.00. The system will check your balance, and it will create the Buy Order because you have sufficient funds to cover the Order. Suppose further that, moments later, as the first Order remains open (that is, unmatched), you attempt to place another Buy Order for $7500.00. The system will again check the balance of your Account, and it will enter the second Buy Order because that balance is still $10,000.00. You now have open Buy Orders totaling $15,000, but you have only $10,000 in your Account. When the second Order is matched, your Account's balance will be negative. This is clearly a violation of the required behavior of this application.

Correcting this flaw requires that you distinguish an Account's total balance from its available balance, the amount of cash in the Account that is not already earmarked for Buy Orders (or some other purpose). This entails adding to the Account class an `availableBalance` attribute and some accessor methods to get and set the attribute's value. It also requires adding code to the Trading System's `enterBuyOrder` method to check and set that value when funding a Buy Order. As in the previous examples, you must implement state changes in the controlled object, Account, and behavioral changes in the controller, Trading System.

Consider adding margin accounts to a future release of this system. Provided certain conditions are met, a margin account can borrow money from the brokerage house to buy stock. This extension requires that you introduce the new type of Account, and that you store the Account's margin requirements (describing under what conditions the Account can borrow money). It also requires that the Trading System's `enterBuyOrder` method now check the type of Account and, based on the result, use either the Account's available balance or margin requirements to fund the Order.

A more extensible allocation of behavior is one in which the Trading System simply tells the Account to fund the Order, as illustrated by the sequence diagram in Figure 7.15. In particular, the Trading System invokes the Account instance's `fundBuy` method, passing the amount of cash required, and receiving a boolean result (`true` in this example) indicating whether the Buy Order could be funded.

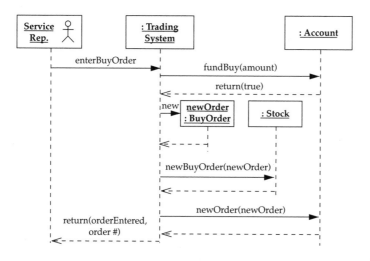

FIGURE 7.15 *An alternative sequence diagram for successfully entering a Buy Order.*

For this specific scenario, you can make both the correction and extension outlined above by modifying only the Account class. To correct the flaw, you alter the `fundBuy` method so that it uses (and sets) the Account's available balance rather than simply checking its balance. Introducing margin accounts entails transforming Account into an abstract class with an abstract `fundBuy` method. Its subclasses, Cash Account and Margin Account, implement the `fundBuy` method in different ways, as shown in Figure 7.16. (The former uses the available balance, whereas the latter may combine the use of available funds and borrowed funds, subject to its margin requirements.)

The Trading System's `enterBuyOrder` method remains the same; it uses an account number to obtain a reference to a generic Account and, then, invokes that Account's `fundBuy` method. In the latter case, of course, that reference is actually to either a Cash Account or a Margin Account, but through the magic of polymorphism, the correct `fundBuy` method will be invoked.

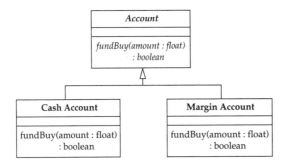

FIGURE 7.16 *Distinguishing between Cash and Margin Accounts.*

These examples illustrate a danger of initially defining a class in terms of its state. Because you've defined all the data, and because you want to encapsulate that data, you feel a temptation to define methods to read and write each data item. As the examples demonstrate, however, concentrating on what an instance of the class must do, rather than the data it must have, will frequently lead you to a more extensible design.

While the co-location of state and behavior in a class is a fundamental principle of object-oriented development, it is only a guideline and is sometimes relaxed. The most typical reason you opt for a controller is to improve system performance. Consider the Match Orders use case. How do you match Buy and Sell Orders? Because Orders have the state information required for matching, your first approach might be to place the matching behavior in the Order class (or in the Buy Order and/or Sell Order subclasses). When attempting to find a matching Buy Order, however, a Sell Order must check every Buy Order in this system (and it's not clear that parallelism can help you in this case). What a "CPU hog" that scheme would be! In addition, matching groups of Orders, such as matching two Sell Orders for 300 shares each to three Buy Orders for 200 shares each, would be extremely complicated (assuming executing only a part of an Order is illegal).

Because the Buy Orders for a particular security can be matched only to Sell Orders for that same security, you can improve the performance of this application by having a security mediate the process of matching its Orders. The Stock class, an instance of which represents a particular security, will therefore be assigned this behavior. This centralizes the matching behavior and thereby improves performance. Take care, however, to understand the implications of introducing controllers in your design.

7.3 Extension Versus Reuse

You typically have an inverse relationship between the extensibility of a design and the reusability of its classes. That is, some of the guidelines that make a design more extensible also make its classes *less* reusable. This may seem counterintuitive at first but consider the Account class in the examples above. To make the stock-trading application extensible, a fundBuy method is assigned to that class. The class also has fundSell, unfundBuy, and unfundSell methods. (The latter two are invoked when an open Buy or Sell Order expires or is canceled, because the assets set aside for that Order must be released.) The Account class is rife with methods specific to the application at hand, stock trading.

This phenomenon is hardly surprising. As you strive to avoid controllers and keep state and behavior together, you are distributing the application logic across more and more classes. The implication, of course, is that as they are assigned that logic, the classes become less reusable in other kinds of applications. The Account class, with methods to fund stock trades and carry out other trading-related activities, cannot easily be reused in a banking application that has nothing to do with stock-trading.

If your goal is developing reusable classes rather than extensible designs, you should apply a somewhat different set of guidelines when allocating behaviors. At a minimum, you want to temper the guidelines outlined in the previous section.

7.3.1 Primitive Class Interfaces

A maximally reusable Account class provides some basic functionality common to all accounts but, otherwise, is as nondescript as possible. In other words, the public interface of that class provides only the basic building blocks common to all Accounts. This concept is similar in philosophy to what Lakos calls a *primitive* interface (Lakos 1996, 557).

A class with a primitive interface need not be an unencapsulated class. If you define an account as something that holds cash, the corresponding Account class has a balance attribute, as well as methods to deposit and withdraw funds and to obtain the balance of the account, as shown in Figure 7.17.

An even more general but complicated Account class is one that holds a portfolio of assets, whether cash or otherwise, each keyed by its asset type. An accompanying pair of Asset classes, one each for indivisible assets (such as pork bellies, which cannot be subdivided) and divisible assets (such as stocks, which through dividend reinvestment plans can be purchased in fractional parts), define those assets, as shown in Figure 7.18. In each case, the reusable classes provide a set of primitive methods to deposit and withdraw assets while still encapsulating the underlying implementation of these assets.

NOTE

Recall from Section 2.3.1, "Qualified Associations," of Chapter 2, "Class Diagramming Notation," that the small rectangles labeled Asset Type in Figure 7.18 are qualifiers. The illustration indicates that an Account instance will use an Asset Type to find a Divisible Asset or an Indivisible Asset. The `depositAsset` *and* `withdrawAsset` *methods are overloaded, accepting either an integer-valued or floating-point argument for an Indivisible and Divisible Asset, respectively.*

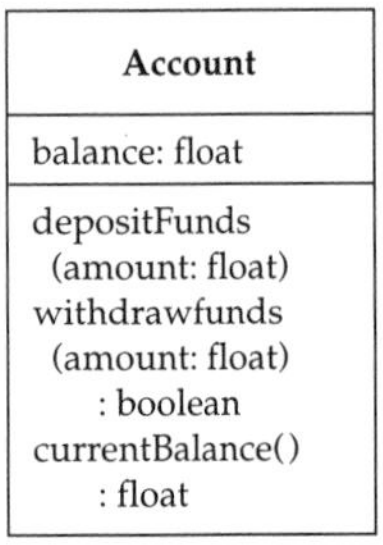

Account
balance: float
depositFunds (amount: float) withdrawfunds (amount: float) : boolean currentBalance() : float

FIGURE 7.17 *A reusable Account class.*

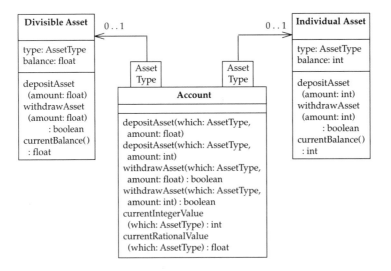

FIGURE 7.18 *A more general reusable Account class.*

7.3.2   Commingling Extension and Reuse

Is it possible to have it both ways? That is, can you define an Account class that is both extensible relative to one application and at the same time reusable across multiple disparate applications? In most cases, this is probably an unreachable goal; nonetheless, you can define a pair of related classes that give you both effects simultaneously.

Figure 7.19 contains a pair of classes that define accounts. The Account class is a generic, reusable class that could be included in a financial class library. It defines only the primitive methods required of an account that holds a single asset (such as cash). The Stock-Trading Account class defines the interfaces that an Account class in a stock-trading application must have. That class makes use of an underlying Account instance to hold its cash. The other classes in the application, such as Trading System and Order, refer only to the Stock-Trading Account class; the Account class and its instances are invisible to those classes (and their instances). Hence, the application-specific Stock-Trading Account class is using a reusable Account class as part of its implementation.

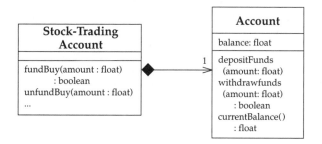

FIGURE 7.19 *A pair of Account classes for extension and reuse.*

This is an example of applying a design pattern—a way of solving a small problem that could be applied to a design in any problem domain. (Design patterns are discussed in more detail in Chapter 9.) Call this the *Have Gunk, Will Travel* pattern. The class diagram for the pattern is given in Figure 7.20. The class named Application-Specific Class in the figure has all the "gunk" required of the application. In particular, it defines the methods (and data) specific to the application, thereby making the application more extensible.

The Trading-System Account class plays that role in the application of the pattern in Figure 7.19. The class labeled Reusable Class is the generic, reusable abstraction and, therefore, "will travel" among applications. The Account class in Figure 7.19 represents this role. The Have Gunk, Will Travel pattern will be revisited in Chapter 9.

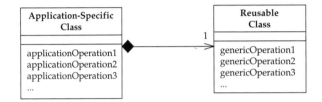

FIGURE 7.20 *The class diagram for the Have Gunk, Will Travel design pattern.*

Observe that while the use of this pattern provides you with additional flexibility, it does so at the price of increased complexity. For every abstraction in your design that must be both extensible and reusable, you must develop two distinct classes (the Reusable Class and the Application-Specific Class). Your design also may suffer some degradation of performance, as an Application-Specific Class instance must often call a method in its Reusable Class instance to carry out its functions. While this price is too steep for many applications, the Have Gunk, Will Travel pattern may be the correct solution in situations where extensibility and reuse are simultaneous development goals.

CHAPTER 8

Architectural Models

The preceding chapters limit themselves to "development in the small" because their examples treat a system or application as a monolithic entity. They ignore system architectural issues such as what subsystems are required, how persistence is achieved, and what hardware boxes will be employed. This chapter addresses many of those issues.

One view of architecture is *decomposition*. An architecture decomposes a system into the set of building blocks that constructs the overall system. This decomposition can either be logical, because each building block defines a conceptual entity, such as a layer or subsystem, or it can be physical, such as describing a system in terms of its hardware boxes or its source or executable files.

The building blocks may be nested, in that one block can be composed of smaller, lower-level blocks. For example, consider the following:

- A physical block may embody a collection of logical blocks. A hardware processor, for example, may contain a set of subsystems running on that machine.

- A logical unit can be composed of physical ones. An example is a subsystem that consists of a set of executable files that together define the subsystem.

- A logical unit can be decomposed into other logical units, such as when a subsystem consists of smaller subsystems.

- A physical unit may be composed of other physical units, which occurs when a hardware processor has several executables running on it, for example.

A complementary view of architecture is as a *composition* mechanism. It groups small pieces into larger, more coherent units. The use cases or classes in an object-oriented system or application, for example, can be grouped in logical units, each of which defines a conceptual building block such as a layer or subsystem. This composition is logical because it employs a logical rather than physical criterion as its guiding hand. An example of this is grouping use cases into subsystems based on functional cohesion; all the use cases in one functional area, such as order entry or inventory management, reside in the subsystem for that area. Classes can also be composed based on physical considerations, such as the hardware on which their instances run, or the executables in which their binaries reside.

When defining architecture by composition, you can employ a process of *superimposition*. You can superimpose a process structure, hardware configuration, and so forth over the static and dynamic views of the design described in Chapters 2 through 7. UML provides basic notation for the architectural building blocks, and it permits the superimposition of those blocks onto other UML diagrams.

This chapter covers the concepts, notation, and process employed to define a system architecture:

- *Logical architecture*: A system can be organized logically, such as into layers or subsystems. This concept is explored, and the use of a *UML package* to model such a group is discussed.

- *Hardware architecture*: Many applications and systems are distributed, meaning that they span multiple hardware boxes. The *deployment diagram*, the UML notation for hardware architecture, is explained.

- *Process architecture*: Many programs are also grouped into a set of *processes* and *threads* (or *tasks*). The UML notation for processes and threads is illustrated. Issues that arise in concurrent applications, such as synchronization and locking, are also discussed.

- *Implementation architecture*: The classes in an application must be grouped into a set of source files, binary files, and executables. The UML notation for that implementation architecture, the *component diagram*, is described.

The chapter also describes how these building blocks (packages, components, hardware nodes, and tasks) can be superimposed onto use case, class, and interaction diagrams.

8.1   Logical Architecture

A system or application, whether object-oriented or not, can be organized into logical units such as layers or subsystems. These are *logical* because the grouping criterion is conceptual. A *layer*, for example, defines one tier or stratum of the system that is typically organized around functional cohesion. Each layer carries out a different functional responsibility and, therefore, is defined by a conceptual boundary.

A common layered system organization (even in applications that are not object-oriented) is the *three-tiered* architecture shown in Figure 8.1. The user interacts with the top tier, the *presentation layer*, which contains the user interface. This interface might be a command line interface or a graphical user interface (GUI). The presentation layer, in turn, makes requests of the *application layer*, which contains the business logic. That layer loads and stores items in persistent storage using a set of data services provided by the *persistence layer*. The number of tiers can be expanded further, resulting in what is referred to as an *N-tiered architecture* in its general form.

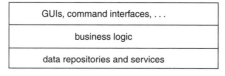

GUIs, command interfaces, . . .	**Presentation Layer**
business logic	**Application Layer**
data repositories and services	**Persistence Layer**

FIGURE **8.1**   *A three-tiered architecture.*

Note

Observe that all the examples in this book (processing catalog orders, loaning books and videos, handling stock trades, and tracking the states of factory machines) are of the application layer. Each example describes the business logic required to carry out that application. Although the presentation and persistence layers are omitted from the examples, they can also be object-oriented. Addressing those subjects is beyond the scope of this book. Refer to Dave Collins' book, Designing Object-Oriented User Interfaces *(Reading Mass.: Benjamin/ Cummings, 1995), for a description of the development of object-oriented GUIs, and Mary Loomis' book,* Object Databases: The Essentials *(Reading, Mass.: Addison Wesley, 1995), for the utility of using an object-oriented database for persistence.*

A layer can be modeled in UML as a *package*, which is a logical grouping of classes or use cases. As such, it can appear in a class diagram or a use case diagram. A package is depicted as a folder labeled with the name of the package. In its closed form, a package includes its name on the folder, but the contents of the package are not visible. Figure 8.2 shows three closed packages corresponding to the three layers in Figure 8.1.

FIGURE 8.2 *Closed UML packages for system layers.*

In its open form, a package exposes the classes or use cases it contains. The folder's tab is labeled with the name of the package. The Application Layer package in Figure 8.2 is shown in its open form in Figures 8.3 and 8.4. In particular, this is the application layer of the stock-trading system described in Section 3.2, "Developing a Class Diagram Using Abstraction," in Chapter 3, "Developing Class Diagrams," and revisited in Section 6.1, "Top-Down Design of System Dynamics," in Chapter 6, "Developing Dynamic Diagrams." The packages in Figure 8.3 and 8.4 contain the use cases and classes, respectively, for the application layer of that system.

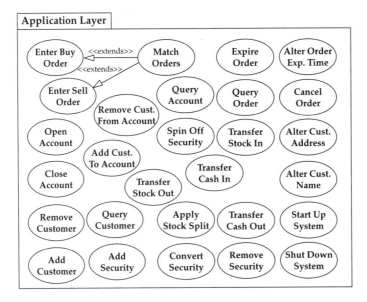

FIGURE 8.3 *A package containing a stock-trading system's use cases.*

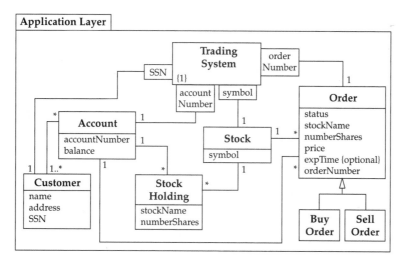

FIGURE 8.4 *A package containing a stock-trading system's classes.*

The package in Figure 8.3 would appear in the use case diagram for the stock-trading system. Likewise, the package in Figure 8.4 would be a part of the system's class diagram. Hence, these packages represent both the decomposition of the system into layers, as well as a composition of classes or use cases to form those layers. You can, therefore, decompose or compose to form layers: You can decompose the system into its layers *a priori*, or you can compose the layers by superimposing packages over the top of an existing use case or class diagram. (Many CASE tools support composition as well as decomposition because they allow you to assign existing classes or use cases to packages you have just created.)

Decomposition is most appropriate in cases where an obvious system organization is apparent from the beginning. If you know up front, for example, that you want a three-tiered architecture or that you have some obvious subsystems, committing to those packages early in the development process poses very little risk. That separation also presents a way to divide the project into teams by assigning a package to each team. Conversely, in cases where preferred system architecture is not readily apparent, deferring the identification of packages until the design of some of the classes has been completed can save development time and frustration.

In most layered architectures, each layer is dependent on the layer immediately below it. In the stock-trading application, for example, the presentation layer (represented by the Service Representative actor class in the original class diagram in Figure 3.7) communicates with the Trading System instance in the application layer. Furthermore, that Trading System instance (or an unspecified helper of that instance) must communicate with the persistence layer to obtain Orders, Accounts, and so forth from the application's database(s).

A dependency relationship between layers (or, more generally, between packages) is depicted in UML using an «imports» dependency. The dependency is directed toward the layer (or package) being accessed. It indicates that one or more entities in the source package must access entities in the destination package. For packages that contain classes, for example, it specifies that some of the classes in the destination package must be visible to one or more classes in the source package. The dependencies described in the previous paragraph are shown in Figure 8.5.

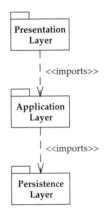

Figure 8.5 *Dependencies among the system layers.*

An «imports» dependency can be refined to begin at and/or terminate at a particular entity in a package. Figure 8.6 is a refinement of Figure 8.5. It indicates specifically that the presentation layer interacts with the Trading System instance, which in turn communicates with the persistence layer. (The other classes in the application layer have been omitted from the figure.)

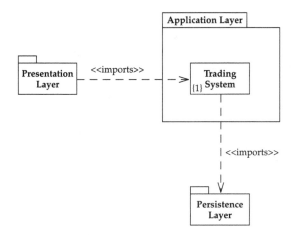

FIGURE 8.6 *Refined dependencies among the system layers.*

Up to this point, all the package examples are of layers. Another logical grouping of classes or use cases is by *subsystem*. A subsystem is a part of the overall system. In a layered system, it is one part, typically one functional area, within a layer. The classes in the application layer of the stock-trading system might be partitioned into separate subsystems for Account Management, Security Management, and Order Management. Figure 8.7 includes the resulting packages. Observe that the three subsystem packages are nested within the application layer package. UML permits the nesting of packages to any desired depth.

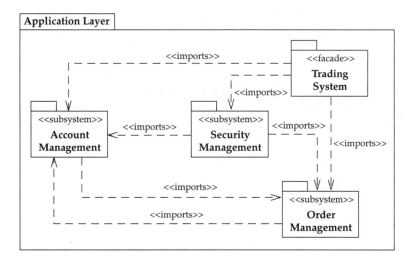

FIGURE 8.7 *The subsystems of the stock trading application layer.*

The package stereotypes employed in Figure 8.7 are both defined by UML. A «facade» package serves as a *façade*: an interface to external clients (Gamma et al. 1995, 185–193). In this example, it contains only the facade class, Trading System. The outside world accesses the subsystem packages only through this package. A «subsystem» package contains a portion of the overall system. In this case, it contains a portion of the application layer, its containing package.

Note

UML states that a «facade» package contains no model elements (Rational Software Corporation 1997, 140). Hence, it cannot contain classes (that is, it is simply an empty package). I find, however, that such a package is a useful container for the actual façade classes, such as the Trading System in Figure 8.7. The Trading System class serves as an interface into the other subsystem packages and, therefore, does not belong in any one of those packages. The alternative is to omit it from any subsystem package, placing the class only within the application layer package that contains those subsystem packages.

When a package is used to group classes, it is not necessary for all of those classes to be available to the external world. Some classes may define internal implementation details rather than constitute a part of the public interface of the package. Burying those classes within the package is a sound design practice because it is a form of information hiding.

You can indicate the visibility of a class by including an access directive before the class name. A plus sign (+) before the class name indicates that the class is accessible by other packages, whereas a class name with a leading minus (–) specifies that the class is hidden within the package. (These are the only two possibilities because a class either is, or is not, visible outside the package.)

Suppose, for example, that the Account Management package in Figure 8.7 contains the Customer, Account, and Stock Holding classes (and, as development proceeds, perhaps some lower-level classes). Suppose, however, that the Stock Holding class is not available to outside entities that import this package. This is indicated in Figure 8.8. (This requires, of course, that you alter the class diagram in Figure 8.4 so that Stock instances access Accounts rather than Stock Holdings.)

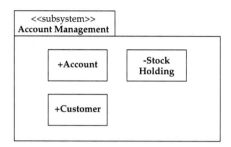

FIGURE 8.8 *Specifying the visibility of classes in a package.*

Until now, the discussion has concentrated on the concepts and notation. Given that a package typically represents a logical grouping, what criteria can you apply to partition your classes? Possible schemes include the following:

- *The partitioning is based on functional cohesion.* That is, each package represents a distinct functional area, and so the classes involved in that activity are placed in that package. The subsystems in Figure 8.7 are examples, as are the layers in Figure 8.2.

- *A package forms a unit of reuse.* That is, it contains several classes that can be reused together. It might represent a component or some other reusable unit. In such a case, you should take care to reduce the relational coupling (that is, the «imports» dependencies) this package has to others. If you want to reuse a package in another application, and that package depends on other packages, you must also drag those other packages into the application.

- *The partitioning is based on access control.* As illustrated by Figure 8.8, you can hide classes within a package. Other classes in the package can access those types, but the types are transparent to the outside world. You might say that the classes in the group are "friends" of one another. The Java programming language takes this one step further, permitting you to hide individual fields and methods of a class in the same way. (If it is public, the class is visible to the outside, but any of its fields and methods that have package access are not.)

- *You could define packages based on delivery units.* A package of classes represents a single salable unit, such as a feature, and the dependencies among packages are feature dependencies.

You might also want to partition your classes based on the physical components on which they run: All the classes in one partition will be allocated to the same physical hardware box. This topic is covered in the following section.

8.2   Hardware Architecture

Many systems are spread across multiple hardware boxes. An important view of such a system is its hardware architecture, defined in terms of the hardware nodes and their interconnections. This is a physical organization because the boundaries are defined by physical entities: computers.

A UML *deployment diagram* defines the hardware architecture of a system or application. The diagram includes a set of nodes depicted as three-dimensional cubes. Each node represents a class of hardware processor and is labeled with the type of the node. The relationships between nodes represent physical connections between the corresponding processors.

Both the nodes and relationships can include cardinality constraints. The cardinality constraint of a node appears in the upper right corner of the node (or anywhere within the node if enclosed with curly braces) and specifies how many instances of this type of processor can be included in a deployment of the system. Relationship cardinalities employ the same syntax and semantics as association cardinalities.

To illustrate the notation, suppose the stock-trading application described in Chapter 3 and above has three hardware layers. You have a set of client machines used largely to host the service representative's client interfaces. The middle hardware layer consists of application servers that handle the business of stock trading. Some of those servers are dedicated to handling account and customer responsibilities, whereas others handle security and order duties. The lower layer consists of servers (or mainframes) that house the account, customer, stock, and order databases.

Figure 8.9 contains deployment diagram for this hardware architecture. The system includes many Entry Client machines on which the service representative's user interfaces run. It also includes several Account Servers (handling customer and account responsibilities) and Order Servers (handling securities and orders). A single Account Database Server holds the customer and account databases, whereas an Order Database Server maintains the order and security databases.

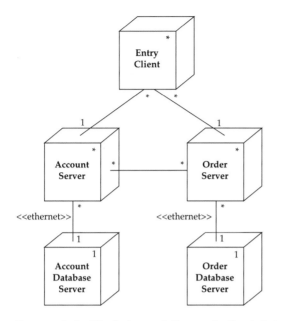

FIGURE 8.9 *The deployment diagram for the stock-trading system.*

The figure also indicates that several Entry Clients are tied to a single Account Server and Order Server, the Account Servers are connected to the Account Database Server, the Order Servers are connected to the Order Database Server, and the Account and Order Servers are connected to each other. Furthermore, the connections to the Database Servers are stereotyped in the diagram to indicate that they are ethernet connections.

The hardware nodes in a deployment diagram can be superimposed onto the classes in a class diagram or the use cases in a use case diagram. The classes or use cases within a node in the diagram reside on that type of hardware processor. Specifically, the instances of those classes, or the behaviors that implement those use cases, run on instances of that type of processor. In Figure 8.10, for example, the Order Server node has been superimposed onto the Stock, Order, Buy Order, and Sell Order classes, indicating that any instances of those classes run on Order Servers. Likewise, in Figure 8.11, the Order Server node has been superimposed onto the Security Management and Order Management subsystem packages, indicating that the classes or use cases in those packages reside on that node.

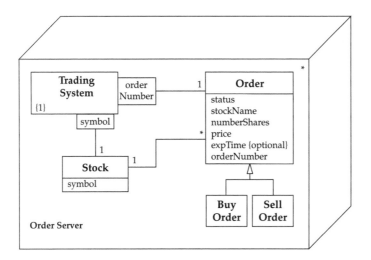

FIGURE 8.10 *Superimposing a hardware node onto a group of classes.*

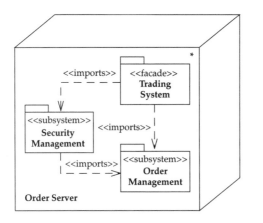

FIGURE 8.11 *Superimposing a hardware node onto packages.*

A deployment diagram is roughly equivalent to a class diagram because it describes all legal hardware configurations for the system. Just as you can draw an object diagram depicting a particular set of objects and links, you can draw a *deployment instance diagram* that describes a particular configuration of node instances and their connections. Figure 8.12 contains such a diagram for a deployment that includes two Order Servers and a single Account Server. The underlining of the name within a node specifies that this is an instance of that node . The asterisk (*) in the upper right corner of the Entry Client instances indicate that possibly many instances are represented by that single cube.

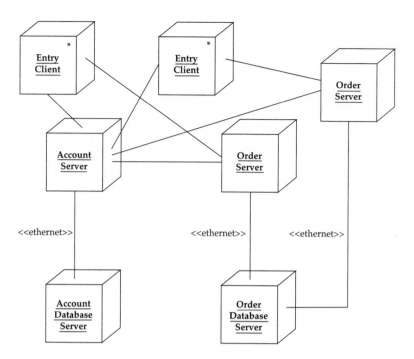

FIGURE 8.12 *A deployment instance diagram for the stock-trading system.*

You can superimpose a deployment instance diagram onto an interaction diagram to show what instances are executing on what hardware nodes. Figure 8.13 contains a collaboration diagram for successfully entering a buy order in the stock-trading system. In this scenario, the customer is placing a buy against account number 113311 for 100 shares of PigSty at $31.25 per share. Figure 8.14 contains the same collaboration diagram, but with the hardware instances superimposed.

Note

An interaction diagram describes scenarios in terms of instances, so Figure 8.14 includes hardware processor instances. Furthermore, observe the underlining, and recall that class instances, or objects, are distinguished from classes by the presence of underlining in the instances. The same convention is employed for hardware nodes.

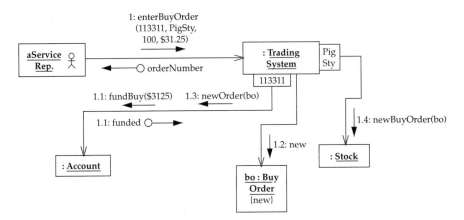

FIGURE 8.13 *A collaboration diagram for entering a buy order.*

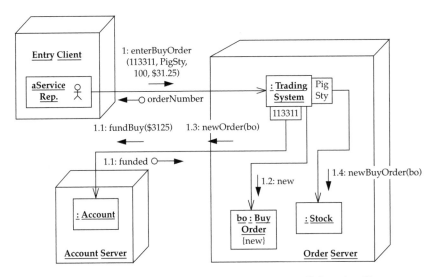

FIGURE 8.14 *Superimposing hardware instances onto a collaboration diagram.*

Because collaboration diagrams are spatially oriented, adding hardware nodes is straightforward. In theory, you can also superimpose hardware nodes onto sequence diagrams, but the results are less appealing. Furthermore, to be effective, this superimposition requires that the objects be adjacent. When objects are created during a scenario, however, they are not listed across the top of the diagram, but rather appear "down the page" when they are instantiated.

Consider the sequence diagram in Figure 8.15, for example. It describes the same scenario as the collaboration diagram in Figure 8.13. Although you could place hardware cubes around the objects at the top of the sequence diagram to indicate in what processors they run, extending a cube to include the Buy Order instance would result in a rather ugly diagram.

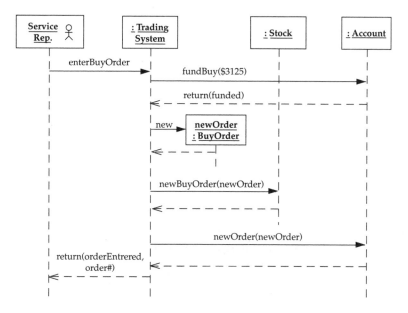

Figure 8.15 *A sequence diagram for entering a buy order.*

You may encounter situations in which an object migrates from one processor to another during the course of a scenario. That is, the object that exists on one processor is shipped to another. Figure 8.16 contains a collaboration diagram for a scenario in which a Service Representative queries the status of an Order, providing an order number, 034467. The Trading System instance asks the Order Store object on the Order Database Server to load the Order from the database, providing the order number. The Order Store loads the Order, then returns it to the Trading System, which then reconstitutes the Order on the Order Server. The migration of the Order from the Order Database Server to the Order Server is depicted using a «becomes» dependency, as shown in the figure. The Order on the Order Database Server *becomes* the Order on the Order Server.

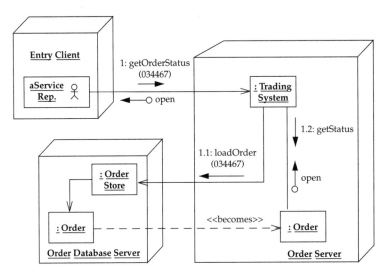

F IGURE 8.16 *Object migration across hardware nodes.*

A pair of connections in Figure 8.9 are stereotyped to indicate special semantics (specifically, that they are ethernet connections). You can also stereotype nodes in a deployment diagram in situations where the nodes have special semantics. A common example is a node that acts as a device, meaning that the node interacts with your system but is not a part of your system per se.

Recall the factory control system described in Section 3.3, "Developing a Class Diagram from Use Cases," in Chapter 3. The class diagram for that system (originally depicted in Figure 3.13 and repeated here as Figure 8.17) includes a Failure Monitor class. An instance of that class represents a sensor attached to a factory machine that monitors the machine and sends an event to the factory control software when the machine fails while in operation. The factory control system treats each Failure Monitor as a "black box." The system interacts with, but does not have software running on, a Failure Monitor.

Figure 8.18 contains a deployment diagram for this system. Observe the Failure Monitor node, which includes the «device» stereotype indicating that it is a device. As this example illustrates, a «device» node in a deployment diagram is on the boundary of the system. Therefore, it typically appears as an actor class in the system's class diagram. Figure 8.19 superimposes that hardware structure onto the class diagram in Figure 8.17. (The cardinalities of the nodes have been omitted from the diagram.)

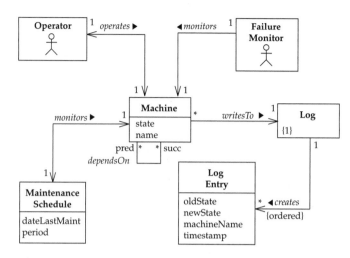

FIGURE 8.17 *The class diagram for the factory control system.*

Note

The interaction between objects on different hardware boxes, such as a Machine's use of a Log File in Figure 8.19, requires a mechanism that supports communication across processor boundaries. Several forms of infrastructure for such communication among distributed objects exist, including CORBA and DCOM. An in-depth discussion of those technologies is beyond the scope of this book. Refer to Thomas Mowbray and William Ruh's book, Inside CORBA: Distributed Object Standards and Applications *(Reading, Mass.: Addison Wesley, 1997) and Don Box's book,* Essential COM *(Reading, Mass.: Addison Wesley, 1998).*

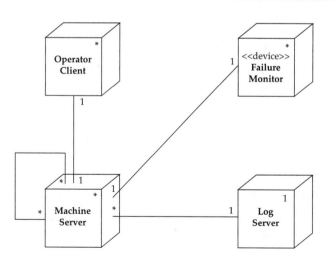

FIGURE 8.18 *The deployment diagram for the factory control system.*

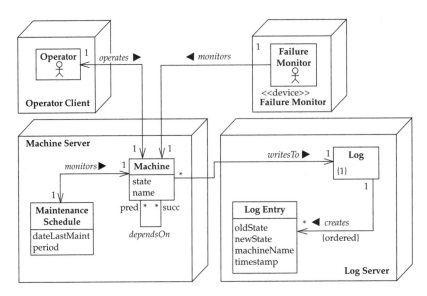

Figure 8.19 *Superimposing the factory control hardware onto the class diagram.*

8.3 Process Architecture

Many applications consist of multiple *processes* and *threads* (or *tasks*) executing concurrently. An application's processes and threads, therefore, form another architectural view of the application because they define a set of constituent building blocks.

The application layer of the stock-trading system, for example, has concurrency in two forms. Multiple Service Representatives can access the same Order Server or Account Server simultaneously. Therefore, to maximize throughput, each Service Representative request must run as a separate process. (To be more precise, each Service Representative mostly likely will have its own Trading System instance running as a separate process.) In addition, recall that an Order can have an expiration time. When that time is reached, the system must initiate a process or thread to expire the Order.

Note

The term concurrent, *as used here, does not necessarily imply true parallelism. Two processes running on a single processor are not truly parallel. However, because they can be interleaved with one another, they are apparently parallel. Those two processes, which could run in parallel given adequate hardware resources, are therefore concurrent.*

A *process* is a thread of control that runs in isolation from other processes. Each process has its own stack, heap space, instruction pointer, and registers. Because these resources are not shared, it is impossible for one process to write into the stack, heap space, or registers of another process. A process, therefore, provides a "fire-wall" around its contents, but switching from one process to another is relatively expensive.

A *thread*, on the other hand, is a thread of control that runs within a process. Each thread has its own stack, instruction pointer, and registers, but the threads within one process share the heap space of that process. It is quite common, therefore, for one thread to update an object on the heap that is accessible to other threads. While threads are relatively unprotected from one another, switching from one thread to another is relatively inexpensive because only the stack pointer, instruction pointer, and registers must be updated.

A *task* in a real-time system is typically analogous to a thread because all the tasks share a heap space, thereby making task switching relatively fast. These systems typically have no processes—with the intuition being that all of the tasks execute in one huge virtual process.

8.3.1 Defining a Process or Thread

Many operating systems provide functions an application can invoke to create a process or thread. Some class libraries also provide classes for this purpose. The Java programming language, for example, includes a Thread class that defines the state and behavior of a thread. A class that specializes the Thread class will, therefore, inherit those thread properties. Client Class in Figure 8.20 specializes the Thread class. It overrides the run method, which will execute when the thread begins. (The default implementation of run in Thread simply returns—not a very interesting behavior!) You start the thread by creating a Client class instance and invoking the start method it inherits from Thread. (That method initializes the thread and then calls run.)

Figure 8.20 also illustrates the UML notation for objects that embody processes, threads, or tasks. Such an object, called an *active object*, has a bold border to distinguish it from normal objects. If not stereotyped, an active object defines a task. However, UML provides the «process» and «thread» stereotypes for active objects that are processes and threads. Although not depicted, this stereotype can also be applied to classes (such as the Thread class in the figure).

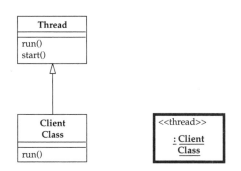

FIGURE 8.20 *Specializing a Thread class.*

An alternative to specializing a Thread or Task class is to link an object to a separate Thread or Task object. The Thread or Task object then calls back to the client object when the task or thread begins. Figure 8.21 illustrates this way of using Java's Thread class. Client Class is associated with Thread. You first create a Client Class instance; then, you create a Thread object with a link to that instance. When you invoke the Thread object's start method, it will initialize itself and then invoke run in the Client Class instance.

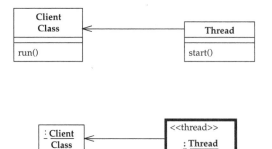

FIGURE 8.21 *Associating with a Thread class.*

8.3.2 Object Synchronization

One source of concurrency in the stock-trading system is the presence of multiple Entry Clients simultaneously accessing the same Order Server or Account Server. This opens the possibility that two Entry Clients (that is, two Service Representatives) might attempt to simultaneously access the same Order or Account instance. Suppose, for example, that one Service Representative is transferring money into an Account while another is removing money from that same Account. Without any locking, the two modifications could conflict; for example, they might both use the initial balance of the Account as their starting point, meaning that one of the transactions will be overwritten by the other.

The need for locking is a common problem in concurrent systems. In general, the level of locking can be any of the following:

- *A class or method is* sequential. When invoked on an instance, a sequential method neither checks nor grabs the lock of that instance. This may mean that the method can execute concurrently with any other method called on the instance. Alternatively, a sequential method may be one that is not guaranteed to operate correct in the presence of concurrency. A sequential class is one in which all methods are sequential.

- *A class or method is* concurrent *(or synchronous in earlier versions of UML).* A concurrent method grabs a lock on the instance on which it was invoked. Then, it holds that lock throughout the duration of the execution of the method. Just before control is returned to the caller, the lock is released. This blocks out requests from all other clients while the method is in progress. If the lock is not available when the method is invoked, the invoking thread or process must wait until the lock becomes available. A concurrent class is one in which all methods are concurrent.

- *A class is* guarded. The class provides methods (such as `lock` and `unlock`, or `seize` and `release`) that a client must invoke on an instance of the class to lock and subsequently unlock that instance. When a class is guarded, the client must invoke `lock` (or `seize`) to obtain the lock on an instance before calling any other methods on the instance. If the instance is already locked by another client when the client invokes `lock`, the client thread or process must wait until the lock becomes available.

Note

Systems that support multi-threading often provide built-in locking mechanisms. The Java programming language, for example, supports both concurrent methods (by declaring the method to be synchronized*) and guarded locking (through the client's use of a* synchronized *statement). Some systems that offer such mechanisms also solve one of the problems of guarded locking (that is, guaranteeing that clients behave correctly) by automatically ensuring that a client invoking a method on a guarded object holds the lock on that object. Java, for example, assigns a lock to a thread and guarantees that the thread invoking a synchronized method on an object holds the lock on that object.*

The synchronization semantics of a class or method is depicted as a property of that entity. The Stock class in Figure 8.22 includes a property indicating its instances are guarded. The class lists the `lock` and `unlock` methods used to lock and unlock a Stock instance. In the Account class in the figure, the `fundBuy` and `fundSell` methods are concurrent, indicating that an Account instance locks itself when one of those methods is invoked. The `balance` method, on the other hand, is sequential. It does no locking, and so it can be invoked on an instance while that instance is simultaneously handling another request. (Because the `balance` method simply returns the balance of the Account, the assumption is that no locking is required.)

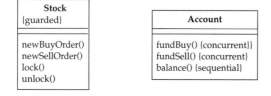

FIGURE 8.22 *Synchronization primitives of classes and methods.*

A concurrent locking scheme is normally preferable to a guarded one for the following several reasons:

- The client code isn't cluttered with calls to the locking and unlocking methods (for example, `lock` and `unlock`). Clients simply invoke the application-specific methods provided by the service object.

- You don't have to depend on clients to behave correctly. With a guarded Stock class, a client must lock a Stock instance before using it. What if a client forgets to do this? What if the client forgets to unlock an instance the client has locked? What if a client unlocks an instance that is currently locked by another client?

- Circular waiting (that is, deadlock) may be easier to prevent. This situation can result when you have a cycle of locking dependencies. For example, suppose Client 1 has locked A and is trying to lock B, while Client 2 has locked B and wants to lock A. Clients 1 and 2 will wait forever on each other. With guarded locking, a client can hold a lock for a long period of time. To prevent deadlock, therefore, you must predict clients' patterns of grabbing and holding locks. With concurrent locking, on the other hand, a lock is held only during the execution of a method. Deadlocks, therefore, are due to circular calling patterns, and these are typically easier to find than deadlocks in guarded schemes.

- Concurrent policies can be changed without the client's knowledge (and, therefore, without altering the client). Suppose you discover that an Account can safely handle a `fundBuy` and a `fundSell` request simultaneously. In an Account class with concurrent locking, that modification is internal to the class. In a guarded Account, however, the `lock` method must be extended to include an argument that indicates how the client intends to use the Account, and the client code must be altered to supply the appropriate value.

On the other hand, a guarded solution is more powerful than a concurrent one. Therefore, despite its disadvantages, it is sometimes required. In particular, a guarded solution is required in cases where a client must invoke multiple methods as a single atomic action. Suppose, for example, that you have a situation in which you must transfer shares of several different securities into an Account as a single, atomic operation. In that case, you must grab and hold a lock on the Account until you complete the transfers.

As another example, consider a stock split. All the Stock Holdings and open Orders for that security must be split as a single atomic operation. One way to achieve that result is to lock all of the Holdings and Orders, and then apply the split to each of them. (Another is to provide a method that handles the multiple operations. But, trying to define all such combinations of operations and then implementing a method for each combination, is impractical and leads to bloated interfaces and incohesive methods.)

Note

This discussion addresses only one locking problem, mutual exclusion. Mutual exclusion requires that each client have exclusive access to an object. Other types of locking problems exist. A notable one is readers and writers, in which multiple clients can hold a read lock, but holding a write lock requires exclusive access to the object. In addition, many implementations of locking exist, including monitors, semaphores, and mutex variables. Refer to Gregory Andrews' book, Concurrent Programming: Principles and Practice *(Reading, Mass.: Benjamin/Cummings, 1991), for an excellent (although procedural rather than object-oriented) description of several locking algorithms and implementations. You can also refer to Doug Lea's book,* Concurrent Programming in Java: Design Principles and Patterns *(Reading, Mass.: Addison Wesley, 1997), for algorithms and implementations in terms of Java.*

How do you determine what locking the instances of a class require? If you have developed a complete list of use cases for the system in question, you can allow that list to guide your analysis. For each class in the system, consider each pair of use cases (including perhaps the same use case being invoked by two different actor instances). Then, ask yourself whether an instance of that class might be compromised if those two use cases executed in parallel.

Recall the list of use cases developed for the stock-trading application in Section 6.1.1, "Identifying Use Cases," in Chapter 6. That list follows:

Enter a buy order

Enter a sell order

Cancel an order

Open a new account

Close an existing account

Transfer cash into an account

Transfer cash out of an account

Transfer stock into an account

Transfer stock out of an account

Query the properties of an account

Query the properties of an order

Query the properties of a customer

Start up the system

Shut down the system

Add a new customer

Remove an existing customer

Change a customer's name

Change a customer's address

Add a customer to an account

Remove a customer from an account

Execute orders (match buy orders to sell orders)

Add a security

Remove an existing security

Spin off a security

Convert one security into another

Expire an order

Change an order's expiration time

Apply a stock split

As an example of that analysis, consider the Order class. If executed concurrently, are there any two uses cases in the above list that might compromise the integrity of an Order instance? Yes, there are several such pairs. For example, a Service Representative might be canceling the Order as the Order is being matched. Alternatively, two different attempts to match (and execute) the Order could occur simultaneously. The Order class, therefore, requires synchronization control.

After you determine that the Order class requires locking, then determine if a concurrent (rather than guarded) locking scheme is sufficient. A concurrent class is preferable for the reasons cited earlier in this section. You can make this determination by inspecting each of the Order's methods, asking yourself if locking *within* the method is sufficient. If such locking is acceptable for all methods, use concurrent locking.

8.3.3 Object Synchronization

The above discussion addresses *object synchronization*. Another form of synchronization is *process synchronization*, which occurs when two or more processes (or tasks or threads) must "meet up" at a particular point in a computation. As a simple example, consider two threads that must synchronize when completing their current processing. That is, neither thread can proceed to the next step until both threads have finished their duties at hand.

Some systems provide mechanisms for process synchronization. For example, the original Solaris thread package included a function, `thr_join`, that is used to force one thread to await the completion of another (Lewis and Berg 1996, 233). The POSIX thread library offers a `pthread_join` function for the same purpose (Norton and Dipasquale 1997, 56).

Many systems require more powerful thread synchronization schemes; so, you may want to implement additional mechanisms. Douglass defines a pattern, Rendezvous, that permits any number of threads to synchronize their computations (Douglass 1999, 278-282). The essence of the pattern is that a Synchronizer object is created for a specific number of client threads. During its initialization, the Synchronizer creates a wait lock for each client. Invoking `lock` on a wait lock suspends the caller until `unlock` is called. When a client (in the client's thread) invokes the Synchronizer's `wait` method, the Synchronizer attempts to grab the lock for that client, thereby suspending the client. When all clients have called `wait`, the Synchronizer unlocks the locks, thus allowing the clients to proceed.

Figure 8.23 contains a sequence diagram for the Rendezvous pattern. In the pictured scenario, three clients must synchronize. Although the wait locks are omitted from the diagram, the Synchronizer creates three locks, one for each client. Then, it calls `lock` on a client's lock when its `wait` method is invoked by that client, thereby suspending the client. Comments in the diagram indicate when each client is blocked. The Synchronizer, in its own thread, determines when all three clients are suspended, at which point it unlocks the locks, which in turn permits each client's `wait` call to return. (As an alternative, the Synchronizer could make this determination as a part of the `wait` method, before calling `lock`, thus eliminating the need for a distinct Synchronizer thread.) The separate Synchronizer lifelines in the diagram depict that object's participation in the different threads.

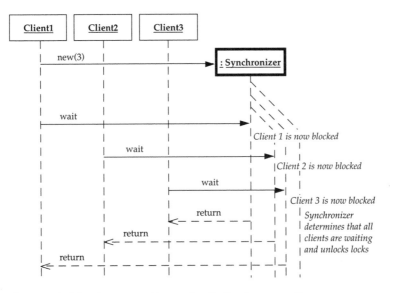

FIGURE 8.23 *A sequence diagram for the Rendezvous pattern.*

8.3.4 Invocation Schemes

When making a request of a service object that will lock that object, a client may have to wait a long time before obtaining the lock. For example, invoking lock on a guarded Stock instance, or invoking a concurrent fundBuy method on an Account instance, could require several minutes. How much waiting is acceptable?

The client object can make a request in a way that limits the waiting time. Four common invocation schemes follow:

- *Asynchronous*: The client object issues the request and then proceeds. (That is, the client is not blocked awaiting the operation to complete.) The service object eventually accepts and processes the request in its own thread or process, then optionally notifies the client when the operation is complete.

- *Synchronous*: The client suspends until the operation is complete and will wait indefinitely. (That is, the client waits as long as required.)

- *Time-out synchronous*: The client suspends awaiting the completion of the operation. When invoking the operation, however, the client specifies a maximum time bound. The operation must start within the stated time bound or else the request is aborted.

- *Balking*: The client suspends awaiting the completion of the operation. The operation must start immediately, however, or the request is aborted. (That is, if the service object is locked by another client, a balking request aborts immediately.)

UML uses different types of arrows to specify what kind of communication is used to send messages between objects in an interaction diagram. It defines arrows for asynchronous and synchronous communication, and it recommends notation for the other two forms, all four of which appear in Figure 8.24. Because balking and time-out synchronous calls are variations of the standard synchronous call, UML recommends that those two forms be modeled as a synchronous arrow with a wait constraint indicating the maximum waiting time. For a balking call, that maximum bound is always zero.

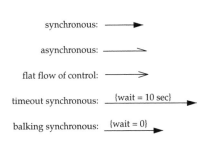

FIGURE 8.24 *UML notation for different forms of communication.*

Figure 8.24 also illustrates the open-headed arrow used to depict a flat flow of control. This type of communication indicates that steps occur in a particular order, but not because of procedure invocation. An example is the signaling employed in normal analog telephony. The calling handset receives and sends signals in the form of tones. You could model this communication as flat flow of control. (This permits you to reserve the use of asynchronous arrows for cases that are truly implemented using asynchronous messages.)

8.3.5 Concurrency in Interaction Diagrams

The notation for active objects, described in Section 8.3.1, "Defining a Process or Thread," of this chapter, as well as the notation for different forms of method invocations, described in Section 8.3.4, "Invocation Schemes," can be employed in a collaboration or sequence diagram. In addition, UML provides a means of specifying that calls can be concurrent.

The sequence diagram in Figure 8.25 depicts the beginning of a scenario for entering a Buy Order in the stock-trading system. (The comment in the diagram indicates that many of the details of the scenario have been omitted.) The sequence diagram shows that, to look up an Account and a Stock using an account number and stock symbol, respectively, the Trading System instance consults an Account List and a Stock List. These are indexed lists (such as hash tables) that store object references and a key for each object being referenced. Each list provides a `find` method that a client can use to look up an object reference for a given key.

Figure 8.25 specifies that, when asked to enter a Buy Order, the Trading System first asks the Account List to find an Account with a given account number. When such an Account reference is returned, the Trading System then asks the Stock List to find a Stock using a stock symbol. It may be more efficient to do the two searches in parallel, however. If the Account List is on a different server, for example, the Trading System could do the two requests in parallel. (One thread could initiate the request to the remote Account List while another thread queried the Stock List.) If either request fails (that is, if no object with that key exists), the result of the other is discarded.

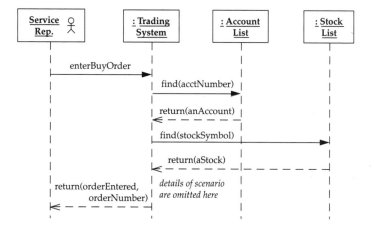

FIGURE 8.25 *A partial sequence diagram for entering a buy order.*

The sequence diagram in Figure 8.26 depicts the same part of the scenario, but with concurrent requests to the two List objects. Concurrent messages are depicted in a sequence diagram using two messages with the same point of origin. The fact that the messages emanate from the same point indicates that no temporal ordering is enforced regarding which message is sent first. Technically, the two find requests in Figure 8.26 could be executed concurrently, or in either order.

The separation of the Trading System object's lifeline in the figure allows the two returns to occur in either order. (If the returns occurred along the same lifeline, one would appear above the other, requiring that that return occur first.) Both lifelines share everything that occurs after the joining of the two lifelines. You could enhance this part of the diagram to show precisely how the Trading System synchronizes with the two returns.

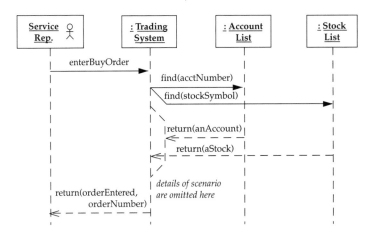

FIGURE 8.26 *A similar sequence diagram with concurrency.*

The sequence diagram in Figure 8.26 specifies only that the two requests *could* be concurrent. You can extend the diagram to depict exactly what processes and threads are involved. Suppose the Trading System and Service Representative run as processes and that the Trading System spawns two threads to find the Account and Stock. The class diagram in Figure 8.27 includes the two required thread classes. The Account Lookup Thread class inherits the state and behavior of a thread from the Thread class. Its constructor requires an account number as an argument.

When an instance of the class is created and its thread is started, it will call the associated Account List object's find method, passing the account number. (Although not illustrated in the figure, it will store the resulting reference to the Account instance with that account number.) The Stock Lookup Thread class carries out the analogous activities to look up a Stock using a stock symbol.

The sequence diagram in Figure 8.28 includes the process and thread structure absent from Figure 8.26. The fact that the Service Representative and Trading System instances run as processes is explicit in the diagram. In addition, the Trading System creates and starts one instance each of the Account Lookup Thread and Stock Lookup Thread classes. Then, those instances make the necessary method calls to find the Account and Stock. (How the Trading System obtains the results from those threads, as well as the remainder of the scenario, is not depicted.)

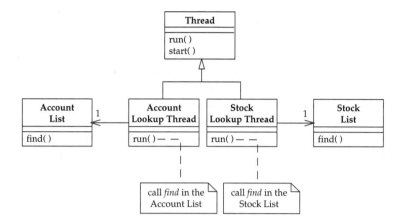

FIGURE 8.27 *The Thread classes for finding Accounts and Stocks.*

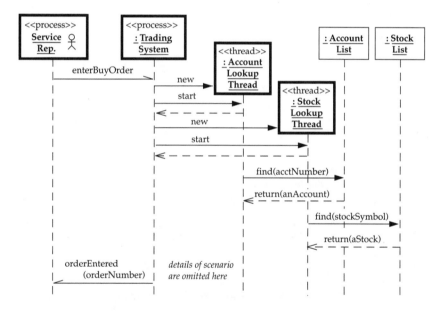

FIGURE 8.28 *Extending the sequence diagram with processes and threads.*

Figure 8.28 also illustrates the use of different arrowheads for different forms of calls. Observe that the Service Representative sends an asynchronous `enterBuyOrder` message to the Trading System, and the Trading System returns an asynchronous acknowledgment when the Order has been entered.

The collaboration diagram in Figure 8.29 describes (the beginning of) the same scenario, as does the sequence diagram in Figure 8.25. Like that sequence diagram, its object interactions are sequential. Figure 8.30 contains the collaboration diagram that is analogous to the sequence diagram in Figure 8.26. In particular, it indicates that the two `find` messages are concurrent (or can occur in either order). This concurrency is indicated using *letters* to specify ordering. Letters have no temporal sequencing relative to one another. Therefore, message 1.1a does not necessarily precede or follow message 1.1b. Otherwise, normal sequence rules apply. Message 1.1a follows message 1, and it precedes messages 1.1a.1 and 2.

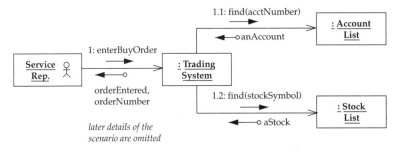

FIGURE 8.29 *A collaboration diagram for entering a buy order.*

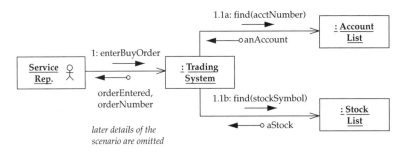

FIGURE 8.30 *A similar collaboration diagram with concurrency.*

You can also *start* a message sequence number with a letter (or letters). In the collaboration diagram in Figure 8.31, the two `find` messages have sequence numbers. In this case, the letters are mnemonics for thread names (ALT, for Account Lookup Thread, and SLT, for Stock Lookup Thread). Again, ALT1 and SLT1 can occur in either order or in parallel. The fact that both must follow message 1, however, is indicated by that number (1) before a slash (/). Hence,

1/Alt1 means that message 1 temporally precedes message 1. Think of what precedes the slash as a pre-condition; in other words, that message must occur before this message can be sent. Of course, the normal sequencing rules apply. ALT1 must precede ALT1.1 and ALT2.

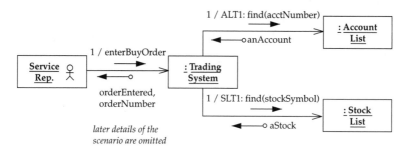

FIGURE 8.31 *An alternative collaboration diagram with concurrency.*

The collaboration diagram in Figure 8.32 is analogous to the sequence diagram in Figure 8.28. It includes the same process and thread indications. The thread instances in Figure 8.32 are declared as transient, indicating that they are created and deleted in this scenario. Although Figures 8.28 and 8.32 depict the creation of the two threads in a particular sequence, the diagrams could be altered to show that the threads are created concurrently (or, more specifically, in either order).

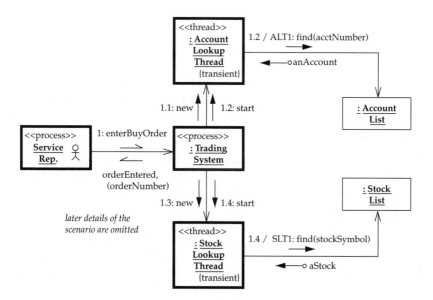

FIGURE 8.32 *Extending the collaboration diagram with processes and threads.*

You can also specify that iteration is to be done in parallel. In the collaboration diagram in Figure 8.33, the Trading System is asked to apply a stock split of factor 2 (that is, one share becomes two) to a stock called PigSty. The Trading System finds the appropriate Stock instance; then, it calls that instance's `applySplit` method (passing the factor). The Stock instance iterates through its Stock Holdings, calling `applySplit` on each. Recall that the asterisk (*) after the message number indicates iteration (with the bound of the iteration enclosed in parentheses). The double bars (| |) after the asterisk indicate that the iteration is to be done in parallel. (The Stock's handling of open Orders is not included in the diagram.)

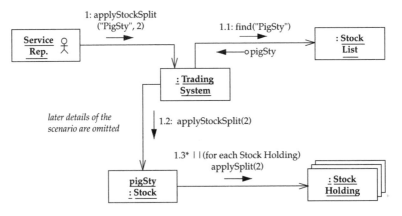

FIGURE 8.33 *Parallel iteration in a collaboration diagram.*

Figure 8.34 contains the analogous sequence diagram. The interactions within the rectangle occur multiple times, for concurrent messages in a sequence diagram (e.g., Figure 8.26) with the bound of the iteration in the upper left corner of the rectangle. The double bars before that bound specify parallel iteration. Unless it includes double bars, iteration in an interaction diagram is assumed to be sequential.

Be aware that the notational conventions for concurrent messages in a sequence diagram (e.g., Figure 8.26) also apply to conditional messages. Recall the catalog order processing system described in Chapter 1, "System Functional Models." Figure 8.35 contains a sequence diagram for a scenario in which an Order is prepared for shipment. An Order can include one or more Shipments (consisting of a group of Line Items being sent to one address).

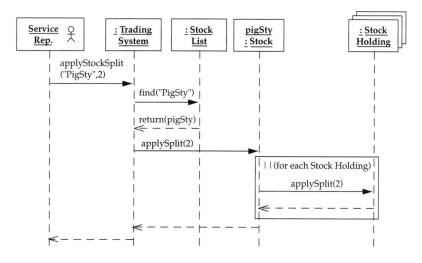

FIGURE 8.34 *Parallel iteration in a sequence diagram.*

In this scenario, the Order has one Shipment. The Order invokes the Shipment's prepareToShip method. If the destination address is international, the Shipment invokes an Address Agent's isDestinationLegal address to ensure that this is an address to which the law permits shipments. If the Shipment has fewer than ten items, it must ask a Shipping Agent to calculate the shipping costs. (For ten or more items, shipping is free.) If both conditions are true, both messages are sent. Furthermore, they are sent concurrently because these two conditional messages have the same point of origin.

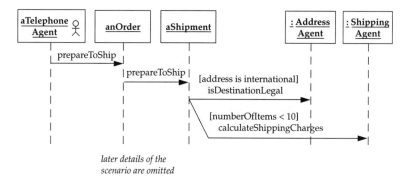

FIGURE 8.35 *Parallel branches in a sequence diagram.*

Figure 8.36 contains the equivalent collaboration diagram. The two conditional messages have sequence numbers that permit concurrency (1.1.1a and 1.1.1b). Therefore, if the two messages are both sent, they are sent concurrently.

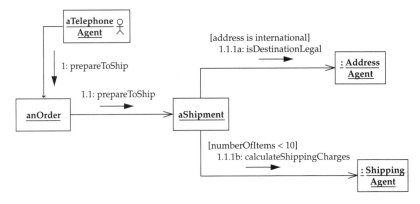

FIGURE 8.36 *Parallel branches in a collaboration diagram.*

You can introduce concurrency in an existing interaction diagram. When using collaboration diagrams, you can first develop sequentially ordered diagrams; then, you can subsequently renumber the messages to permit concurrency. To introduce concurrency in a sequence diagram, you must join the origins of the concurrent messages. For both diagrams, you can also introduce specific tasks, processes, and threads as necessary.

Examples in Section 8.2, "Hardware Architecture," earlier in this chapter illustrated the superimposition of a hardware architecture onto sequence and, particularly, collaboration diagrams. That process can be interleaved with the introduction of concurrency. For example, you can develop sequential collaboration diagrams first, then superimpose the hardware architecture on them, and finally superimpose the process structure on the result. Alternatively, you can add the process structure first, followed by the hardware architecture. Figure 8.37 illustrates the superimposition of hardware onto the sequence diagram from Figure 8.32.

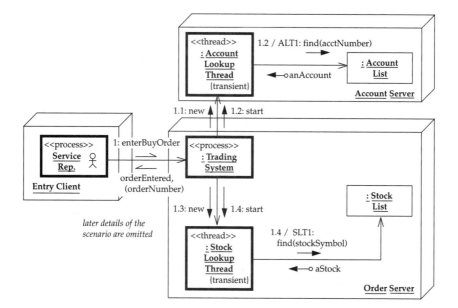

F I G U R E 8.37 *Superimposing hardware on a collaboration diagram with concurrency.*

Note

Obviously, the introduction of hardware distribution and especially concurrency in interaction diagrams greatly complicates the diagrams. You should, therefore, use these mechanisms judiciously. Some applications may employ concurrency in a relatively simple way that doesn't justify complicated graphical depictions. In situations where describing a system's concurrency is critically important, however, having a documented notation for those descriptions is invaluable.

8.3.6 Process Scheduling

When multiple processes, tasks, or threads are running on a single processor, the scheduling of those entities is also an issue. In general, a scheduling policy arbitrates two things:

- How long a process, thread, or task executes

- Which process, thread, or task executes next when the current one is no longer executing

Regarding the first question, how long a process executes, the two basic schemes are preemptive and non-preemptive scheduling. In a *non-preemptive* policy, a process (or task, or thread) executes either until it explicitly relinquishes the processor (typically by making a system call or by terminating), or until it attempts to grab a resource that some other process has locked. In contrast, in a *preemptive* scheme, a process can be interrupted at any moment.

With respect to the second question, two basic approaches dominate. One is a *priority-based* policy in which each process has a priority and preference is given to the highest priority process. In a non-preemptive, priority-based scheme, a process executes as long as it can (that is, until it completes its execution or becomes blocked awaiting a message or resource), after which the unblocked process with the highest priority is scheduled next.

In a *preemptive* environment, a process executes as long as it has the highest priority among all unblocked processes. If a process with a higher (or perhaps equal) priority appears or becomes unblocked, however, the currently executing process will be suspended in favor of the one with a higher priority.

As an additional wrinkle, priority assignment can be static, meaning that when it is created, a process is given a priority that never changes, or it can be dynamic, in which case the priority of a process can be adjusted during the execution of the process.

The alternative to priority-based scheduling is a *round-robin* (or cyclic) policy. Conceptually, the processes are arranged in a circle. When the currently executing process surrenders the processor, the next process in the circle is assigned the CPU. With non-preemptive scheduling, a process executes as long as it can, after which the next process in the circle executes. In a preemptive scheme, each process receives a fixed time slice.

Some scheduling policies combine priority-based and round-robin approaches. For example, in a priority-based scheme, all of the processes with the same priority may be scheduled using a round-robin algorithm. Furthermore, these are not the only policies possible, but surveying other, less common schemes, or further elaborating these common approaches, are beyond the scope of this book.

Be aware, however, that scheduling policies sometimes affect your design. For example, in a non-preemptive environment, you typically need very little locking because a process can make any set of operations atomic simply by refusing to yield the CPU. Conversely, in a preemptive environment, you must be aware of the issues associated with being preempted at any time.

8.4   Implementation Architecture

One physical view of a system or application is its hardware architecture. Another physical view is the system's *implementation architecture*. The focus of this view is on the source, binary, and executable files that define the system. UML provides a special diagram, the *component diagram*, to describe the implementation architecture.

The primary node in a component diagram is the component. A component is a unit during the compilation, linking, or execution of the system. As such, it might correspond to a source file (including either a code or header file in C++), a binary file, or an executable file. A component is depicted as shown in Figure 8.38. Each component is labeled with its name. To specify a particular type of component (such as a header file), you can either suffix the name (for example, with a *.h* to indicate a header file), or you can add a property to the component (for example, {header}).

component
name

FIGURE 8.38   *The UML notation for a component.*

Components can have dependencies upon one another. The semantics of such a dependency is a function of what a component is. Figure 8.39 shows an example of a C++ compilation dependency. Specifically, it indicates that when being compiled, the Stock code file must include (import) the header files for Account and Order.

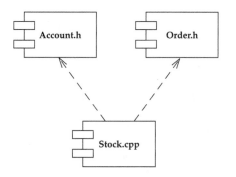

FIGURE 8.39   *A compilation dependency.*

Figure 8.40 illustrates another example of a dependency between components. The two lollypops indicate that the Customer component exports two interfaces, Customer and Account. These interfaces might be defined in terms of CORBA or DCOM IDL, for example. The Order component communicates with the Customer component, but only through the Account interface.

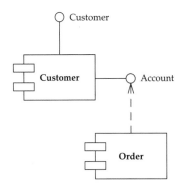

FIGURE 8.40 *An interface dependency.*

You can superimpose your hardware architecture onto your component architecture, as shown in Figure 8.41. The figure specifies that the Customer component runs on the Account server, while the Order component resides on the Order Server.

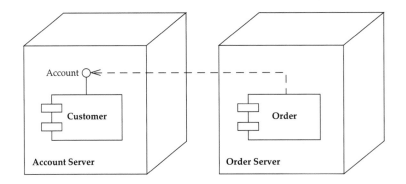

FIGURE 8.41 *Superimposing hardware nodes onto component diagrams.*

Components will be revisited in the next chapter. Describing guidelines for the mapping of classes to components is a very broad topic and beyond the scope of this book. Refer to John Lakos' book, *Large-Scale C++ Software Design* (Reading, Mass.: Addison Wesley, 1996), for a set of rules guiding the physical design of C++ programs. Refer to Desmond D'Souza and Alan Wills' book, *Objects, Components, and Frameworks with UML: The Catalysis Approach* (Reading, Mass.: Addison Wesley, 1999), for a process for developing reusable, customizable components that are irrespective of programming language.

CHAPTER **9**

Reuse: Libraries, Frameworks, Components, and Patterns

Reuse of design and code is often cited as a principle benefit of object-oriented development. When arguing for object technology, for example, Adele Goldberg and Kenneth Rubin state that objects are natural units of reuse (1995, 55). Ivar Jacobson, Martin Gris, and Patrik Jonsson devote a book to the subject of how and why to design and use reusable code in object-oriented systems (1997).

Although design and code reuse is not a panacea, if it is properly executed, it can shorten development time and increase product quality. Reusing existing code can obviously reduce the development time of a project. If that code has already been thoroughly tested, its reuse can also shorten testing time while avoiding errors that might have been introduced if the code had been written from scratch.

Reuse is not a single concept; it comes in different sizes and shapes. The scale of the reusable item can be anything from a single class to a large component consisting internally of hundreds of classes. The form also varies because reuse of classes, components, and frameworks is implementation-based reuse, whereas the application of a pattern reuses a general idea rather than code. In addition, components are used as is, whereas frameworks typically must be extended to be of value.

This chapter describes several forms of reuse in object-oriented development. It also explains UML notation that aids in documenting reuse:

- *Reuse of classes*: The simplest form of reuse is the use of a single class from a class library. This form is explained through a pair of examples, and the reuse of generic classes (such as C++ template classes) is also discussed.

- *Reuse of components*: Components represent an attempt to reuse code on a very large scale. In some ways, a component is similar to a very overweight class. Component-based design is examined.

- *Reuse of frameworks*: A framework is a group of classes that work together to solve a general problem. Two types of frameworks, white-box and black-box frameworks, are explained through examples. Role-based design, a tool for developing black-box frameworks, is also outlined.

- *Reuse of patterns*: A pattern is a way of solving a problem. Analysis, architectural, and design patterns are explained, and the latter two are illustrated with examples.

In many cases, successful reuse requires careful management. This chapter does not address management issues, such as the economic and sociological aspects of reuse. Jacobson, Gris, and Jonsson devote several chapters throughout their book to these topics (1997); Goldberg and Rubin discuss these subjects as well (1995, 203–276).

9.1 Reuse of Classes

The simplest and probably most common form of reuse is the reuse of individual classes. These classes are packaged in the form of a *class library* (or *package* in Java). Classes are typically grouped in terms of functional cohesion; in other words, all the classes in one functional area are placed in one library. You might have a data structures class library, for example, that includes classes for linked lists, stacks, queues, and so forth.

Suppose you are building financial applications, and you have a class library of financial classes. One such class is the Account class shown in Figure 9.1. This class defines the interface and implementation of a basic cash-bearing account. An Account instance maintains a cash balance, and it has methods to deposit cash in itself, withdraw cash from itself, and return an indication of its current balance.

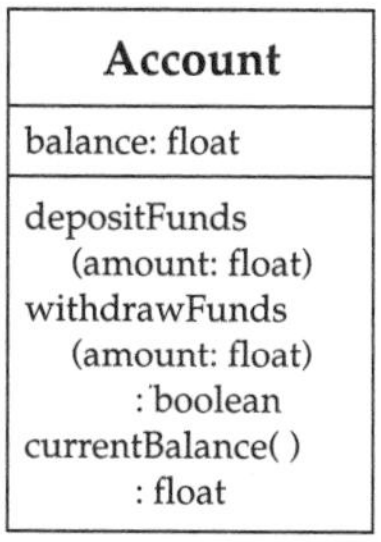

Account
balance: float

depositFunds
    (amount: float)
withdrawFunds
    (amount: float)
    : boolean
currentBalance( )
    : float

FIGURE 9.1 *A reusable Account class.*

If you are developing a banking system, you may be able to use the Account class, as it stands, in your application. That is, for a vanilla-flavored bank account, you can create an instance of the existing Account class. This is class-based reuse in its most effective form; the abstraction defined in the class library is precisely the abstraction you require in your application.

For the stock-trading application discussed in previous chapters, the Account class has only a subset of the required features. Like an Account instance, a stock-trading account holds cash assets. In addition, however, a stock-trading account holds various stock securities that are bought and sold for cash. When defining a Stock-Trading Account class, therefore, you can employ the existing Account class, but you must augment it with the features unique to Stock-Trading Accounts, such as the ability to deposit and withdraw securities, the ability to fund Buy and Sell Orders, and so forth.

You can define the Stock-Trading Account class in two different ways. One is to aggregate an instance of that class with an instance of the Account class, as discussed in Section 7.3.2, "Commingling Extension and Reuse," in Chapter 7, "Flexibility Guidelines for Dynamic Diagrams." The resulting structure was depicted in Figure 7.19 and is repeated here as Figure 9.2. When a Stock-Trading Account object is created, it creates an underlying Account instance. That Account instance maintains the cash part of the Account, whereas the Stock-Trading Account instance handles the other assets. The Account instance is invisible to the application; other objects in the application talk only to the Stock-Trading Account.

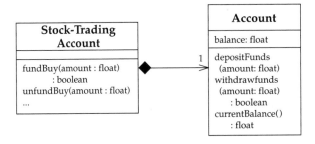

FIGURE 9.2 *Aggregating a Stock-Trading Account with a reusable Account.*

Figure 9.3 contains an alternative definition of the Stock-Trading Account class. In this approach, Stock-Trading Account uses inheritance rather than aggregation (and delegation) to obtain the features of the Account class. Stock-Trading Account extends the Account class by adding features unique to the application.

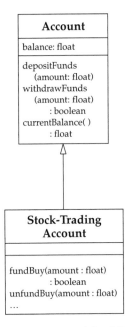

FIGURE 9.3 *A Stock-Trading Account class derived from a reusable Account.*

Which of the two approaches is better? Using class specialization, as in Figure 9.3, is often easier to implement. When using aggregation, as in Figure 9.2, you must duplicate the interface of the Account class in Stock-Trading Account. The Stock-Trading Account class must include `withdrawFunds`, `depositFunds`, and `currentBalance` methods. (At a minimum, those methods will simply call the analogous methods in the underlying Account.) If you use specialization, however, the Stock-Trading class inherits those three methods. It must redefine the methods (by overriding them) only in cases where it needs to extend the methods' behaviors.

On the other hand, using class specialization also has some disadvantages. Assuming you are using what C++ calls public inheritance, the public methods in Account must be public in Stock-Trading Account. If you want to hide any of the public methods of the reused class, aggregation is the preferred solution. In addition, when you use specialization, the client classes must be aware of the Account superclass. This increases coupling because changing the public interface of the Account class requires that all clients be recompiled. It also permits a client to treat a Stock-Trading Account as a generic Account (by using type promotion) which can lead to confusion.

Employing class specialization also assumes that the subclass (Stock-Trading Account) will have exactly *one* copy of the superclass (Account). Suppose that a Stock-Trading Account can have multiple cash repositories (each keyed by some identifier, such as a repository name). In that situation, you should use aggregation because it allows a Stock-Trading Account to have multiple Account parts (one for each repository). The section "Inheritance Coupling" in Chapter 4, "Flexibility Guidelines for Class Diagrams," also discusses this topic.

In some cases, class specialization is the only way to make use of a class from a class library. Recall the discussion of guarded locking in Section 8.3.2, "Object Synchronization," in Chapter 8, "Architectural Models." To lock and unlock a guarded entity, a client must explicitly invoke methods, such as `lock` and `unlock`, on that entity. Figure 9.4 contains a Guarded Entity class that defines those methods. The `lock` method returns a unique Key instance. The Guarded Entity class also provides a protected method, `isValidKey`, that a subclass can use to determine whether the Key exhibited by a client is the Key that is currently valid for this instance.

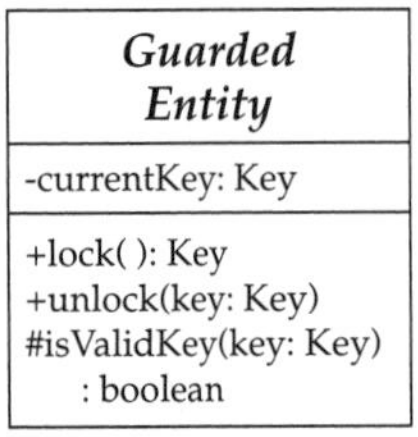

Guarded Entity
-currentKey: Key
+lock( ): Key
+unlock(key: Key)
#isValidKey(key: Key) : boolean

FIGURE 9.4 *A reusable abstract superclass.*

The Guarded Entity class is abstract and will be reused only through specialization, as exemplified in Figure 9.5. The Stock class in the figure inherits its guarded locking behavior from the Guarded Entity class. Its methods that require locking, such as the `applyStockSplit` method included in the figure, take a Key as an argument. As part of their implementation, those methods invoke the `isValidKey` method to ensure that the client calling `applyStockSplit` has the valid Key for the stock instance.

Guarded Entity
-currentKey: Key
+lock( ): Key
+unlock(key: Key)
#isValidKey(key: Key) : boolean
Stock
symbol
applyStockSplit (factor: float, key: Key)

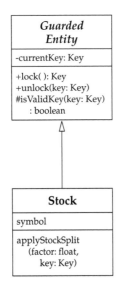

FIGURE 9.5 *Reusing an abstract superclass through specialization.*

Some programming languages extend class-based reuse by supporting the definition of generic classes. An example is the *template* mechanism in C++. The following C++ code fragment defines a template class, Queue, in terms of a generic Type. The Queue's methods, such as first and append, are defined in terms of that Type. Figure 9.6 includes the UML notation for the Queue template that follows:

```
template<class Type>
    class Queue {
        public:
            Type first();
            void append(const Type&);
            /* ... */
    }
```

To instantiate the Queue template, you define a class or an instance that is derived from the template but provides a specific type to be substituted for Type. Any occurrence of Type in the template class is replaced in the instantiation by the specific type. Figure 9.6 depicts a Message Queue class derived from the Queue template by replacing Type with Message. The C++ declaration of that class is

```
typedef Queue<Message> MessageQueue;
```

The explicit «bind» dependency in the figure is a stereotype defined by UML. It indicates the mapping of specific types to generic types during template instantiation. The first and append methods of the Message Queue class return as a result and accept as an argument, respectively, a reference to Message instance.

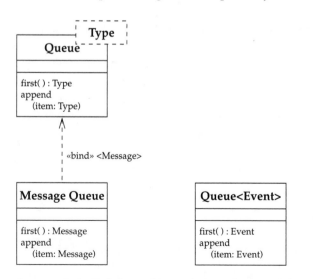

FIGURE 9.6 *Defining and instantiating a Queue template class.*

Figure 9.6 also shows the specification of an unnamed class that defines a Queue of Events. In this case, the derivation and binding are implicit, but the effect is the same as that of the «bind» dependency. The first and append methods of the resulting class return and accept references to Event instances.

Class-based reuse is very commonplace. The Java programming language includes several packages that contain hundreds of classes for everything from containers such as stacks and lists to network widgets such as sockets and packets. Commercial class libraries are also available for many languages, and C++ includes a standard template library (commonly referred to as the C++ STL) that is packaged with many C++ class libraries (American National Standards Institute 1998, 459–564).

The disadvantage of class-based reuse is that the scale of reuse is very small. This is the toolkit approach to reuse because you are reusing individual classes that you must piece together. Furthermore, to be of general use, those classes must be primitive. For application-independent concepts, such as containers and GUI widgets, the approach is very efficacious. For more application-specific abstractions, such as accounts and orders, however, defining the class becomes problematic. Much of the state and behavior of such a class is specific to the application, but as you add those features, you make the class less reusable in other domains. (The Have Gunk, Will Travel design pattern, introduced in Section 7.3.2, "Commingling Extension and Reuse," in Chapter 7 provides a solution to this problem.)

9.2 Reuse of Components

Whereas a class is a relatively small reusable part, a *component* is a large-scale building block that, like a class, is reused as a single unit. An object-oriented application is a composite of classes whose execution-time instances (objects) work together. In an analogous way, an application can include a set of components whose execution-time instances (binaries) collaborate by invoking operations in one another. As noted, however, a component's scale is much larger than that of a class. For example, a component may be composed of many classes internally.

What exactly is a component? How do you recognize one when you see it? Philippe Kruchten provides two complementary characterizations of a component:

> A component is a non-trivial, nearly independent, and replaceable part of a system that fulfills a clear function in the context of a well-defined architecture. A component conforms to and provides the physical realization of a set of interfaces (1999, 89).

> Components offer one or more interfaces and are dependent only on the interfaces of other components (153).

Desmond D'Souza and Alan Wills state that a component is

> ...a coherent package of software artifacts that can be independently developed and delivered as a unit and that can be composed, unchanged, with other components to build something larger (1999, 386).

They state further that a *code component* is

> ...a coherent package of software implementation that (a) can be independently developed and delivered, (b) has explicit and well-specified interfaces for the services it provides, (c) has explicit and well-specified interfaces for services it expects from others, and (d) can be composed with other components, perhaps customizing some of their properties, without modifying the components themselves (387).

A common thread through these definitions is the notion that a component exposes and implements a well-defined interface. In that sense, a component is like a class. A client invokes methods in the component's interface without knowledge of the component's internal implementation details. In fact, it is a component's analogy to a class that, in many organizations, makes component-based design a popular extension of object-oriented design.

Figure 9.7 contains an Inventory Control component that could be used in a sales order processing application, such as the DryGoods.com system described in Chapter 1, "System Functional Models." The component exposes five methods:

- allocateFromInventory: It accepts as arguments a product number and a quantity. It attempts to allocate the specified quantity of the specified product and returns an indication of whether it was able to do so.

- `addToInventory`: It accepts as arguments a product number and a quantity. It adds the specified quantity to the inventory of the specified product and returns nothing.

- `currentInventory`: It accepts as an argument a product number and returns the current inventory level of the specified product.

- `defineInventoryItem`: It accepts as an argument a product number. It creates an inventory entry for a product with that number, the initial inventory level of which is zero. It returns nothing.

- `removeInventoryItem`: It accepts as an argument a product number. It removes the inventory entry for the product with that number. It returns nothing.

Calls to some of these methods may raise error conditions. For example, attempting to add an inventory item for a product number that already exists should raise an error condition. Although they are not included here, the definitions of those error conditions, as well as a statement of what methods raise what error conditions in what situations, would also be an important part of the specification of the component's interface.

In languages that support exceptions, such as C++ and Java, an error in a component method should throw an exception. The component's specification should include a definition of the exception classes used by the component. For each method that throws an exception, the specification of that method should indicate what exception is thrown as well as the conditions under which it is thrown. For languages that do not support exceptions, such as Smalltalk or Visual Basic, another mechanism must be employed (such as returning an error status or logging an error in a defined location).

Note

The «component» package stereotype that appears in Figure 9.7 is not one of the defined stereotypes in UML. It is introduced here as a means of interjecting components into class diagrams, rather than just into component diagrams.

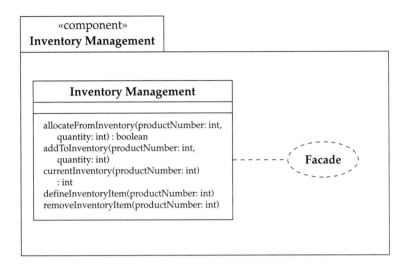

FIGURE 9.7 *An Inventory Management component.*

A client application can use the Inventory Management component to handle the maintenance of inventory levels of any product. Furthermore, defining the component with a facade divorces the client of any knowledge of how products and their inventory levels are defined (Gamma et al. 1995, 185–193). Nonetheless, Figure 9.8 depicts one possible (and simple) implementation of the Inventory Management component. This particular implementation employs an Inventory Item class that defines the inventory for a single item, as well as an Item Registry class that registers and looks up an Inventory Item based on a product number.

To be applied effectively, a component must have a well-defined interface. The definition of the interface should include not only the method signatures (that is, their names, parameter types, and return types), as shown in Figure 9.7, but also a complete description of the *contract* of the component (Meyer 1997, 341–342). That contract consists of the method signatures together with

- Any *invariants* that the component maintains
- The *effects* of invoking the methods in the component's interface

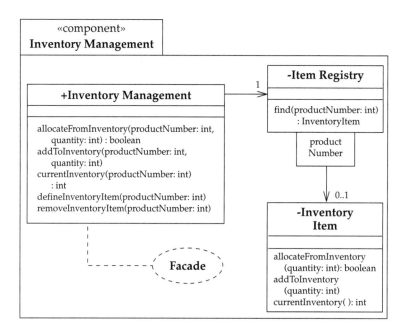

FIGURE 9.8 *A possible implementation of the Inventory Management component.*

The component's contract can be included in a class diagram in the form of a «responsibility» stereotyped comment, as shown in Figure 9.9. In general, such a comment specifies the responsibilities (such as the contract) of the class to which it is attached. In this case, the comment is attached to the Inventory Management facade class that provides the clients' only access to the component.

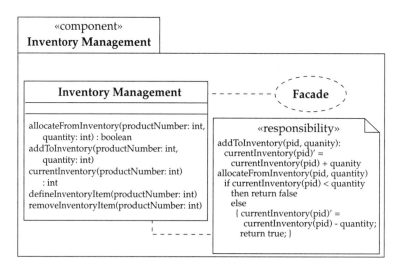

FIGURE 9.9 *Specifying the contract of the Inventory Management component.*

The comment in the figure specifies the effects of calling the `allocateFromInventory` and `addToInventory` methods. The prime mark (`'`) indicates a value after the call. To paraphrase the comment, the effect of calling `addToInventory` with a *specified product number* (pid) and quantity is as follows:

> If you invoke `currentInventory` by passing the product number before you call `addToInventory`, and then if you invoke `currentInventory` for the same product number after the `addToInventory` call, the value returned for the second invocation is greater by the specified quantity than the value returned for the first one.

A paraphrasing of the specification of the `allocateFromInventory` method is as follows:

> If, when calling `allocateFromInventory` for a product number and quantity, the result of a `currentInventory` call for that product number would yield a result smaller than the specified quantity, the method returns `false`. Otherwise, the method returns `true` and calling `currentInventory` for that product number after the `allocateFromInventory` call would yield a result that is smaller by the specified quantity than the first `currentInventory` call.

Observe that these effects are specified only in terms of *externally observable results* (such as the result of calling `currentInventory` for a specific product number). The implementation of the component has not been exposed. Observe also that, due to space limitations, the comment in the figure contains only a part of the contract of the class. The complete specification also includes

```
invariant: currentInventory(pid) >= 0,
                for any product number pid

defineInventoryItem(pid):
        currentInventory'(pid) = 0
```

The first portion states that, as an invariant, `currentInventory` will never return a negative number (and therefore, the inventory level of a product can never fall below zero). The second part specifies that, after a product is introduced using `defineInventoryItem`, its initial inventory level, as obtained by calling `currentInventory` and passing the product number, is zero.

The Inventory Management component described in Figures 9.7 through 9.9 hides all underlying types from the client. Only the Inventory Management facade class is visible to the outside world. Although this de-couples the client from *all* details of the component, such an extreme solution may not always be practical. (For example, accessing a component through a façade results in a level of indirection, thereby decreasing execution speed.) Figure 9.10 depicts an alternative Inventory Management component that exposes both a facade and an Inventory Item interface class. This interface class is an abstract type because it defines only a set of abstract methods that some hidden class implements. A client goes through the facade to obtain an Inventory Item reference for a specified product number and then invokes methods directly on that reference.

Note

Both CORBA and DCOM provide mechanisms for defining the interfaces of and accessing components. In both technologies, a component's externally visible interface is defined in terms of an Interface Definition Language (IDL). (While sharing a name, however, CORBA's IDL and DCOM's IDL are different languages.) See Thomas Mowbray and William Ruh, Inside CORBA: Distributed Object Standards and Applications *(1997), and Don Box,* Essential COM *(1998), for information about CORBA and DCOM, respectively.*

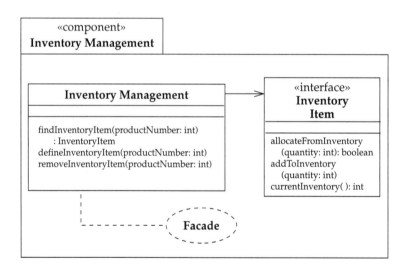

FIGURE 9.10 *An alternative Inventory Management component.*

9.3 Reuse of Frameworks

A component represents an attempt to achieve large-scale reuse. For the most part, however, a component is a monolithic entity. Customization is typically achieved by adding *external* behavior and by composing components together. A *framework*, on the other hand, is a set of classes that work together to achieve a purpose but that must be specialized internally by the designer.

A framework defines a family of related applications in a general way. It contains the elements that are common to those applications. Handling sales orders and service orders, for example, are very similar activities that act on very similar entities. An order-processing framework casts those similarities in the form of a collection of interacting classes. Each specific order processing application is a specialization of that framework because it uses the classes in the framework while adding whatever is specific to the application.

One dichotomy among frameworks is the distinction between a white-box and a black-box framework. A *white-box framework* consists of a set of classes that define *abstractions*. Each class defines both the interface and the implementation of its abstraction. When you specialize a white-box framework, you define subclasses that inherit that abstraction. Therefore, a primary mechanism at play is inheritance of implementation; this is white-box specialization because you must understand the implementation details of the classes in the framework.

In contrast, a *black-box framework* consists of a set of classes that operate on specific interfaces. Each interface defines a *role*. Specializing the framework entails introducing classes that play those roles by implementing the interfaces. You are, thus, relying on interface inheritance and polymorphism as the principle specialization mechanisms. Because you are "plugging in" classes to a set of interfaces (which requires only that you understand those interfaces), this is black-box specialization.

9.3.1   An Example of a White-Box Framework

Figure 9.11 contains a portion of a white-box framework for order processing. The classes in the framework define the interface and implementation common to those abstractions shared by various order processing applications. An Order, for example, has an order number, a time it was placed, and a status (pending, fulfilled, canceled, and so forth). It also has a set of Order Line Items as parts, and it is associated with Accounts, Funding Transactions, and a Line Item Factory. It can cancel and commit itself, add and remove Line Items to and from itself, and determine its price.

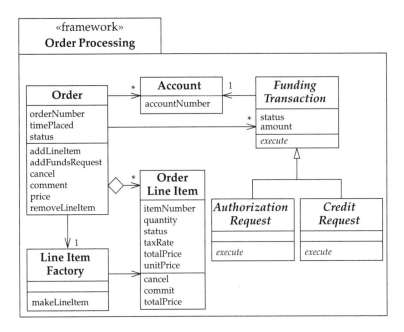

FIGURE 9.11 *An order processing white-box framework.*

These classes (and their instances) interact with each other to handle basic order processing tasks. When asked to add a Line Item, an Order uses the Line Item Factory to create a Line Item instance. The factory object simply manufactures the appropriate Line Item object. An Order can be funded from any number of Accounts (such as from multiple credit cards). When asked to add a funds request, an Order creates an Authorization Request. This too will probably involve a factory that isn't included in the figure. An Authorization Request removes money from an Account when asked to execute, whereas a Credit Request credits funds to its Account.

You specialize a white-box framework by introducing the appropriate subclasses for the application under development. Those subclasses add any state and behavior specific to the application. While some of the framework's classes are abstract, many are concrete and, in some cases, can be used "as is" (rather than specialized).

The class diagram in Figure 9.12 illustrates the specialization of a part of the order-processing framework for handling sales orders, such as the catalog sales orders of DryGoods.com. This application requires that different Line Items be billed to different Accounts and shipped to different addresses. The Sales Order variant of an Order, therefore, consists of a set of Billables, a group of Line

Items billed to one Account, and a collection of Shipments, a group of Line Items shipped to one address. Although it is not included in the figure, a Shipment includes a reference to a Customer object from which the shipping address is obtained.

For this application, items in a Sales Order must be allocated from internal inventory. The Sales Line Item subclass, therefore, overrides the commit and cancel methods to allocate the item from, and return the item to, inventory. (Those methods also call the overridden methods in the Order Line Item superclass.) The Line Item Factory is also specialized to create Sales Order Line Items (which it returns as generic Order Line Items). In fact, a Sales Order's reference to a Line Item Factory will refer to a Sales Line Item Factory instance.

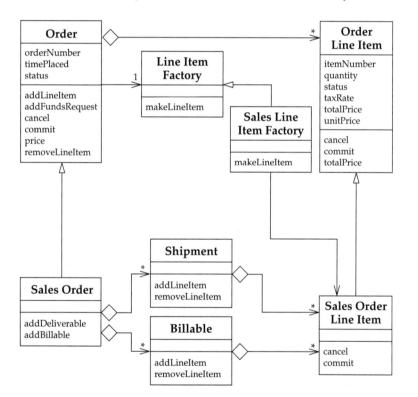

FIGURE 9.12   *A partial specialization of the order processing white-box framework.*

Figure 9.13 illustrates the specialization of the part of the framework that handles funds. In this application, Sales Orders are funded only from credit cards. An instance of the Account class will hold a credit card number as its account number. A Billable is funded through a list of Funding Transactions; each of which is, in fact, a Credit Card Authorization Request or a Credit Card Refund Request. The Credit Card Authorization Request class implements its `execute` method by performing a credit authorization against the credit card number in its related Account. Although not shown in the figure, it will store any relevant results, such as an authorization number. A Credit Card Refund Request executes itself by issuing a credit to the credit card (and retaining any important results).

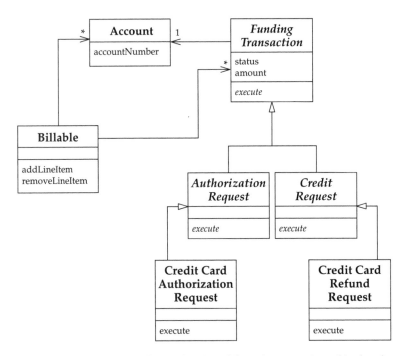

FIGURE 9.13 *Additional specialization of the order processing white-box framework.*

Figures 9.14 and 9.15 depict another specialization of this framework; this time it is for Service Orders. As shown in Figure 9.14, a Service Order consists of two different types of Order Line Items: Parts Line Items and Service Line Items. The Service Order Line Item Factory will create the appropriate type of Line Item given an item number. When committing or canceling itself, a Parts Line Item must allocate or release parts, whereas a Service Line Item must schedule or cancel a technician's time. (Which technician is assigned to do the service is omitted from the figure.)

In this application, a Service Order is also tied to a Contract. To obtain service, a customer must first establish a Contract. Although not specified in the figure, a Contract might include a set of terms, such as a negotiated price and a maximum response time (the interval between the time the customer requests service and the time the service is completed).

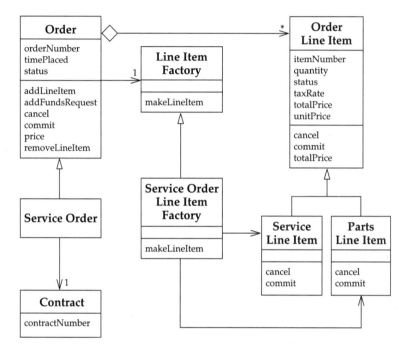

F I G U R E 9.14 *Another partial specialization of the order-processing framework.*

Each Contract is related to an Account, as shown in Figure 9.15. The Account defines the way the customer pays for service (which, although not shown, might be through a purchase order or a credit card). The Funding Transaction specializations, included in Figure 9.15, merely ask the Account to authorize or credit funds. Although not shown in the figure, Credit Authorization Requests and Credit Refund Requests refer directly to a Service Account (to allow them to invoke the methods defined in Service Account).

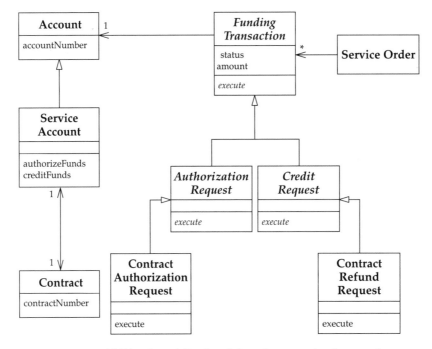

Figure 9.15 *Additional specialization of the order-processing framework.*

In both of these examples, specializing the framework requires using some classes directly and creating subclasses of others. The framework's classes define common abstractions. The Order class, for example, defines the properties orders share across various order-processing applications. In other words, Sales Orders and Service Orders are very similar, and those similarities are the properties of the Order class.

As these examples illustrate, specializing even a relatively simple white-box framework is a complicated process. It requires that you understand the internals of all the classes, as well as how the instances of those classes interact with one another. The payoff is that you have defined the implementation those classes share across a family of applications. Therefore, you can reuse that implementation in each application.

9.3.2 An Example of a Black-Box Framework

Whereas a white-box framework defines common abstractions as classes, a black-box framework specifies common roles as interface classes. As discussed in Section 4.2.3, "Subclass Coupling," of Chapter 4, an interface class is a class (or Java interface) that has only public, abstract methods. That is, it has no implementation of state or behavior. Specializing a black-box framework requires specializing those interface classes by implementing their abstract methods.

Figure 9.16 illustrates a very small black-box framework for a particular type of scheduling problem. A Scheduler instance maintains a list of references to Measurables and a single reference to a Handler. As the note in the figure indicates, a Scheduler's scheduleMeasurable method first iterates through its Measurables, invoking computeMetric on each, then selects the Measurable with the highest metric, and finally invokes the Handler's handle method, passing that Measurable.

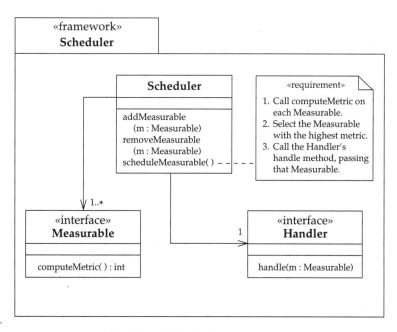

FIGURE 9.16 *A black-box scheduling framework.*

The two interface classes in the figure, distinguished by the «interface» stereotype, define the two roles on which a Scheduler relies. A Measurable must implement a computeMetric method that returns an integer-valued metric, and a Handler must implement a handle method that takes a Measurable as an argument (and handles it in some way).

As an example of an application of this framework, suppose you are using a group of Queues to collect items that are to be sent to a remote site. Periodically, you want to select the longest Queue and stream its contents to that site. (This might be a multi-threaded application, for example, where each client thread has its own Queue instance.) Figure 9.17 shows the specialization of the Scheduler framework for that application. The Queue class implements the Measurable interface by defining a computeMetric method that returns the length of the Queue. (The dashed specialization arrow denotes what UML calls a *realization relationship*, in which a class implements an abstract type. The class in the relationship inherits only interface.) A Streamer is a Handler that implements handle by turning the Measurable reference into a Queue reference (through down-casting), and removing and streaming the Queue's contents.

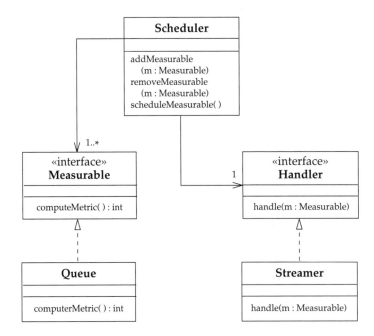

FIGURE 9.17 *A specialization of the black-box scheduling framework.*

Figure 9.18 illustrates another specialization of the framework. In this example, Command instances are being pooled for eventual execution. Each Command has a priority that is returned by its `computeMetric` method, and that priority may change frequently as the Command awaits execution. A Command Processor implements the `handle` method by casting the Measurable as a Command and then executing it. When asked to schedule a Measurable, therefore, the Scheduler will select the Command with the highest priority and pass it to the Command Processor for execution.

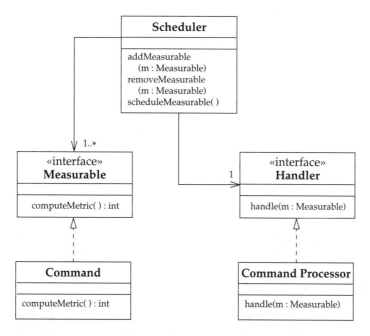

FIGURE 9.18 *Another specialization of the black-box scheduling framework.*

These two examples underscore the fact that the Measurable and Handler interface classes define roles. A Queue and a Command are not similar in any way except that both implement a `computeMetric` method (thereby playing the Measurable role). A Streamer and a Command Processor are also dissimilar except that each implements a method to handle a Measurable (and, therefore, plays the Handler role).

You can think of a black-box framework as a form of plug-compatible software. An interface class defines a receptacle. Any client class that provides a matching plug can "plug into" the receptacle. A service class implements a receptacle by inheriting from the interface class, implementing any inherited abstract methods.

> **Note**
>
> *While they sound similar, implementing an abstract type and inheriting from an abstract class are distinct concepts. An abstract type defines only an interface (and, in some languages, a contract). When a class implements an abstract type, such as the Queue class implementing the abstract type defined by the Measurable interface, it inherits only the interface (and, in some languages, the contract) of that type. An abstract class, on the other hand, can include implementation. When an Automobile class inherits from an abstract Vehicle class, therefore, it inherits all of the interface and implementation of that superclass.*

A black-box framework is typically easier to use than a white-box framework because you must understand only interfaces. This assumes, of course, that the interfaces provided by the framework are exactly what you need. If not, you may have to develop a new framework to meet your needs.

9.3.3   Role-Based Design

Designing white-box frameworks requires that you look for common abstractions across related applications. To build the order-processing framework described earlier, for example, you might examine sales order and service order applications, searching for the common abstractions such as Order and Line Item. To design a black-box framework, however, you must concentrate on the *roles* required by the framework. Doing so often requires a fundamentally different way of approaching a problem.

The following example illustrates the difference in thought process. Consider this problem:

> You have several types of devices in a system. Some devices can be reset; the `reset` method takes no arguments and returns nothing. Some devices can be paused and resumed. The `pause` and `resume` methods each take no arguments and return nothing. Some devices can be polled; the `poll` method takes no arguments and returns an instance of a generic Token class.
>
> As an example, D1 devices can be reset, paused/resumed, and polled. D2 devices can be reset and paused/resumed (but not polled). D3 devices can be reset and polled (but not paused/resumed). D4 devices can be paused/resumed and polled (but not reset).
>
> Some clients reset devices, some clients pause and resume devices, and some clients poll devices.

If you adopt an abstraction-based approach to this problem, you leap immediately toward defining a Device superclass from which the specific device classes (such as D1) are derived. The class diagram in Figure 9.19 is this type of design. Clients hold Device references. So, the Device class defines the four methods those clients must invoke. Those methods could be abstract, or they could hold empty implementations. The design in the figure uses the latter approach. Therefore, the reset, pause, and resume methods simply return, whereas the poll method returns an empty Token. Each subclass then overrides the methods for the behaviors it must provide. (The D1 class overrides all four methods, for example, as a D1 device can be reset, paused and resumed, and polled.)

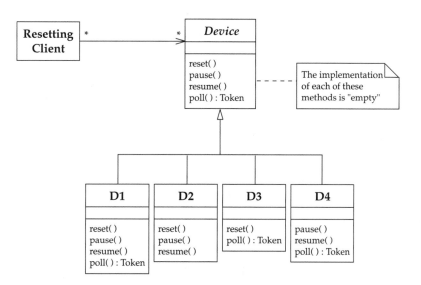

FIGURE 9.19   *An abstraction-based design of the device problem.*

This solution has at least three disadvantages, listed from the least to the most significant:

- Some devices have interfaces for behaviors that they don't really support. For example, a client can invoke poll on a D2 instance even though D2 devices don't define any polling behavior. This capability is probably harmless in most cases, but it complicates the design.

- Clients can see more than they need to see. The Resetting Client in Figure 9.19, for example, invokes only the reset method. Nonetheless, that client is exposed to all four methods defined in the Device class. Reducing a client's coupling to a service object is one of the principle goals of a good design. Exposing more than is necessary can also have implications regarding recompilation. In C++, for example, a Resetting Client must be recompiled if anything in the Device's header file changes, even if the reset method itself is unaltered.

- A client is coupled to the Device abstraction, and so those clients must adapt when adding new abstractions that are not Devices. Suppose, for example, you subsequently discover that when the Resetting Client in Figure 9.19 resets the network it must also reset Probes. Suppose further that these are *software* Probes (rather than physical probes) and, therefore, are not Devices. (Perhaps the Device class defines some properties that do not apply to Probes.) To handle Probes, the Resetting Client class must be extended to include a list of Probes as well as the list of Devices, as shown in Figure 9.20. Furthermore, its resetting code must be modified to iterate over that new list (calling reset on each Probe).

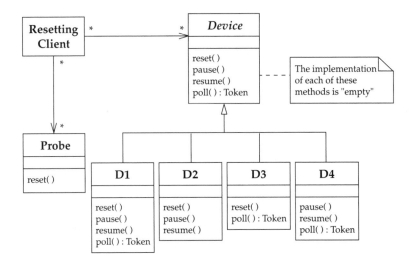

FIGURE 9.20 *Adding a resettable probe to the abstraction-based design.*

As an alternative, consider the roles that each device plays in its relationships with different clients. To a resetting client, a D1 device is a resettable (that is, something that can be reset). To a client that pauses and resumes devices, it is a pausable. To a polling client, it is a pollable. Defining an interface class for each such role results in the design shown in Figure 9.21.

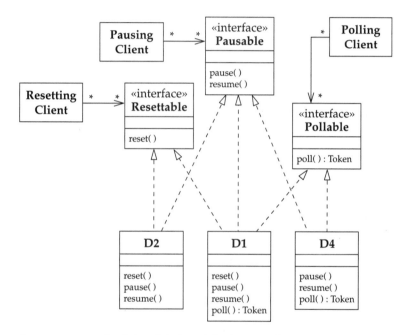

FIGURE 9.21   *A role-based design of the device problem.*

The device classes inherit only from the interface classes that represent the roles those devices play. The D1 class inherits from all three because it plays all three roles. A D2 device cannot be polled, however. Therefore, the D2 class does not inherit from the Pollable interface class. This design corrects all three of the following problems cited with the abstraction-based solution:

- A device has only interfaces for behaviors it truly provides. The D2 class does not inherit from Pollable. So, a D2 device has no `poll` method.

- A client can see only what it needs to see. The Resetting Client sees only the Resettable interface class and its `reset` method. Altering the Pollable interface class will not affect that client (or require that the client be recompiled).

- A client is coupled to a role rather than to an abstraction and, therefore, can interact with any object that plays that role. Adding a resettable Probe, for example, requires only that the Probe class inherit from the Resettable interface class, as shown in Figure 9.22. The Resetting Client requires no changes because it maintains a list of Resettable references (and a Probe can be cast as a Resettable).

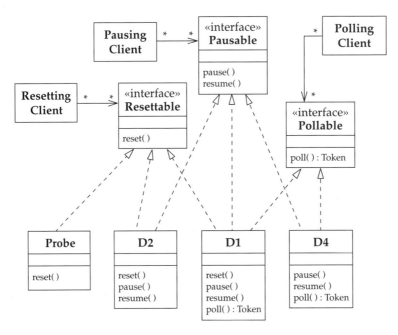

FIGURE 9.22 *Adding a resettable Probe to the role-based design.*

The device subclasses compose interfaces (or roles) through multiple inheritance. However, this multiple inheritance of interface does not suffer from the problems that plague multiple inheritance of implementation. Many of the difficulties with the latter stem from the inheritance of conflicting implementations. When a subclass inherits two methods with the same signature (name and parameter types) but with different effects, for example, those two implementations are in conflict. If a class inherits two *abstract* methods with the same signature, on the other hand, it is essentially inheriting the same method interface twice. The class must implement that method, and the same implementation suffices for both inherited interfaces.

Note

Multiple inheritance of an interface has its pitfalls, too. A problem arises when you inherit two abstract methods with the same signature but with different intended effects. For example, if you specify the interface's contact and the two methods have different pre-conditions and post-conditions, their effects are different. In such a case, no single implementation will satisfy both method declarations. (An exception is when one method's pre-conditions imply the other's pre-conditions, and the second method's post-conditions imply the post-conditions of the first. In that case, the second method's contract subsumes that of the first. So, an implementation of the second method suffices as an implementation of the first.) Bertrand Meyer provides an excellent discussion of satisfying class contracts in the presence of inheritance (1997, 569–580).

Most programming languages do not provide any mechanism for specifying the contract of a class or interface. Nonetheless, if one of your classes inherits two abstract methods with the same signature but with different intended effects, you have a problem. Different clients of your class will expect that method's implementation to fulfill each of the conflicting effects.

Observe that, even though they inherit from the various interface classes, the D1, D2, and D3 classes can inherit from a common Device superclass. If all devices have a device identity and name, for example, a Device class could define the implementation of those attributes. A class cannot inherit conflicting implementations if it specializes just one non-interface class.

Role-based design is an important tool when developing black-box frameworks. As the device example illustrates, however, it can also be a useful approach when designing an application (rather than a framework).

9.4   Reuse of Patterns

The reuse of classes, components, and frameworks differ in the scale and mechanism of reuse, but the three share one important property: In all three cases, you are reusing *code*. The codification and application of patterns, on the other hand, is an attempt to reuse *knowledge*. A pattern is a way of solving a problem. Patterns form a part of the lore that an experienced designer accumulates—those interesting ways of solving problems that recur over time.

A pattern typically promotes a design principle while solving a problem. Some patterns strengthen encapsulation. Others reduce various types of coupling, whereas others increase cohesion. From that standpoint, employing a pattern not only provides a solution that you might not have formulated on your own, but it also makes your design more flexible.

Because a pattern embodies the reuse of knowledge rather than code, developing catalogs of patterns has become an important point of emphasis in the object-oriented design community. The book, *Design Patterns: Elements of Reusable Object-Oriented Software*, by the "gang of four," Erich Gamma, Richard Helm, Ralph Johnson, and John Vlissides, was the first textbook on object-oriented software patterns and describes twenty-three common design patterns (1995). Several other books also describe specific patterns, including:

Pattern-Oriented Software Architecture: A System of Patterns by Frank Buschmann, Regine Meunier, Hans Rohnert, Peter Sommerlad, and Michael Stal (1996)

Object Models: Strategies, Patterns, and Applications by Peter Coad, David North, and Mark Mayfield (1995)

Analysis Patterns: Reusable Object Models by Martin Fowler (1997)

Patterns in Java, Volume I by Mark Grand (1998)

CORBA Design Patterns by Thomas Mowbray and Raphael Malveau (1997)

Design Patterns for Object-Oriented Software Development by Wolfgang Pree (1995)

Hatching Patterns: Design Patterns Applied by John Vlissides (1998)

The proceedings of the Pattern Languages of Program Design (PLoP) conferences also describe specific patterns:

Pattern Languages of Program Design edited by James Coplien and Douglas Schmidt (1995)

Pattern Languages of Program Design 2 edited by John Vlissides, James Coplien, and Norman Kerth (1996)

Pattern Languages of Program Design 3 edited by Robert Martin, Dirk Riehle, and Frank Buschmann (1997).

Patterns come in different flavors. An *analysis pattern* is a way of solving a problem in a particular problem domain. Fowler has cataloged several such patterns in accounting, securities trading, and other domains (1997). Because they are specific to a problem domain and require an understanding of the domain, analysis patterns are not discussed in detail here. Architectural and design patterns, on the other hand, are independent of any problem domain and illustrated with examples in this section.

9.4.1 Architectural Patterns

An *architectural pattern* is a problem-independent way of organizing a system or subsystem. It describes a structure by which the different parts of a system are organized or interact.

Buschmann, Meunier, Rohnert, Sommerlad, and Stal have been pioneers in cataloging architectural patterns such as Pipes and Filters (1996, 53–70) and Blackboards (71–95). When organized using the Pipes and Filters pattern, for example, an application consists of a set of *filters* that communicate with one another using data streams, or *pipes*. Each filter reads data from one or more input pipes, transforms that data, and then writes its results to one or more output pipes. In most cases, an output pipe of one filter is an input filter of another. A general form of this pattern is illustrated in Figure 9.23.

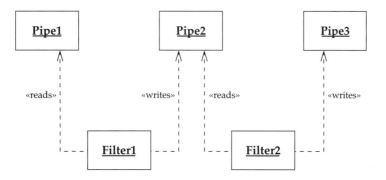

FIGURE 9.23 *The pipes and filters architectural pattern.*

An example of an application that might be organized in this way is a signal processing system. The first pipe holds an analog representation of the signal. The first filter converts the signal to a digital form, which it writes to the second pipe. The second filter reads from that second pipe, removes noise from the signal, and writes its result to the third pipe. Such a system might have several filters that remove different kinds of noise.

9.4.2 Design Patterns

A *design pattern* is a solution to a small problem that is independent of any problem domain. It represents an attractive solution to a design problem that could occur in any kind of application. The same design pattern can be applied in areas as diverse as order processing, factory control, and meeting room scheduling.

As an illustration of what a pattern is and how it is applied, consider the following problem:

> Your company sells both simple products and product bundles. A simple product is a stand-alone item, whereas a product bundle is a packaged collection of other products.
>
> All products have a name and description. When you request the description of a product bundle, you should receive its description followed by the name of each of its parts.
>
> You must be able to determine the price of a product. Simple products have a fixed unit price. The price of a product bundle is calculated by taking the sum of the prices of the bundle's parts and applying some discount rate (for example, 10 percent for some, 15 percent for others).
>
> You must implement a product catalog that, given a product code, returns a reference that can be used to obtain the name, description, and price of the product.

An initial analysis of this problem indicates that you have three Product classes. A Product superclass will hold the properties common to all products, such as the name, description, and product code. Two Product subclasses, Simple Product and Product Bundle, define the properties specific to those types of Products (for example, a unit price for a Simple Product, and a discount rate and a parts list for Product Bundles). A Product Catalog uses a product code to obtain a Product reference.

Figure 9.24 depicts an initial class design for this problem. The figure omits most of the properties of the classes. In this design, a Product Bundle has as parts to two or more Simple Products.

This design has a limitation that precludes a Product Bundle from having other Product Bundles as parts: A Product Bundle can be composed only of Simple Products. For example, an office supply company may want to sell a home office package that includes another bundle as one of its parts such as, a printer package consisting of a printer, printer cables, and a box of paper. The design in Figure 9.24 prevents such groupings, and I can assure you that one month after this application is on line, sales and marketing will want bundles of bundles.

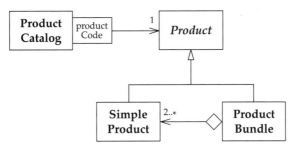

FIGURE 9.24 *A first solution to the product problem.*

The brute force approach to correcting this deficiency is simply to add another aggregation relationship, as shown in Figure 9.25. A Product Bundle now has two parts lists, one of Simple Products and the other of Product Bundles. Observe that the lower bound of the cardinality constraint on each relationship is zero. A Product Bundle does not need any Simple Products as parts because it could be composed entirely of other Product Bundles. Likewise, if it consists only of Simple Products, it will not have any Product Bundles as parts. However, it must have at least two parts of some variety. Therefore, the class diagram includes a constraint stating that requirement.

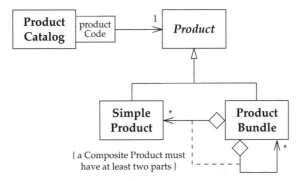

FIGURE 9.25 *A first attempt at allowing bundles of bundles.*

The problem with this solution is that a Product Bundle must maintain and operate on two lists. For example, when asked to compute its price, it must iterate through both lists and total the prices of the elements of each. Furthermore, if you introduced another class of products of which Product Bundles could be composed, you would have to extend the Product Bundle class to manipulate yet another list.

Applying the Composite pattern produces a better design (Gamma et al. 1995, 163–173). This pattern produces a tree-structured, whole-part hierarchy of instances that can span any depth. Figure 9.26 contains a class diagram for the pattern. A Composite is a whole that has a combination of Leaf and Composite instances as parts. However, its parts list is a collection of Component references, and the Leaf and Composite classes are derived from the Component superclass.

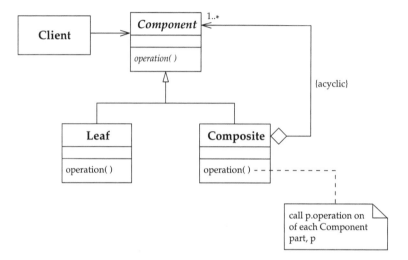

Figure 9.26 *A class diagram for the Composite design pattern.*

Figure 9.27 contains the class diagram for a design using the Composite pattern. The class structure in this design mimics that in the Figure 9.26. Like the Composite class in the pattern, the Product Bundle class maintains a list of references to its superclass as its parts. It implements its price method by invoking the price method on each of its Product parts and then applying a discount to the sum. It overrides Product's description method by calling that method, then invoking the name method on each of its parts, and finally returning the concatenation of those results.

UML provides syntax to document the application of a pattern. Figure 9.28 illustrates that notation. The name of the pattern appears in the dashed oval in the figure. Recall from Section 5.4, "Collaborations Provide the Glue," in Chapter 5, "Dynamic Diagramming Notation," that such an oval depicts a collaboration. A collaboration is a "society" of classes or objects that fulfill some overall purpose. Because it defines how a group of classes solve a small problem together, a pattern is a particular type of collaboration.

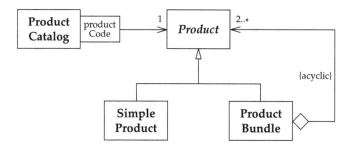

FIGURE 9.27   *A better way to allow bundles of bundles.*

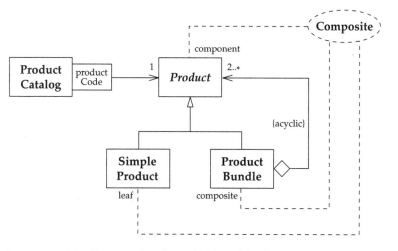

FIGURE 9.28   *Documenting the application of the Composite pattern.*

The dependencies between the oval and the classes in the figure indicate exactly what classes participate in the pattern. The intersection of a dependency and a class is labeled with the role that class plays in the pattern. Figure 9.28 states that the Product class is playing the component role (that is, the role defined by the Component class in the pattern's description), whereas the Simple Product and Product Bundle classes play the leaf and composite roles, respectively.

Figure 9.29 includes the final class diagram for the design. That diagram includes the attributes and methods omitted from the previous diagrams.

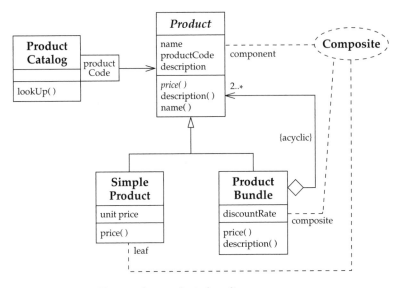

FIGURE 9.29 *The complete product class diagram.*

A design pattern such as Composite can be applied to designs for any problem domain. For example, consider the following problem:

> You must allow client programs to reset parts of a system consisting of subsystems and cards. Each subsystem consists of at least one subsystem and/or card. The system currently has three different kinds of cards: C1, C2, and C3.

> Resetting a subsystem requires resetting each of its constituent parts. The cards share a common reset interface, but different cards may implement that interface differently.

Obviously you need a Card superclass with C1, C2, and C3 as subclasses. That superclass defines an abstract reset method that the three subclasses implement in different ways. You also require a Subsystem class with a reset method that will reset all of the parts of a Subsystem. All that remains is to define the whole-part relationship between a Subsystem and its constituent Subsystem and Card parts.

The brute force solution is to define two aggregation relationships, one from Subsystem to itself and the other from Subsystem to Card, as illustrated by Figure 9.30. This solution has all the disadvantages of the design in Figure 9.25, however. The Subsystem code must manipulate two lists, and adding a new type of part entails extending the Subsystem class to handle a list of that new type. Later, if you wish to permit a Subsystem to include Probes and Connections, both of which must be reset when their containing Subsystem is reset, you must add code to the Subsystem class to define and iterate through those two new parts lists.

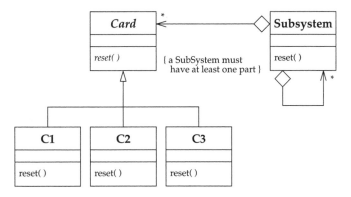

FIGURE 9.30 *A first solution to the Subsystem problem.*

Although this problem bears no resemblance to the Product Bundle problem above, the Composite pattern applies to both problems in essentially the same way. The Subsystem and Card classes specialize a System Node class, as shown in Figure 9.31. That superclass defines an abstract `reset` method. A Subsystem's parts list consists of System Node references. When a Subsystem is reset, it iterates through its parts list, invoking `reset` of each of those references.

Figure 9.32 illustrates the simplicity of adding a new Subsystem component, such as a Probe, to this design. The Probe class is a subclass of System Node. Therefore, a Probe reference can be assigned (as a System Node reference) to a Subsystem's parts list. The Subsystem class requires no modifications to allow this new type of part.

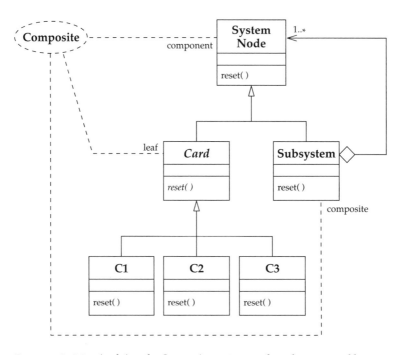

FIGURE 9.31 *Applying the Composite pattern to the subsystem problem.*

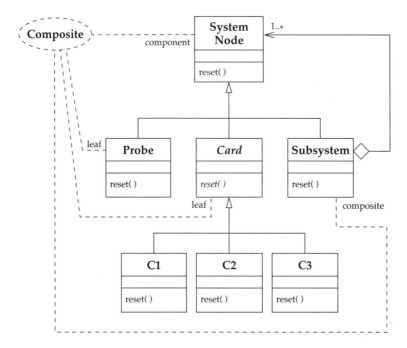

FIGURE 9.32 *Adding Probes to the design of the subsystem problem.*

Different design patterns solve different kinds of problems. A pattern that appears in many designs is Proxy (Gamma et al. 1995, 207–217). A proxy serves as a surrogate for another object, the ultimate subject. To a client, the proxy appears to be the subject because both the proxy and real subject implement the same interface. The client accesses the real subject through the proxy, and the proxy controls the client's access to the subject.

Figure 9.33 contains the generic class diagram for the Proxy pattern. The Subject class defines the interface shared by the real subject and the proxy. The Proxy subclass implements that interface by taking some action before and/or after calling that method in the associated Real Subject instance.

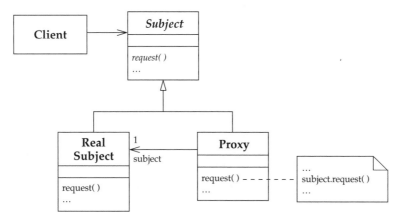

FIGURE 9.33 *A class diagram for the Proxy pattern.*

As an example of the application of this pattern, suppose you have a reusable Account class in a class library. You would like to use this class in an application, but the application demands that an Account instance have concurrent locking. Recall from Section 8.3.2, "Object Synchronization," in Chapter 8, that when an object implements concurrent locking, its methods must lock the object during their execution.

One way you can implement the required locking behavior is through the introduction of a locking proxy. The Account Proxy class in Figure 9.34 implements the same interface as does Account. In the body of each of its methods, an Account Proxy first locks its Account instance, then calls the corresponding method in that instance, and then releases the lock. Because the Account class already exists and is not derived from any other class, and because a goal is to use the class without modification, that class plays the role of both the subject and the real subject. The client expects to be given a reference to an Account but actually holds a reference to an Account Proxy.

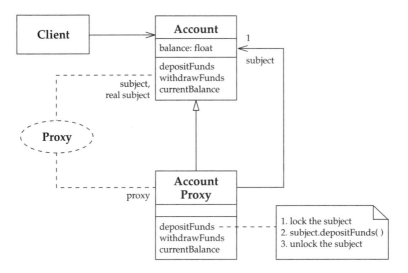

FIGURE 9.34 *An application of a locking proxy.*

Proxies have many other uses beyond locking. When the real subject is on a remote machine, a client may use a local proxy that shields it from the knowledge of where the real subject resides and how to contact it. When the real subject is in persistent storage and you want to materialize it only when a client accesses it, you can give the client a reference to a proxy that handles that materialization on demand. Gamma, Helm, Johnson, and Vlissides outline other applications (1995, 208–209).

Numerous design patterns are cataloged in other books and papers, many of which are cited in this chapter. A pattern first presented in this book is the Have Gunk, Will Travel pattern introduced in Section 7.3.2, "Commingling Extension and Reuse," in Chapter 7. This pattern applies to situations in which your goals include both reusable classes and an extensible application. You might be developing the reusable classes yourself, or you may be pulling them from existing class libraries.

As explained in Section 7.3, "Extension Versus Reuse," in Chapter 7, a tension exists between reuse and extension. For instance, to make the sample stock-trading application as extensible as possible, you want a stock-trading Account to carry out application-specific activities, such as funding orders and retaining shares of securities. To maximize its reuse, however, the Account class should be void of any application-specific behavior.

The Have Gunk, Will Travel pattern is a solution to this problem in which two distinct variants of an abstraction are developed. The *application-specific* version has those properties specific to the application at hand, and it uses the *application-independent* reusable variant of the class as part of its implementation. The class diagram for this pattern was presented in Figure 7.20 and is repeated here in Figure 9.35.

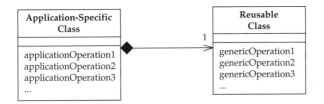

FIGURE 9.35   *The class diagram for the Have Gunk, Will Travel design pattern.*

You use this pattern when both of the following conditions are true:

- You have access to, or are developing, a generic, reusable class for an abstraction.

- You wish to use that class in an application where the class must have application-specific behavior to promote extensibility.

The application of this pattern to the stock-trading application was illustrated in Figure 7.19 and is repeated here as Figure 9.36. Unlike Figure 7.19, however, Figure 9.36 specifically depicts the application of the pattern using the notation explained earlier in this section.

The examples in this section illustrate two benefits of design patterns cited early in the section. First, when you apply a pattern, you are reusing a solution to a small problem. This typically saves you time because you do not have to formulate the solution yourself. Second, most patterns promote design flexibility in some way. In the Composite pattern, for example, a composite's coupling to its parts is generalized, thereby allowing you to add new composites and leaves relatively easily. A proxy in the Proxy pattern encapsulates a means of controlling a client object's access to a service object. The use of a proxy permits you to change the service object or the control mechanism without affecting the client. The Have Gunk, Will Travel pattern provides for both extensibility and class reuse in a single design.

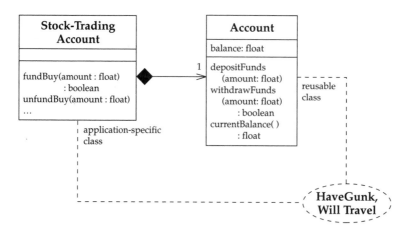

FIGURE 9.36 *The application of the pattern to a Stock-Trading Account.*

CHAPTER 10

Putting It All Together

This book does not prescribe a particular process for developing object-oriented software. Rather, it describes a set of approaches that can be put together in different ways under various process models. The lack of emphasis on process is not an indication that process is not important. Even though many object-oriented design books attempt to explain the topic within the framework of an overall process, no single process is correct for every project.

The choice of a process is driven by several factors, such as the size of the project, the degree of risk that is acceptable, whether it is a project for a single customer, whether project members are domain experts, and so forth. Nonetheless, having *some* process is a key ingredient in any successful development project, and this chapter provides some general guidance on that subject.

This chapter addresses process at four different levels:

- *General process models*: Developing software requires a general process model that defines which activities will occur when. Some common process models are described.

- *The artifacts of development*: Through its different diagrams, UML supports several views of an object-oriented system. The question, "What should a complete analysis and design document include?" is examined.

- *Combining development strategies*: Previous chapters describe various approaches for identifying use cases, finding classes, and developing the dynamic aspects of a design. These strategies can be applied in different sequences, some of which are outlined.

- *The Process of design refinement*: As you develop an object-oriented design, you follow a process of refinement through elaboration in which you refine abstract elements of the design into more detailed elements. The process is described and examples of particular refinements are given.

10.1 General Process Models

When you develop a software system or application, you employ a *process model* that, at a minimum, dictates what development activities should take place in what order. A process model provides a skeletal framework for organizing activities. That framework can be tailored to add new activities and to refine a general activity into a set of finer-grained activities.

One of the oldest software process models is the *waterfall model*. Under this model, development is a sequence of phases. Each phase flows into the next, and the direction is always downstream. In other words, once a phase is completed, it is never revisited. The number of phases could be anything from two or three (perhaps analysis, design, and implementation) to ten or more.

Figure 10.1 contains an activity diagram for a deployment of the waterfall model in which development consists of six activities:

1. *Business analysis:* During this phase, project members work with marketing to determine if a business case for the product exists and, if so, what the core requirements of the product are.

2. *System analysis:* This phase entails dividing the system into a set of subsystems and defining the major interfaces between those subsystems. The project team also determines any system-wide requirements (such as overall performance requirements).

3. *Subsystem analysis:* This is a more detailed analysis phase, during which the team establishes the requirements of each subsystem.

4. *High-level design:* Assuming this is an object-oriented development project, the team identifies the problem domain classes, their general properties, and the general interaction sequences for each subsystem.

5. *Low-level design:* During this phase, project members refine the design, working through the details of static structures and dynamic interactions. This activity includes the introduction of design classes and specific data structures to promote cohesion, the development of algorithms and methods, and a final determination of the exact signature of each method.

6. *Implementation and test:* Project members translate the low-level design into an implementation.

Observe from the activity diagram in the figure that subsystem analysis and its subsequent phases occur for each subsystem in this variant of the waterfall model. Furthermore, subsystem analysis on those subsystems begins in parallel. Once overall system analysis is complete, the project might be broken into smaller teams, each tackling the analysis and design of a single subsystem.

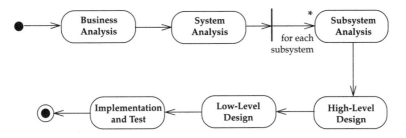

FIGURE 10.1 *An activity diagram for a waterfall process.*

The major selling point of the waterfall model is the apparent ease of scheduling and tracking its activities. Projects using this model often have *Project Evaluation and Review Technique (PERT)* charts that cover the walls of a conference room. The model also offers a sense of security because the team is always monotonically marching toward the goal (the completion of the product).

One major flaw in the waterfall model is its assumption that requirements never change. For a large project, many months may pass between the end of the requirements analysis phase and the completion of the implementation. Any changes in market conditions or customer whims during that time cannot be reflected in the project's consideration of requirements, because once requirement analysis is complete that phase is never revisited. Likewise, if you discover during implementation that a portion of the design is incorrect or inadequate, you have no provision in this process model for redesigning that part of the system.

Another of the waterfall model's disadvantages is the fact that all implementation occurs in one massive explosion of activity just before the "ship the pig" date. As a manager or customer, you hope that the final pig will look like the pig described by the analysis and design specifications, and of course you trust that your understanding of those documents coincides with the authors' intentions.

To reduce the risk inherent in the waterfall model while retaining the model's advantages, many projects adopt an *incremental development model*. In this model, a team goes through a series of *builds*, each of which is a mini-waterfall model. This process is also sometimes called *evolutionary development* because the product evolves over that series of builds. Generally, the features of highest priority or of greatest risk are addressed in the initial builds.

Figure 10.2 contains an activity diagram for an incremental development process. Recall that the «trace» dependency indicates a refinement and points away from the refinement. Hence, the activity diagram in the lower portion of the figure is a refinement of the Build Cycle activity in the upper part. The figure indicates that after system analysis, the project undertakes a series of build cycles. In this particular rendering of the incremental model, each of those cycles consists of feature analysis, high-level design, low-level design, and implementation and test.

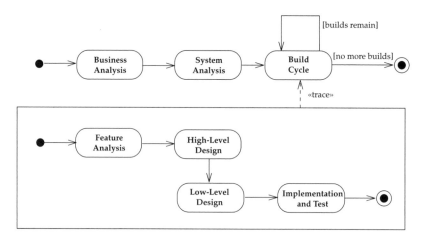

FIGURE 10.2 *An activity diagram for an incremental process.*

The activity diagram in Figure 10.3 describes a somewhat different incremental process. In this model, every build cycle includes an analysis of business conditions and requirements for the portion of the system under construction during that cycle. As Figures 10.2 and 10.3 illustrate, an overall process model can be specialized in various ways.

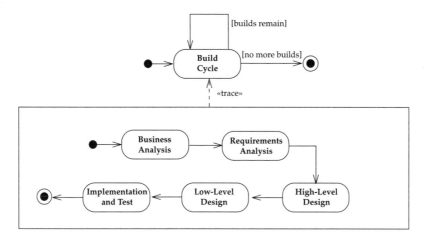

FIGURE 10.3 *An activity diagram for an alternative incremental process.*

A complementary view of incremental development is illustrated in Barry Boehm's *spiral model* pictured in Figure 10.4 (1998, 61–72). The model in the figure parcels development into four phases even though you can have as many phases as you want. You start at the center of the spiral, and each trip around the spiral is one build cycle.

Note

Boehm's original formulation of the spiral model is somewhat more complex than the simple incremental model presented here. Boehm allows different trips through the spiral to include different activities. One implication of this fact is that a single build might include multiple trips through the spiral. Boehm also populates the spiral with a prescribed set of activities that include prototyping.

The major contribution of his model, which is captured here, is its definition of development as an incremental process in which each step culminates with a validation of the results from that step.

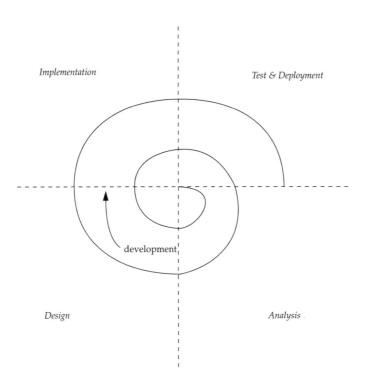

FIGURE 10.4 *A spiral development model.*

Note

Some authors refer to the model above as iterative, while others call it both incremental and itera-tive. I have labeled it as incremental. Is it iterative or incremental? Any definition of iterative devel-opment is driven by what is being iterated. Authors that refer to the above (incremental) model as iterative development view the process as the body of the iteration. That is, you iterate over a set of development steps.

I adopt the same view here as does Alistair Cockburn (1998, 123). To me, development is iterative if you allow for the reworking of a part of the system. That is, you iterate over the product itself. Therefore, incremental development improves the process (by dividing development into phased builds), whereas iterative development improves the product (by providing for the reworking of any part of the design or implementation that is flawed).

An *iterative model* is one that provides for the re-analysis or re-design of a por-tion of the system. This model admits the possibility of discovering that some-thing you have already completed must be reworked. The necessity for such alterations could be due to various factors, such as changing requirements or a flaw in the original analysis or design.

The incremental model can also be iterative if some build cycles are devoted to redeveloping elements from earlier cycles. Suppose, for example, that the fourth and eighth builds are dedicated to correcting mistakes or deficiencies in previous builds. This model is incremental because you are developing the system in pieces, and it is iterative because it sets aside time to rework parts of the design and implementation.

In a purely iterative style, there are no phases per se. A developer jumps around between the analysis, design, and implementation of a piece of code instead. This purer form permits a quick response to changes and deficiencies, and it may mirror the way designers think about problems. Unfortunately, it is somewhat chaotic because it is void of any defined structure and is, therefore, difficult to plan and track. Furthermore, because you may take large steps backward, you do not monotonically approach the goal of product completion. (Picture the scene that ensues when your manager asks you on a Friday afternoon, "How much closer are you to being finished today than you were last Friday?" and you reply, "Actually, I think I'm farther away from completion." I assure you that you will make this mistake only once.)

Murray Cantor describes a process model for *rapid application development (RAD)* that is very similar to the purely iterative development style described above (1998, 96). In this model, after the requirements and high-level architectural design are completed, the system is developed piecemeal in a series of *time boxes*. The model is incremental because as you iterate through time boxes, you are repeating the same development step on a new part of the product. It is also iterative because the developer may jump around between analysis, design, and implementation of a piece of the system within a time box. Figure 10.5 contains an activity diagram describing such a model.

Observe the similarities between Figures 10.2 and 10.5. The general control flows are essentially the same in the two models, and the fact that both models are incremental is obvious. In each case, the model reapplies an activity in which one part of the application is developed. The primary difference between the two models is that a time box in the RAD model is not structured as distinct phases, whereas a build cycle in Figure 10.2 is an ordered sequence of activities.

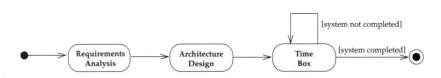

FIGURE 10.5 *An activity diagram for a rapid application development model.*

These four process models are not, by any means, the only software process models that have been proposed, and they are not the only ones in use. Other models do exist, and these models can be tailored to produce countless variations. For example, you can incorporate prototyping, increase or decrease the number of phases, and release parts of the system to customers at different times. Steve McConnell provides an extensive discussion of process models and their variations (1996, 133–162, 425–574).

10.2 The Artifacts of Development

UML defines seven distinct diagrams for describing an object-oriented application, all of which are explained in this book. Each type of diagram that follows has a somewhat different purpose:

- *Use case diagram*: It shows the basic functionality of a system or subsystem.

- *Activity diagram*: It describes a *workflow view* of the dynamics of a business process, use case, and so forth.

- *Class diagram*: It shows the static structure of classes and their relationships. (An object diagram, or instance diagram, depicts a particular configuration of objects and their links.)

- *Interaction diagram*: One of these depicts the dynamics of object interactions in a scenario. An interaction diagram is either a collaboration diagram or a sequence diagram.

- *State transition diagram*: It shows the state-based dynamics of a class of instances.

- *Component diagram*: It specifies compilation, link, and execution units (such as files) and their dependencies.

- *Deployment diagram*: This describes the hardware architecture of the system in terms of hardware nodes and their connections.

Taken together, these diagrams form several views of the system that should be documented as development proceeds. The following is one enumeration of the views of a system and their constituent diagrams:

- *A functional view (or model)*: This view includes a use case diagram. It typically includes a description of each use case in terms of a textual specification, an activity diagram, or pre- and post-conditions, as described in Section 5.1, "Describing Use Cases," in Chapter 5, "Dynamic Diagramming Notation." If your application requires that the use cases be executed in a specific order, the functional view can include a specification of that use case sequencing in terms of an activity diagram (in which the activities are use cases) or perhaps a regular expression (where the terms are use case names).

- *A static view (or model)*: This view defines the static class structure of the application and tells you what objects and links you can have during the application's execution. It includes a class diagram and may also include any interesting object diagrams. For example, you might want to include an object diagram depicting the initial configuration when the system is powered up or when a user signs on.

- *A dynamic view (or model)*: For this view, you include one or more scenarios for each use case, as well as an interaction diagram for each scenario. Writing a textual description of a scenario is often a good idea because it can include actions not present in interaction diagrams, such as the internal actions within objects. This view also may include a state transition diagram for each class with state-based behavior.

- *An architectural view (or model)*: This view may include a specification of packages and their dependencies, where a package represents a system building block such as a subsystem, component, or class library. It may also include a component diagram that describes dependencies among source files, binaries, and executables. For a distributed application, it normally includes a deployment diagram to show the hardware architecture of the system.

Philippe Kruchten adopts a slightly different set of system perspectives in his "4+1 view" of system architecture (1999, 83–85). Because he is concentrating on architecture rather than the overall design, his five views are aimed at the developers' and end users' views of general system organization:

- *Use case view*: This model includes use cases and scenarios.

- *Logical view*: This model describes the system's major building blocks, such as subsystems and packages.

- *Process view*: This model outlines the processes, threads, and tasks and their interactions.

- *Deployment view*: This model defines the hardware architecture, as well as what execution components run on what processors.

- *Implementation view*: This final perspective identifies the system's source files and executables and their relationships.

The deployment and implementation views correspond to UML's deployment and component diagrams, respectively, whereas the logical and process views are formed in part by a portion of the class diagram and interaction diagrams, respectively.

Regardless of the views you depict or the diagrams you employ, you must strive for a level of detail that is appropriate for your current phase of development. In the earliest analysis phase, for example, you should omit many details regarding exactly how certain features will be realized. Your goal at that stage is to model the essence of the application domain. As you near the end of design, however, you must decide on, and describe, those very details. At any stage of development, you must find a balance between sketchy artifacts that omit significant information and writing such detailed documentation that you make a career of it.

10.3 Combining Development Strategies

Assume you want to document the functional, static, dynamic, and architectural models described above. Constructing the functional view entails applying one of the use case identification approaches outlined in Section 6.1.1, "Identifying Use Cases," of Chapter 6, "Developing Dynamic Diagrams." Recall that the three approaches discussed are

- Identifying the actors, and then analyzing their interactions with the system

- Assuming you have a class diagram, analyzing the lifecycles of each class (that is, considering what use cases cause an instance of each class to be created, destroyed, or to change)

- Analyzing the action-oriented verb phrases in a problem specification

To build the static model, you can use one of the class diagramming approaches described in Chapter 3, "Developing Class Diagrams." Those approaches are

- Using noun phrases from a problem specification

- Abstracting from your problem domain expertise, perhaps with the aid of a set of identification keys (for example, tangible things, roles, events, and interactions)

- Analyzing use cases

When developing the dynamic view, you can employ either of the two following approaches described in Section 6.1, "Top-Down Design of System Dynamics," and in Section 6.2, "Bottom-Up Design of System Dynamics," of Chapter 6:

- *Top-down approach*: Start with use cases and work down through scenarios to individual class properties.

- *Bottom-up approach*: First identify class responsibilities and then proceed upward, using scenarios for validation.

These approaches can be applied in various combinations to construct an overall design. The preferred combination depends upon several factors, including

- The breadth and depth of your domain knowledge

- Whether you are developing a system from scratch

- Whether you have an initial problem specification

- How many people are on the team (and their experience level)

- Customer expectations

- The scope and complexity of the project

Suppose that you are building an application from the ground up, and you are somewhat uncertain about exactly what functions are required of the application at the outset of the project. In such a situation, analyzing use cases and constructing a functional model first is almost imperative. Because you have not yet identified classes, the use cases must be derived either from the actors and their interactions with the system, or from the verb phrases in a system specification (assuming that such a document exists).

Once you identify the use cases, you can analyze those use cases to find classes (as described in Section 3.3, "Developing a Class Diagram from Use Cases," in Chapter 3) and to produce a dynamic model (as discussed in Section 6.1, "Top-Down Design of System Dynamics," in Chapter 6). The activity diagram in Figure 10.6 describes this process flow. As shown in the figure, the creation of the static and dynamic models can occur in parallel even though the two models must be consistent with one another.

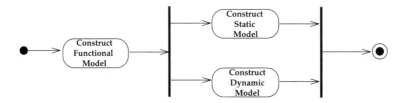

FIGURE 10.6 *A process flow driven by functional requirements.*

In some development efforts, you may elect to start with a class diagram first. Perhaps you have built a very similar system previously, and you already understand the functional requirements and basic system structure. Maybe you are collaborating with business analysts who are comfortable working with a business object model. You might have an existing data model from which to start.

To build the initial class diagram, you can use either noun phrases from a system specification (as described in Section 3.1, "Developing a Class Diagram from Noun Phrases," in Chapter 3) or abstraction (as discussed in Section 3.2, "Develop a Class Diagram Using Abstraction," in Chapter 3). Then, you can identify use cases by analyzing the life cycles of each class (as described in Section 6.1.1, "Identifying Use Cases," in Chapter 6). Finally, those use cases are used to drive the top-down approach for the design of system dynamics. This class-driven process flow is depicted in Figure 10.7.

FIGURE 10.7 *A process flow driven by the class diagram.*

When you employ the bottom-up, responsibility-driven approach for analyzing system dynamics, as described in Section 6.2, "Bottom-Up Design of System Dynamics," in Chapter 6, the development of an explicit functional model is almost an after-thought. The fundamental steps in the process follow:

1. Identify classes, perhaps using abstraction or noun phrases.

2. Attempt to list the responsibilities (the state and behavior) of each class.

3. Either identify attributes and methods from noun phrases and verb phrases, respectively, or use abstraction.

4. Employ scenarios to validate and modify what you have.

This process flow is illustrated in Figure 10.8. The development of a functional model is not present in that figure, but you could choose to create it to help you identify scenarios.

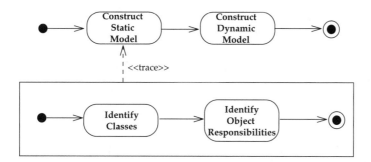

FIGURE 10.8 *A process flow driven by class responsibilities.*

The process flows in Figures 10.6 through 10.8 include some feedback loops that are not depicted in the figures. As you develop the static and dynamic models, you must keep the two consistent. For example, as you introduce new objects and messages in your interaction diagrams, you must add the corresponding classes, methods, and associations to your class diagram. Likewise, changes to your class diagram may require modifications to your interaction diagrams.

10.4   The Process of Design Refinement

Object-oriented development is a process of refinement through elaboration. Your first class diagram includes classes from the problem domain, perhaps together with packages that define the system's major layers and subsystems. Your initial interaction diagrams may describe only the coarsest of interactions between those layers and subsystems. As development proceeds, however, you refine those diagrams by adding detail about particular classes required by your design, about specific interactions between objects, and so forth.

Consider the class diagram for the factory control system developed in Section 3.3, "Developing a Class Diagram from Use Cases," in Chapter 3. That class diagram, originally included as Figure 3.13, is repeated here as Figure 10.9. The diagram is an analysis-level model because it includes only classes and class properties defined in the problem domain.

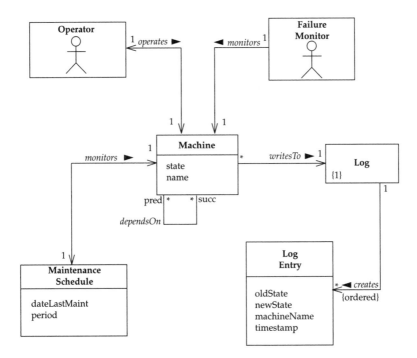

FIGURE 10.9 *The class diagram for the factory control system.*

One of the use cases for this problem, Machine Now Running, requires that a waiting Machine instance recognize that it can run again. Recall that a waiting Machine can run only if *all* of its predecessor Machines are also running. How does a waiting Machine make this determination? These details were deferred during the initial analysis of this problem.

The class diagram indicates that predecessor and successor Machines are linked together in some way. One possible design is to have each Machine maintain a count of its non-running predecessors. Consider the following:

1. When a predecessor Machine stops running (because it is down for maintenance, off, or waiting on one of its predecessors), it invokes a `predecessorNotRunning` method in each of its successors.

2. When it begins running again, a predecessor invokes a `predecessorNowRunning` method in each successor.

3. A successor Machine increments and decrements its count of non-running predecessors when its `predecessorNotRunning` and `predecessorNowRunning` methods, respectively, are invoked.

4. When that count is zero, the successor Machine can run.

This design has two advantages, the more obvious of which is its simplicity. Implementing this design requires only a few lines of code. A second, and perhaps more significant, advantage is the fact that a successor Machine is completely de-coupled from its predecessor Machines. The successor has no knowledge of who its predecessor Machines are or even of how many predecessors it has. It simply responds to messages (or method invocations) by incrementing and decrementing a counter.

The obvious disadvantage of this solution is its lack of robustness. Predecessors and communication channels must behave perfectly if this design is to work correctly. If a predecessor inadvertently sends the same message twice or neglects to send a message, or if a message is lost en route, the successor Machine will not run or wait as required.

This design also assumes a particular waiting behavior. In particular, it assumes that a successor Machine waits on *any* predecessor. Suppose some Machines must wait only if *all* predecessor Machines are not running. (Such a Machine processes the same material from each predecessor in the same way. Therefore, if any single predecessor continues to run, the successor should also run.) A counting scheme could also be employed to achieve this waiting behavior, but it must be a mirror image of the scheme described above.

Consider a situation in which a successor can run only if two particular predecessor Machines are running, as well as any one from a group of three other predecessors. A simple counting scheme cannot handle this case because knowing that three predecessors are running is insufficient. The successor Machine must know *which* predecessors are running.

If faulty behavior is possible, or if the more complicated waiting behavior is required, then you must find an alternative design. At least two other solutions come to mind:

- A successor Machine could periodically poll its predecessor Machines to determine whether they are running.

- When informing its successors that it is running or not running, a predecessor Machine includes its name. A successor Machine maintains a list of its predecessor Machines and their current states.

In some sense, these two solutions are equivalent. One is the polling version, and the other is the interrupt-driven version of the same basic design. In both cases, a successor must collect knowledge about the running status of its predecessor Machines. The polling solution is a little messier because you must determine when a successor should poll its predecessors, and you must deal with the case where a predecessor that has already been polled suddenly changes its state.

The class diagram in Figure 10.10 includes the extensions required to allow a successor Machine to maintain a list of its predecessor Machines' states. Observe that the dependency association is now directed from the predecessor toward the successor. The Machine class includes an attribute, predecessorStates, for the list of predecessor states, as well as methods through which a predecessor can inform a successor of a relevant state change.

This is obviously an elaboration of the original design. This refinement is still somewhat unappealing, however, because it requires that a successor Machine maintain information about the states of its predecessors. Figure 10.11 contains an instance diagram that illustrates this arrangement. Forcing one object to keep track of another is rather ugly business. Furthermore, if two Machines have exactly the same waiting behavior (that is, if they wait in exactly the same way on the same predecessors), together they will have two copies of the same list and waiting constraints.

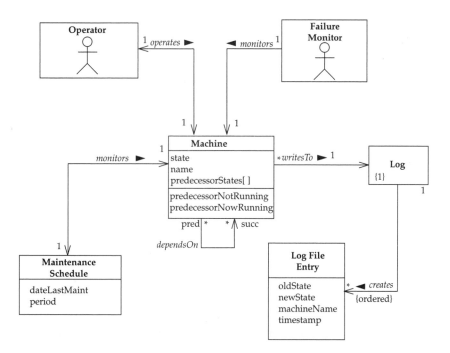

FIGURE 10.10 *A class diagram allowing successor Machines to track predecessors.*

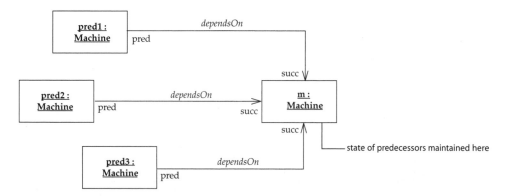

FIGURE 10.11 *An instance diagram for the initial design.*

You can produce a more cohesive Machine class by moving the waiting behavior into a separate class. An instance of that class sits between a successor Machine and its predecessors. It is responsible for maintaining the list of states of a group of predecessor Machines and informing its successor Machine(s) when to run and when to wait.

Such an object is an example of the application of the Mediator design pattern (Gamma et al. 1995, 273–282). A mediator encapsulates a set of interactions among other objects. In this case, a successor Machine can wait or run only if it has received a particular sequence of messages from its predecessor Machines. (It remembers that sequence in the form of a list of what it believes are the current states of its predecessors.) Rather than having the successor Machine remember the history of messages, a mediator object maintains that history.

Figure 10.12 contains the additions to the class diagram required for this solution, including an explicit indication that the Mediator pattern has been applied:

1. A predecessor Machine will inform its Waiting Mediators when it starts or ceases to run.

2. A Waiting Mediator will track the states of its predecessor Machines and tell its successor Machines to run or wait.

A Waiting Mediator can have multiple successors so that if several Machines share the same waiting behavior, the behavior will exist in a single Mediator instance.

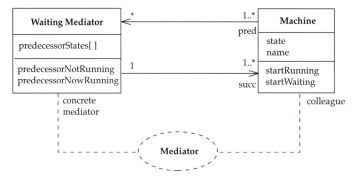

FIGURE 10.12 *Class diagram modifications for the Mediator class.*

The instance diagram in Figure 10.13 shows a modification of the configuration in Figure 10.11 that reflects the inclusion of a Mediator object. The Machine instances in the figure are more cohesive because they are no longer responsible for maintaining information about the states of their predecessors.

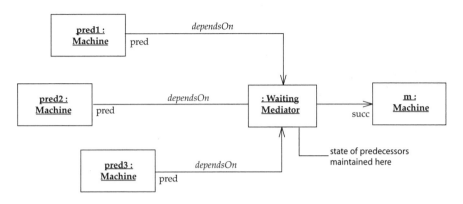

FIGURE 10.13 *An instance diagram for a design with Mediators.*

The introduction of the Waiting Mediator class is another example of a design refinement through elaboration. The Mediator class is not a part of the problem per se, but rather is a mechanism added to facilitate a particular design. You carry out a series of such elaboration throughout the design process. Yet another possible refinement in this design is the introduction of a specific container class to implement the one-to-many relationship between the Log and its Log Entries, such as the one depicted in Figure 10.14. The «trace» relationship is an explicit representation of the refinement.

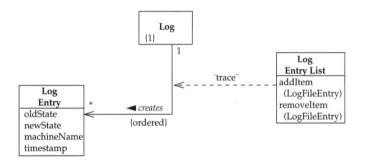

FIGURE 10.14 *A refinement of an association.*

Object-oriented technology enables design by refinement (or elaboration) through what I call *representational continuity*. This continuity exists in two forms. The first is the fact that you draw the same kinds of diagrams throughout the development process. During the earliest analysis phase, for example, you typically draw a class diagram and perhaps some high-level interaction diagrams. As you proceed through analysis and design, you continue to draw those same diagrams. Contrast this with *structured analysis and structured design (SA/SD)* in which you draw data flow diagrams during analysis and structure charts during design.

The fact that the same kinds of diagrams span the entire development process is important, but that alone provides you with very little power. The second form of representational continuity is the fact that the actual elements appearing in your analysis models continue to exist throughout the development process. As noted previously, the class diagram in Figure 10.9 is an analysis-level diagram. Nonetheless, the classes and class properties in that diagram will appear throughout the design and in the implementation of the factory control system. In other words, the analysis becomes the design. The analysis is not transformed by some magic into a design that bears little resemblance to the analysis.

References

American National Standards Institute. 1998. *International Standard ISO/IEC 14882*.

Andrews, Gregory. 1991. *Concurrent Programming: Principles and Practice*. Reading, Mass.: Benjamin/Cummings.

Arnold, Ken, and James Gosling. 1998. *The Java Programming Language*. 2d ed. Reading, Mass.: Addison Wesley.

Bellin, D. and S. Simone. 1997. *The CRC Card Book*. Reading, Mass.: Addison Wesley.

Boehm, Barry. 1998. A Spiral Model of Software Development and Enhancement. *IEEE Computer*, May, 61–72.

Booch, Grady. 1994. *Object-Oriented Analysis and Design with Applications*. Reading, Mass.: Benjamin/Cummings.

Booch, Grady, James Rumbaugh, and Ivar Jacobson. 1999. *The Unified Modeling Language User Guide*. Reading, Mass.: Addison Wesley.

Box, Don. 1998. *Essential COM*. Reading, Mass.: Addison Wesley.

Buschmann, Frank, Regine Meunier, Hans Rohnert, Peter Sommerlad, and Michael Stal. 1996. *Pattern-Oriented Software Architecture: A System of Patterns*. New York: John Wiley and Sons.

Cantor, Murray. 1998. *Object-Oriented Project Management with UML*. New York: John Wiley and Sons.

Coad, Peter, David North, and Mark Mayfield. 1995. *Object Models: Strategies, Patterns, and Applications*. Upper Saddle River, New Jersey: Yourdon Press.

Coad, Peter, and Edward Yourdon. 1991. *Object-Oriented Analysis*. 2d ed. Upper Saddle River, New Jersey: Yourdon Press.

Cockburn, Alistair. 1998. *Surviving Object-Oriented Projects: A Manager's Guide*. Reading, Mass.: Addison Wesley.

Coleman, Derek, Patrick Arnold, and Stephanie Bodoff. 1994. *Object-Oriented Development: The Fusion Method*. Upper Saddle River, New Jersey: Prentice Hall.

Collins, Dave. 1995. *Designing Object-Oriented User Interfaces*. Reading, Mass.: Benjamin/Cummings.

Coplien, James, and Douglas Schmidt, eds. 1995. *Pattern Languages of Program Design*. Reading, Mass.: Addison Wesley.

de Champeaux, Dennis, Douglas Lea, and Penelope Faure. 1993. *Object-Oriented System Development*. Reading, Mass.: Addison Wesley.

Douglass, Bruce Powel. 1999. *Doing Hard Time: Developing Real-Time Systems with UML, Objects, Frameworks, and Patterns*. Reading, Mass.: Addison Wesley.

D'Souza, Desmond and Alan Wills. 1999. *Objects, Components, and Frameworks with UML: The Catalysis Approach*. Reading, Mass.: Addison Wesley.

Fowler, Martin. 1997. *Analysis Patterns: Reusable Object Models*. Reading, Mass.: Addison Wesley.

Fowler, Martin, and Kendall Scott. 1997. *UML Distilled: Applying the Standard Object Modeling Language*. Reading, Mass.: Addison Wesley.

Gamma, Erich, Richard Helm, Ralph Johnson, and John Vlissides. 1995. *Design Patterns: Elements of Reusable Object-Oriented Software*. Reading, Mass.: Addison Wesley.

Goldberg, Adele, and Kenneth Rubin. 1995. *Succeeding with Objects: Decision Frameworks for Project Management*. Reading, Mass.: Addison Wesley.

Grand, Mark. 1998. *Patterns in Java, Volume I*. New York: Wiley.

Harel, David. 1987. Statecharts: A Visual Formalism for Complex Systems. *Science of Computer Programming* 8.

Harmon, Paul, and Mark Watson. 1988. *Understanding UML: The Developer's Guide*. San Francisco: Morgan Kaufmann.

Jacobson, Ivar, Magnus Christerson, Patrick Jonsson, and Gunnar Övergaard. 1992. *Object-Oriented Software Engineering: A Use Case Driven Approach*. Reading, Mass.: Addison Wesley.

Jacobson, Ivar, Maria Ericsson, and Agneta Jacobson. 1994. *The Object Advantage: Business Process Reengineering with Object Technology*. Reading, Mass.: Addison Wesley.

Jacobson, Ivar, Martin Gris, and Patrik Jonsson. 1997. *Software Reuse: Architecture, Process, and Organization for Business Success*. Reading, Mass.: Addison Wesley.

Kruchten, Philippe. 1999. *The Rational Unified Process: An Introduction*. Reading, Mass.: Addison Wesley.

Lakos, John. 1996. *Large-Scale C++ Software Design*. Reading, Mass.: Addison Wesley.

Larman, Craig. 1998. *Applying UML and Patterns: An Introduction to Object-Oriented Analysis and Design*. Upper Saddle River, New Jersey: Prentice Hall.

Lea, Doug. 1997. *Concurrent Programming in Java: Design Principles and Patterns*. Reading, Mass.: Addison Wesley.

Lewis, Bill and Daniel Berg. 1996. *Threads Primer: A Guide to Multithreaded Programming*. Upper Saddle River, New Jersey: Prentice Hall.

Loomis, Mary. 1995. *Object Databases: The Essentials*. Reading, Mass.: Addison Wesley.

Martin, Robert C. 1995. *Designing Object-Oriented C++ Applications Using the Booch Method*. Upper Saddle River, New Jersey: Prentice Hall.

Martin, Robert, Dirk Riehle, and Frank Buschmann eds. 1997. *Pattern Languages of Program Design 3*. Reading, Mass.: Addison Wesley.

McConnell, Steve. 1996. *Rapid Development: Taming Wild Software Schedules*. New York: Microsoft Press.

Meyer, Bertrand. 1997. *Object-Oriented Software Construction*. 2d ed. Upper Saddle River, New Jersey: Prentice Hall.

Meyers, Scott. 1995. *Effective C++: 50 Specific Ways to Improve Your Programs and Designs*. Reading, Mass.: Addison Wesley.

Mowbray, Thomas and Raphael Malveau. 1997. *CORBA Design Patterns*. New York: Wiley.

Mowbray, Thomas and William Ruh. 1997. *Inside CORBA: Distributed Object Standards and Applications*. Reading, Mass.: Addison Wesley.

Norton, Scott and Mark Dipasquale. 1997. *Thread Time: The Multithreaded Programming Guide*. Upper Saddle River, New Jersey: Prentice Hall.

Object Management Group. 1998. *OMG Unified Modeling Language Specification*. (www.omg.org)

Pree, Wolfgang. 1995. *Design Patterns for Object-Oriented Software Development*. Reading, Mass.: Addison Wesley.

Rational Software Corporation. 1997. *UML Extension for Business Modeling Version 1.1*. www.rational.com

—. 1997. *The Unified Modeling Language Notation Guide Version 1.1*. www.rational.com

—. 1997. *The Unified Modeling Language Semantics: Version 1.1*. www.rational.com

Riel, Arthur. 1996. *Object-Oriented Design Heuristics*. Reading, Mass.: Addison Wesley.

Rumbaugh, James, Ivar Jacobson, and Grady Booch. 1999. *The Unified Modeling Language Reference Manual*. Reading, Mass.: Addison Wesley.

Rumbaugh, James, Michael Blaha, William Premerlani, Frederick Eddy, and William Lorensen. 1991. *Object-Oriented Modeling and Design*. Upper Saddle River, New Jersey: Prentice Hall.

Shlaer, Sally, and Stephen Mellor. 1988. *Object-Oriented Systems Analysis: Modeling the World in Data*. Upper Saddle River, New Jersey: Yourdon Press.

Taylor, David. 1995. *Business Engineering with Object Technology*. New York: John Wiley & Sons.

Vlissides, John. 1998. *Hatching Patterns: Design Patterns Applied*. Reading, Mass.: Addison Wesley.

Vlissides, John, James Coplien, and Norman Kerth, eds. 1996. *Pattern Languages of Program Design 2*. Reading, Mass.: Addison Wesley.

Warmer, Jos, and Anneke Kleppe. 1999. *The Object Constraint Language: Precise Modeling with UML*. Reading, Mass.: Addison Wesley.

Wilkinson, N. 1995. *Using CRC Cards: An Informal Approach to Object-Oriented Development*. New York: SIGS Books.

Wirfs-Brock, R., Brian Wilkerson, and Lauren Wiener. 1990. *Designing Object-Oriented Software*. Upper Saddle River, New Jersey: Prentice Hall.

Yourdon, Edward and Larry Constantine. 1978. *Structured Design: Fundamentals of a Discipline of Computer Program and Systems Design*, 2d Ed. Upper Saddle River, New Jersey: Yourdon Press.

Index

Symbols

I

O